THE
FIFTH GENERATION
FALLACY

THE
FIFTH GENERATION
FALLACY

Why Japan Is Betting Its Future on Artificial Intelligence

J. Marshall Unger

New York   Oxford
OXFORD UNIVERSITY PRESS
1987

Oxford University Press

Oxford New York Toronto
Delhi Bombay Calcutta Madras Karachi
Petaling Jaya Singapore Hong Kong Tokyo
Nairobi Dar es Salaam Cape Town
Melbourne Auckland

and associated companies in
Beirut Berlin Ibadan Nicosia

Library of Congress Cataloging-in-Publication Data
Unger, J. Marshall.
The fifth generation fallacy.
Bibliography: p.   Includes index.   1. Fifth generation computers.
2. Artificial intelligence.   3. Word processing.
4. Japanese language—Data processing.   I. Title.
QA76.85.U54   1987   006.3'0952   86-23771
ISBN 0-19-504939-X

1 3 5 7 9 8 6 4 2
Printed in the United States of America
on acid-free paper

For Mutsuyo

Acknowledgments

Research for this book was made possible by a fellowship from the Japan Foundation for 1985 and support during the first half of 1986 from the Japan Studies Endowment of the University of Hawaii Foundation, funded by a grant from the Japanese government. During 1985 the author was a visiting scholar at the University of Tôkyô and wishes to thank Kumon Shunpei of the Faculty of Liberal Arts for his assistance in providing access to the university's facilities.

Much of the material in Part III is based on or was confirmed through interviews and conversations with Japanese engaged in advanced computer science research and visiting foreigners close to the R&D scene, including Aiso Hideo, Nicholas Bond, Alex Conn, Sidney Fernbach, Fuchi Kazuhiro, Fujiwara Yuzuru, Gotô Eiichi, Karatsu Hajime, Kimura Shigeru, Kusama Hiroyuki, John D. Lamb, George Lindamood, Edward Louie, Morita Masasuke, Ronald Morse, Nagao Makoto, Derek Paddon, Sakamura Ken, and Yamada Hisao. Some will probably be unhappy with the author's final conclusions, but all deserve thanks for their cooperation. Valuable information on linguistic and historical matters was provided by Amanuma Yasuo, Robert A. Brown, John DeFrancis, Hubert Dreyfus, Kabashima Tadao, Samuel Martin, Jiří Neustupný, Ôtsuka Haruo, Richard Rubinger, Shibata Takeshi, Shiraishi Daiji, Yamazaki Seikô, and many others.

Finally, the author wishes to thank Joseph Berston, Willem Grootaers, Ikeda Tetsurô, Ikegami Chizuko, Komai Akira, Mitsuhashi Setsuko, and Tokugawa Munemasa for their kind help in making his stay in Japan an especially productive one.

Honolulu, Hawaii   J. M. U.
March 1987

Contents

THE
FIFTH GENERATION
FALLACY

Introduction

This book is about two things that, at first, may not seem to have much in common: the Japanese writing system and the "state of the art" in computer science. In fact, there is a deep and unexpected connection between them, a connection that everyone interested in the future of industrialized society should know more about, and that, simply as a piece of human history, is fascinating in its own right.

The idea of telling the story of this connection was born about six years ago, when *Japan As Number One: Lessons for Americans* (Vogel 1979) and *Theory Z: How American Business Can Meet the Japanese Challenge* (Ouchi 1981) were bestsellers. Certainly, neither Vogel nor Ouchi intended to arouse anti-Japanese feelings among U.S. businessmen and politicians; but their blend of admiration and admonition—praise for Japan and warnings for America—heralded a growing concern over Japan's economic power that has culminated in a spate of books such as *The Eastasia Edge* (Hofheinz & Calder 1982) and *The Japanese Conspiracy* (Wolf 1983), ominous-sounding newspaper articles (e.g., Lohr 1984, Marcom & Bowning 1984), and, most recently, moves in Congress to pass protectionist tariff legislation. Less well known but perhaps equally important is the sudden eagerness of government and private industry in the United States and Europe to jump into the highly speculative field of Artificial Intelligence (AI) lest the Japanese take the lead in this allegedly vital area of computer technology.

The book that deserves the most credit for creating anxiety on this score is *The Fifth Generation* by Edward A. Feigenbaum, a "founding father" of AI who teaches at Stanford, and Pamela McCorduck, the title of whose earlier *Machines Who Think* (1979) makes it clear where she stands on the complex philosophical issues surrounding AI research. Although criticized when it appeared by some experts, such as Terry Winograd (quoted in Batt 1983), also at Stanford, *The Fifth*

3

Generation won general acclaim (see, e.g., Bairstow 1983), and sold well enough to merit a "revised and updated" paperback edition in 1984. Professors at MIT, another university heavily involved with AI research, have called it "extremely influential" and, misguided by it, have asserted flatly that "[t]he Fifth Generation Project is Japan's ambitious plan to seize worldwide leadership in the computing industry" (Winston & Prendergast 1984: 288).

Artificial Intelligence is more of a catchword than a clearly defined subfield of computer science; the distinction between "strong AI" and "weak AI" introduced by the philosopher John R. Searle (1980) helps greatly to clarify things. By weak AI is meant the use of computers as tools for modelling and testing theories of human cognition in an effort to understand how the brain works, how perception occurs, how memories are stored and retrieved, and so on. Few would quarrel with research in this direction, for although it involves computers, it does not assume that the mind is nothing but a computer. The problem is with strong AI—the claim that computer programs are themselves instantiations of intelligence or, in other words, that everything we call intelligence can be reduced to the formal manipulation of symbolic information. From this perspective, the human organism performs no role in intelligent behavior that cannot be reproduced or simulated by a properly designed and programmed computer. It is strong AI to which Feigenbaum and McCorduck subscribe, and it is in the rhetoric of strong AI that most explanations of the Fifth Generation project are couched. What the Japanese have in mind when they speak of AI, however, turns out to be something else yet again, and unless one dispels the fog of strong-AI hyperbole that surrounds the Fifth Generation project, it is impossible to appreciate its true significance.

Feigenbaum and McCorduck's book is subtitled *Artificial Intelligence and Japan's Computer Challenge to the World,* but it hardly provides any insight into the Japanese aspects of the Fifth Generation project. The authors concentrate on advancing their own ideas about AI, ridiculing any and all who disagree with them along the way. They clearly belong to that cavalier band of AI specialists whom MIT scientist Joseph Weizenbaum (1976) wittily dubbed "the artificial intelligentsia." The following passage is typical:

> It is a distinct pleasure to report that while the Japanese have put a lot of planning into their Fifth Generation project, they've spent no time at all in those arid little debates so beloved by Western intellectuals, debates centered on the question whether a machine really can be said

to think. They regard our obsession with this topic the same way we regard their eating raw fish—an odd, puzzling, but harmless cultural quirk. Instead, their debates are about the best way to design an intelligent machine, truly a new generation, the engine that will produce the new wealth of nations. (Feigenbaum & McCorduck 1983: 17)

As this sample suggests, the authors treat the cultural and historical differences between Japan and the West as lightly as they do the opinions of AI skeptics. It never occurs to them that, despite Japan's newfound affluence, its intellectual climate continues to suffer from such fundamental conditions as geographical and linguistic isolation, academic factionalism, and the overweening influence of government bureaucracy and giant corporations. All of these things, as we shall see, can be at least indirectly linked to Japan's rush into AI, where even IBM fears to tread; but Feigenbaum and McCorduck choose to overlook these factors. They take note of the unhappiness of many Japanese manufacturers at being bullied by the Ministry of International Trade and Industry (MITI) into cooperating with the Fifth Generation effort (108–110); they remark on the shortcomings of the Japanese educational system (121, 144–147); yet never do they acknowledge that such things might be anything more than minor obstacles to Fifth Generation success.

In fairness, it must be pointed out that Feigenbaum and McCorduck make no attempt to conceal the fact that their interest in Japan begins and ends with Japanese interest in their brand of AI optimism:

Here come the Japanese, aiming to give us computers that anyone can use, even, in principle, the illiterate, because these machines can show and tell and understand in voice and pictures. They'll be computers that do a lot more than count: they'll reason, guess, understand, behave, intelligently. It happens to be the Japanese who have announced something called the Fifth Generation. But the central idea of the Fifth Generation is not specifically Japanese; on the contrary, it's specifically human. It might have come from any number of sources. Who first brings it to us is, in the long run, beside the point. (In the short run, who has it first is a matter of significant economic consequence.) For our children's children, intelligent machines will be a fact of life as books and television are facts of ours. (Feigenbaum & McCorduck 1983: 58)

Only in the context of urging support for strong-AI research and development in the United States and Europe are they eager to talk about

Japan, and then they do not shy away from melodrama and scare tactics:

> Feigenbaum offered the Stanford campus as a neutral ground where industry and academic knowledge might be pooled. But would Texas Instruments, which takes the Japanese symbolic inference machine seriously, be willing to cooperate with Digital Equipment, which also takes it seriously, even at Stanford? Would Hewlett-Packard confide in Control Data Corporation? Would Honeywell? Then again, would an industrial project intrude on academic freedom? And where would the money come from? No single corporation has the kind of money to spend on a long-term project like the Japanese have received from MITI. Everyone could see the problems, but nobody could see any solutions.
>
> Later, McCorduck drove her rented Toyota back to the airport and heard a popular song: "those certainly depressin', low-down, mind-messin', workin' at the carwash blues." That seemed to sum up a plausible future for her country. On board she sat next to a representative of Kirin Beer. In New York, at last, she called her husband, hoping he hadn't yet had supper, and discovered that he and a colleague were about to go to Midtown for sushi. Under the watchful eye of a Manhattan sushi master, she ate her dinner and pondered the day's events. Were they all corny improbabilities, or is it the end, the wimpish end, of the American century? (Feigenbaum & McCorduck 1983: 185)

And so it goes: a patchwork of rosy promises about the computerized future and dark warnings of an imminent Japanese takeover of the world economy. One cannot help being reminded of government assurances about atomic energy in the 1950s: A teaspoon of uranium will do the work of train-loads of coal. Smokestacks will vanish from the landscape. It was a fantasy world in which reactor meltdowns and nuclear waste disposal simply did not exist. Indeed, substitute "strategic" for "economic" in "who has it first is a matter of significant economic consequence," and the parallel is complete: Feigenbaum and McCorduck could be pleading for the next generation of bomber rather than computer. And indeed they go out of their way to advocate the development of AI for military purposes (215–220)—something that the Japanese, to their very great credit, are *not* doing—even suggesting that using "national defense" as a pretext for channeling federal money into AI research is ethically acceptable (229–230). (No urging is necessary: the U.S. Defense Department is champing at the bit [Raloff 1984a: 333].)

The truth is that international economic competitiveness is just one, and hardly the most important, of the many reasons for MITI's commitment of money to the Fifth Generation project. In a section entitled "Why Are the Japanese Doing All This?" Feigenbaum and McCorduck mention in passing a much more important factor:

[T]he Japanese have suffered from low productivity in white-collar work. So has nearly everyone else, but the Japanese feel it especially because their language doesn't lend itself easily to mechanical means of reproduction such as typewriters. The first writing the Japanese ever saw was Chinese, and though their language had practically no relationship whatever to Chinese, the Japanese adopted that form of writing and have had to live with it ever since. (Feigenbaum & McCorduck 1983: 133)

Improving white-collar productivity was indeed at the top of the Fifth Generation's 1981 list of long-range goals, and Feigenbaum and McCorduck correctly analyze why it is there. It is true that Japanese office workers routinely put in overtime, but it is not true that they do so strictly out of a sense of loyalty; often, it is simply a question of compensating for the inefficiencies built into the preparation, copying, filing, and utilization of Japanese documents. Unfortunately, Feigenbaum and McCorduck fail to probe the matter further because they assume that the script problem, which has defied all previous attempts at solution, will somehow yield to Fifth Generation machines. For them, AI computers will be the future means for achieving all ends.

[P]erhaps the best answer to the question of why the Japanese are doing all this comes from Sozeburo [Sôzaburô] Okamatsu, a MITI official who told an American journalist: "Because we have only limited resources, we need a Japanese technological lead to earn money for food, oil, and coal. Until recently we chased foreign technology, but this time we'll pioneer a second computer revolution. If we don't, we won't survive." (Feigenbaum & McCorduck 1983: 135)

But what does this explain? From a Japanese perspective, the important thing is to start creating new technologies at home instead of constantly trying to catch up with the United States and Western Europe. Okamatsu might just as well have been talking about nuclear fusion, genetic engineering, optoelectronics, new ceramic materials, or ultrafast "supercomputers" (not to be confused with "intelligent" Fifth Generation machines). MITI supports a wide range of projects: why *specifically* was it decided that Artificial Intelligence was worthy of support?

A small part of the answer is that there's no harm in experimenting: even if the project does not succeed, something will have been learned. But this is hardly a specific justification; moreover, it does not account for the fact that several distinguished Japanese computer scientists (e.g., Professors Gotô Eiichi and Kunii Toshiyasu[1] of the University of Tôkyô) are vocal critics of the Fifth Generation project. It also ignores the fact that many of the Japanese writers who have written favorably about the project clearly do not believe that failure is a real possibility. A somewhat larger part of the answer has to do with nontechnical goals, such as encouraging basic research, fostering industry/university cooperation, and so on, which can be reached through the vehicle of the Fifth Generation project (Lindamood 1983, 1984a). In terms of these goals, the project has to a considerable extent already succeeded. These nontechnical successes may serve to cushion the blow of any later disappointments, but do not account for decisions regarding the specific content and strategy of Fifth Generation research. No national R&D project is free of politics, but the rather cynical explanation that the Japanese are just using AI as a cover for accomplishing other things is at best half the story.

The thesis of this book is that the Japanese commitment to strong-AI research is intimately related to the nature of the Japanese writing system. Unless a new, fundamentally different kind of computer can be built, the inefficiency of using traditional script in computer environments will become intolerable as the scope and number of computer applications grow. Unpleasant questions concerning national script and education policies that the Japanese thought they had laid to rest more than thirty years ago will have to be reopened. Should the schools encourage the use of romanized Japanese beyond the token level to which it is now relegated? Should documents in romanized Japanese be legally valid? The list could easily be expanded. Bigger and faster supercomputers cannot forestall this crisis. The only hope is the possibility of a computer that can actually think and behave like a human being.

As a matter of fact, in order to serve as a Japanese amanuensis, a computer would have to *outperform* a human being. One stenographer, at the National Diet for thirty years, estimates that an hour of Japanese speech translates into about 15,000 characters of text and takes twelve to thirteen hours to transcribe by hand (Sakamoto 1984: 62). He notes that it is possible to work "several times" faster from tape recordings using a computer word-processor, but his own typing speed of "more than a 100 characters per minute" (about twice the rate most Japanese users attain) is achieved by preprogramming his machine to accept the stenographic abbreviations he has mastered during his long years of experience (63–64). Furthermore, part of the improvement is undoubtedly the result of being able to control the tape, not the result of using the word-processor. Considering that a good touch typist can aim for 100 *words* (roughly 500 characters) per minute in English, it is clear that, even under the most favorable conditions, transcribing Japanese is an onerous task. A Japanese "robot stenographer" attempting to match the human expertise involved would have to possess, in addition to algorithms for analyzing speech (which would be the "easy" part), some way to simulate the human ability for choosing among the thousands of individual characters used in everyday writing. This would require not only powerful procedures for syntactic analysis (comparable to those needed for translating between languages), but also massive databases of real-life information for making semantic judgments. Moreover, unlike the human stenographer, who has some leeway on the many occasions when the rules of Japanese orthography allow for alternatives, the robot would have to try to produce the exact characters the user had in mind. Only strong-AI enthusiasts have ever promised a machine like this.

No MITI bureaucrat or university scientist consciously decided to support the Fifth Generation concept because he saw it as a way around script reform.[2] The chain of causality was much more subtle: the technically oriented planners of the Fifth Generation project saw VLSI (very large-scale integration) microcircuit technology as an opportunity to build computers of new, fundamentally different architecture, so-called non-von Neumann machines, incorporating vast arrays of parallel processors. Such hardware experimentation, once only a theoretical dream, became feasible with the advent of VLSI, and was closely associated with AI research in the United States and Europe. Fifth Generation planners with a more public orientation saw that a consensus could be built around "thinking" machines as long-range remedies for low white-collar productivity, poor performance in software development, and other domestic social and economic problems. Thus the rhetoric of AI became tied to a set of ambitious social goals that were somehow to be reached through a new kind of computer power. The Institute for New Generation Computer Technology (ICOT), headquarters for the Fifth Generation project, is indeed building "inference engines," "knowledge processors," and other hardware bearing strong-AI labels, but ICOT officials take pains to stress that AI is not their ultimate target. The Japanese aim was, and remains, not so much to develop computers that will justify strong-AI theory as to create "machines for the 1990s" that will cure Japan's perennial productivity ills.

Feigenbaum and McCorduck miss this important point because they are too anxious to extol Japanese indifference to the controversy that has been swirling around AI research in the West for more than twenty years. They do not realize that Japanese aggressiveness stems more from ignorance than understanding. Almost entirely absent from the Japanese literature is any mention of the debate on AI theory, in which one side (e.g., Raphael 1976, Bogen 1977, etc.) hails AI as the natural "next step" in computer science while the other (e.g., Dreyfus 1979, Searle 1980, etc.) relentlessly attacks its theoretical foundations. Not many Japanese have tried to see AI within the broader context of cognitive science (as have Hunt [1982] and Gardner [1985]) or have considered the social responsibilities of AI researchers (as have Weizenbaum [1976] and the Dreyfus brothers [1986]). Fewer still look at AI from a historical or philosophical perspective (Barrett 1986, Roszak 1986). Many of the leading lights of AI research in the United States are now trying to distance themselves from exaggerated strong-AI claims (see, e.g., McDermott et al. 1985), but one would never guess this from recent Japanese books on AI (e.g., Yokoi 1985, Nagao 1986), which barely touch on the deep questions about the nature of ideas and knowledge that strong-AI theory raises.

Because of their lack of interest in these issues, Japanese generally describe the significance of the Fifth Generation project for the nation in rather vague, futuristic terms. Like fish in an aquarium, they do not notice the water so obvious to an outside observer. Whether it is translating by machine, boosting white-collar productivity, writing software automatically, or providing the social services of the future, one common theme runs through the list of things that Fifth Generation machines are supposed to do: the Japanese want to be able to use their own language (actually, not *language* but *script*) on computers with complete freedom.

Contrary to what Feigenbaum and McCorduck think, Japanese indifference to the ramifications of AI is not just a "harmless cultural quirk." It is closely related to the larger indifference Japanese show toward the effects of their writing system on their daily lives. This blind spot makes it hard for them to see that their accustomed mode of writing is itself the cause of their problems in software development and low white-collar productivity, and predisposes them to accept the epistemology of strong AI uncritically. On a superficial level, they take the complexities of the writing system for granted, confuse language and writing, and assume that the maintenance of Japanese culture depends on the maintenance of the orthographic status quo. On a deeper level, they are conditioned by the study of Chinese characters and their myriad usages to look favorably on the idea that all knowledge is reducible to a finite number of symbols and formal rules governing their manipulation. (Of course, there is emotional attachment to habits acquired through many years of practice—but it is easy to make too much of this.) It is because most Japanese see their writing system as an immutable fixture of Japanese culture rather than as an evolving piece of technology that they have so willingly embraced the idea of "intelligent" machinery.

A few AI apologists have recognized that the handling of Chinese and Japanese characters is an acid test of strong-AI claims (e.g., Hofstadter 1979: 602). Feigenbaum and McCorduck are headed in the right direction when they talk about the Fifth Generation emphasis on "intelligent interfaces—the ability the machines will have to listen, see, understand, and reply to human users" (118), but the closest they come to addressing the script problem is in knocking down the strawman of "Japanese is an illogical language" (141–142). The issue for the Japanese, however, is not whether there is anything in Japanese culture that will prevent the success of the Fifth Generation project, but rather whether science will make it possible for them to use computers with the same freedom and ease enjoyed by those who have a simple alphabetic script. Will Artificial Intelligence be the *deus ex machina* that rescues the Japanese writing system?

To repeat, few Japanese have consciously read the problem through to this point. Indeed, Japanese computer manufacturers, who are doing a brisk domestic business in office automation equipment, don't believe that there is any script problem at all. As long as consumers buy, they would ask rhetorically, where's the problem? But this is the wrong question. "The question is not whether Japanese script can be handled *at all* on computers—no one ever doubted that—but whether it can be handled in a way comparable in cost and efficiency to what would suffice if alphabetic writing were used instead" (Unger 1984a: 240–241). This may seem to smack of cultural imperialism—why should the Japanese compromise their traditions for the sake of computers?—but it is useless to pretend that all human scripts are equally well suited to digital computing.

In a broad sense, over the centuries, Japanese script has "worked." Japanese culture has not flourished *because of* the complexities of its

writing system, but it has undeniably flourished in spite of them. This
has been possible because of certain human cognitive capacities that
come into play in the traditional usage of Chinese characters. Human
beings learn to live with this large, open-ended set of characters, with
their countless variations, even though they do so in, by computer
standards, highly unsystematic and unreliable ways. People are adept
at perceiving contexts and guessing at the meaning of unfamiliar characters without the guidance of hard and fast rules; they easily tolerate
ambiguity in both language and writing, and usually have to exercise
some conscious effort to see an ambiguity as a specific violation of a
precise rule of usage. Significantly, these are just the kinds of things
that no one has programmed a computer to do, and which may not be
programmable even in principle. It is especially ironic that Japan, of
all countries, should be in the vanguard of strong AI, for Japanese writing, as a living system that has evolved over centuries to meet the
needs of human communication, is a compelling piece of evidence that
challenges the central dogma of strong-AI theory: that intelligence is
nothing but formal symbol manipulation. Japanese writing is not
defective in any sense per se, but the computer has placed it in a technological environment in which it must grow and change. In short, the
issue is one of technological adaptation, not cultural assimilation.

If this is so obvious, why haven't the Japanese seen it themselves?
Some have. As early as 1972, the well-known anthropologist Umesao
Tadao, in a remarkably prescient article, discussed many of the problems of the writing system that make it ill-suited for use on computers.
But why not the engineers, academics, and bureaucrats who came up
with the Fifth Generation concept? It is tempting to answer this question by pointing to the obsessive concern with language and education
that characterizes so much of modern Japanese life, but here again, as
when assessing the importance of emotional attachments to traditional
script, one must be cautious. The connection between the difficulties
of the Japanese writing system and Japan's peculiar enthusiasm for AI
is not a simple cause-and-effect relationship, but a complex series of
links in which cultural blind spots play a major role. We must try to
identify the specific points at which Japanese ideas about writing, education, knowledge, language, and information meet and interact.

It is a major contention of this book that the experience of learning
the Japanese writing system itself is largely responsible for the content
and maintenance of many of the ideas about cultural "uniqueness"
that are circulating in Japan today. No elaborate psychosocial theories
are needed to explain this. It is only necessary to recognize that the

educational reforms introduced during the Occupation have altered the demographics of literacy in Japan, the demands it places on the individual, and its social meaning. Limited script reforms were undertaken around the same time, but the combined effect of educational and script reforms was actually to increase rather than reduce the burden of literacy for the average Japanese. As if overnight, the intellectual demands once placed on a small, elite group of students now became the norm for all Japanese youth. The full weight of the traditional writing system previously had been borne only by a minority within a small minority—the less talented sons of the well-to-do who had access to the higher schools and universities because of their families' social standing. (Young men of humbler origins who broke into the educational elite *had* to be intellectually outstanding; and education for women beyond the elementary level was generally not approved of.) Today, more than 90 percent of all Japanese students, regardless of economic background or sex, go on to some sort of high school (Rohlen 1983: 82), where the curriculum is designed on the assumption that, already in junior high, they have mastered at least the 1,945 Chinese characters prescribed by the Ministry of Education. Small wonder that the average Japanese, though often better educated than his American counterpart in science and mathematics, should have such a hard time seeing that writing is merely a reflection of spoken language. His father or grandfather likely saw nothing especially unfair in the prewar policy of forcing Asians under Imperial control to learn Japanese, yet he himself may feel bewildered upon meeting a foreigner who, after only a few years of study, can speak Japanese fluently.

That the average Japanese can rattle off a half dozen reasons for the absolute necessity of using Chinese characters on computers is neither a refutation of the plain fact that spoken language exists independently of writing nor evidence of deepseated, unchangeable cultural forces. The simple truth is that computer technology and the current Japanese writing system are not fully compatible; that very modest innovations in orthography for purposes of data processing could correct the situation without any sacrifice of cultural identity; and that waiting for machine intelligence to come to the rescue is a policy of questionable wisdom. These three propositions are respectively the principal themes of Parts I, II, and III of this book.

Each part is divided into two chapters. Chapters 1 through 3 deal primarily with the writing system: what it is, how it affects the writing-related aspects of daily life, and where resistance to reforming it comes from. Chapters 4 through 6 shift the focus to AI: why computers cannot solve the problems of Japanese script, how the Japanese are struggling to avoid a script-reform compromise in data processing, and what role the Fifth Generation is playing in this losing battle. The chapters are arranged for the convenience of readers who have no familiarity with the Japanese language. Those who know Japanese may prefer to start with Part III; they may find it too brief and opinionated but will find supporting arguments in earlier pages, particularly Chapters 2 and 4. If you begin with Chapter 1, be patient: to judge for yourself whether the author's indictment of the Fifth Generation concept in Chapter 6 is valid, the background information in the preceding five chapters is essential.

One final word: Although this book is critical of the Fifth Generation project, its object is not to censure Japan for undertaking it, but to explain how, in the case of Japan, it was possible for the cockeyed optimism of strong AI to subvert rational judgment. The Japanese have no monopoly on woolly thinking. If we cannot see how covert cultural biases interfere with the advance of presumably objective science in another, markedly different culture, how can we hope to diagnose our own failings?

I

LINGUISTICS
AND
ORTHOGRAPHY

1

LINGUISTICS
AND
ORTHOGRAPHY

1

Current Writing Practice in Japan

Strictly speaking, digital computers are just arithmetic machines. They are, as engineers are fond of reminding us, profoundly stupid. This is compensated for by the fact that they are designed to execute millions of elementary calculations at blinding speed and keep track of them flawlessly. What lends computers an aura of intelligence is that we, their designers and users, can coordinate these myriad calculations both hierarchically and over time into complex structures, which we are free to interpret as meaningful symbols far removed from the abstract dance of billions of electronic impulses. Meaning originates in us, and we are totally responsible for what the machine does, not just at the level of the circuitry, but at all higher levels as well. Thus, human language and the techniques of writing must occupy a central position in any discussion of our growing dependence on computers in nearly every aspect of daily life.

Since we are interested in Japan's Fifth Generation project, we have to look at the Japanese language.

Nothing contributes more to the popular impression that Japanese is an exotic language of unapproachable difficulty than the complex appearance of Japanese script. Japanese is certainly more difficult to learn for the ordinary native speaker of English than languages such as Spanish or German, but this is largely due to the unfamiliarity of grammatical distinctions and cultural assumptions in Japanese that, in themselves, are not hard to understand. Native speakers of Korean find that spoken Japanese is a cinch on both counts, although they may have a bit of trouble with pronunciation. In fact, Japanese is not too hard to pronounce compared to languages the world round, makes use of only a few, highly regular inflectional paradigms, and has a syntax that, though radically different from that of most European languages, is simple when compared with the grammars of the few that are similar (e.g., Hungarian, Finnish). In the final analysis, it is the customary

17

method of writing Japanese that is primarily responsible for its formidable reputation, and many Japanese themselves acknowledge this
point. The well-known linguist Kindaichi Haruhiko put it this way:

> But actually, when I talk about the "difficulty of Japanese" in the true
> sense of that expression, I do not have in mind this "difficulty in teach-
> ing the Japanese language to foreigners." In Europe it is an accepted fact
> that the Basque language is a difficult language. . . . [T]he Basque lan-
> guage is very much isolated from the other European languages. This is
> why Basque is difficult for Europeans. In other words, we really ought to
> discount the actual difficulty of Basque. And if Japanese were difficult
> only in the same way that Basque is difficult, in other words, if its diffi-
> culty consisted only in the fact that it is difficult for foreigners, then we
> could not really claim that Japanese is truly a difficult language. But the
> fact of the matter is that the difficulty of Japanese is not simply some-
> thing involved with the difficulties that foreigners have learning our lan-
> guage. Japanese is quite equally as difficult for the Japanese themselves
> to learn. In Europe, school children spend different periods of time mas-
> tering their native languages. In Italy only two years, and in Germany
> only three years are needed for this purpose. Even in England, where the
> most time is spent on this, a child masters reading and writing in five
> years. But in Japan, even after six years in elementary school and three
> years in middle school, a student still cannot read a newspaper satisfac-
> torily. And we all agree that even when a student has graduated from
> high school, he or she will not be able to write Japanese prose that cor-
> rectly makes use of the phonetic syllabaries and Chinese characters.
> (Kindaichi 1957: 4–5 as translated in Miller 1982: 176–177; for another
> rendition, see Kindaichi 1978: 22–23)

The truth is, of course, that the Japanese *language,* that is, speech,
is no more (or less) difficult in absolute terms than any other human
language. Indeed, an *absolute* scale of language difficulty is a logical
impossibility: every human being, unless handicapped, successfully
learns his or her mother tongue, no matter what it may be. The only
reason that Kindaichi and other Japanese think that Japanese is excep-
tionally hard is because they tacitly assume that learning how to write
a language is the same thing as learning the language itself. As millions
of blind persons can testify, this is not so. Get rid of this false premise,
and the whole argument falls apart.

Writing is merely an imperfect reflection of what has been or might
have been said. Once invented, it becomes encrusted with conventions
and acquires a lore of its own, but it never transcends its ultimate
dependence on the living, ever-changing communal fabric of (spoken)

language. A written tradition may, so to speak, embroider and strengthen the fabric, but it is not part of the warp and weft itself. Perhaps the most striking proof of this is the scientific reconstruction, through careful analysis of extant languages and dialects, of the linguistic prehistory of parts of the world, such as North America and the Pacific, in which writing was virtually nonexistent until modern times. But the primacy of speech is just as valid when we look at language in the here-and-now as when we study it historically.[1] As we shall see, the Japanese failure to acknowledge the paramount importance of speech in language, exemplified by Kindaichi's comments, lies at the heart of Japan's computer dilemma.

Kana and Romanization

The phonetic syllabaries to which Kindaichi refers are sets of letters called *kana*. Two phonetically equivalent but graphically distinct sets, *hiragana* and *katakana,* are used in modern Japanese writing, together with hundreds of Chinese characters, or *kanji,* in accordance with rules (some obligatory, some optional) that prescribe when each sort of character is to be used. These complications contribute little or nothing to the accuracy or content of Japanese writing, and in telegrams and much computer work it is standard practice to use only katakana or roman letters *(rômaji).*[2]

From a computational viewpoint, the kanji (Chinese characters) are the problem, but we cannot evaluate the design of Japanese-language computer systems intelligently without understanding the kana syllabaries. This in turn requires some knowledge of the sound structure, or phonology, of Japanese. A clear understanding of how rômaji, kana, and the Japanese sound system are related is essential for three reasons. First, rômaji and kana are the basis for almost all Japanese computer input. The discussion of Japanese typing in Part III requires knowing something about both these techniques of writing. Second, the air must be cleared of any idea that only kana accurately reflect the pronunciation of Japanese, or that Japanese simply cannot be written with roman letters alone. Claims of this kind can be found even in language textbooks and purportedly scientific papers but are totally groundless. Finally, and most important, we need to put some flesh on the bones of the assertion that, in Japan as elsewhere, writing is only a secondary manifestation of language. For this purpose, the kind of romanization used in this and many other English books on Japan provides the easiest point of departure.

Hepburn Romanization

One well-known anthology of Japanese literature offers the reader the following few lines of advice on the reading of Japanese names:

> The pronunciation of Japanese in transcription is very simple. The consonants are pronounced as in English (with *g* always hard), the vowels as in Italian. There are no silent letters. Thus, the name Mine is pronounced "mee-nay." In general, long vowels have been indicated by macrons, but in some stories they have been omitted, as likely to seem pedanticisms. (Keene 1956: 7)

Needless to say, there is a substantial amount of detail missing from this summary. Still, it is surprisingly comprehensive. Japanese pronunciation is indeed very simple.

Japanese speech flows along with an even meter, a steady stream of pulses all more or less equal in prominence. Every vowel counts one beat; syllables contain one or two vowels (with rare exceptions), and the mixture of long and short syllables gives words and phrases a characteristic rhythm.[3] The pitch of the voice rises and falls at certain points in the stream of syllables, producing a melodic effect called, rather misleadingly, *akusento* 'accent'.[4] At any rate, only the syllables matter in most computer applications and in the kind of romanization Keene has in mind in his guide to pronunciation above. We will now describe this romanization scheme in slightly greater detail.

Table 1 shows the basic one-beat syllables or *moras* of Japanese, arranged in alphabetical order. These are the building blocks from

Table 1. Japanese Moras Arranged Alphabetically: Hepburn Romanization

a	e	i	o	u					
a	e	i	o	u	mya			myo	myu
ba	be	bi	bo	bu	na	ne	ni	no	nu
bya			byo	byu	nya			nyo	nyu
cha		chi	cho	chu	pa	pe	pi	po	pu
da	de		do		pya			pyo	pyu
				fu	ra	re	ri	ro	ru
ga	ge	gi	go	gu	rya			ryo	ryu
gya			gyo	gyu	sa	se		so	su
ha	he	hi	ho		sha		shi	sho	shu
hya			hyo	hyu	ta	te		to	
ja		ji	jo	ju					tsu
ka	ke	ki	ko	ku	wa				
kya			kyo	kyu	ya			yo	yu
ma	me	mi	mo	mu	za	ze		zo	zu

which all Japanese utterances are formed. They are supplemented by two other moras which, from the perspective of English orthography, seem to be consonants but function as vowels in the Japanese sound system. In technical notation, they are frequently written Q and N.

Q occurs only before certain moras and is more customarily romanized as a double consonant rather than with its own cover symbol; thus

$$Qk \quad Qs \quad Qsh \quad Qt \quad Qts \quad Qch \quad Qp$$

are written

$$kk \quad ss \quad ssh \quad tt \quad tts \quad tch \quad pp$$

The difference between Japanese -*kk*- and -*k*-, for example, is roughly the same as the difference you hear in English between *black card* and *placard;* Japanese -*pp*- versus -*p*- might be compared with the difference heard in English *hip pocket* and *Hippocrates*; and so on.

Like Q, N assimilates to the sound it precedes, but it can occur before any of the moras shown in Table 1 or at the end of a word. It is usually written just as *n*, with a following apostrophe whenever confusion might arise (viz., before a vowel or *y*). Thus, both *konyakku* 'cognac' and *kon'yaku* 'wedding engagement' have four moras (*ko nya k ku* and *ko n ya ku*).

A final refinement is the substitution of a single vowel with a macron (stroke) or circumflex for certain vowel combinations:

$$aa > â \qquad uu > û$$
$$ii > î \qquad ee > ê$$
$$oo > ô$$

When to use this notation and when not technically depends on etymology; writing out every vowel heard is a perfectly acceptable alternative. Since many typewriters and computers do not support diacritic marks, there is often no choice.

Table 1 plus Q, N, and circumflex give us the system of transcription set forth in 1885 by the Rômaji Association and named after James Curtis Hepburn, who adopted it in the third edition of his Japanese-English dictionary.[5] The actual sounds of Japanese are somewhat different from their nearest equivalents in Italian and English: Hepburn Romanization, like any efficient method for reducing speech to writing, merely provides symbols for the distinctive sound units (phonemes) within a particular language. It isn't concerned with phonetic variations that make no difference in meaning, and such variations can also be ignored in computer applications, except as they affect voice recognition (Chapter 5).[6] The fact that certain familiar spelling conventions happen to be followed in this particular system is not nearly as important as the fact that it provides a unique, unambiguous representation for each of the phonemes of Japanese.

Hepburn romanization is tailor-made for educated speakers of English. If Dr. Hepburn had been German, perhaps we would be writing *Chingaschi* 'east' and *Jatzu* 'eight' instead of *higashi* and *yattsu* as we do today. Letters, after all, can have any values we wish, and we are free to set up whatever special rules for interpreting combinations of letters we please. For example, we can save some ink by writing x in Table 1 everywhere the combination *sh* appears as long as we remember what x stands for. This would not add to or subtract from the number of moras shown or alter the number of basic sounds that make up those moras. What counts, in other words, are the phonemes, the elemental sounds that make up moras, syllables, and eventually words and phrases of Japanese, not the letters one happens to use to represent them.

Cabinet Romanization

There are in fact many good reasons for making certain revisions in Table 1 besides saving ink—reasons having to do with the structure of the language itself.

Japanese vocabulary can be divided into three types of words: native words *(Yamato-kotoba)*, words borrowed from Chinese or made up from Sino-Japanese roots *(kango)*, and recent loanwords from other languages *(gairaigo)*. (The second and third play a key role in Japanese word processing, so we will be using the handy terms kango and gairaigo frequently.) The moras of Table 1 suffice for native words and kango, but not for gairaigo, which may also include the italicized syllables seen in Table 2. Because they are confined to gairaigo like *pâtî* 'party' and *firipin* 'Phillipine[s]', we'll call these moras *innovative*.[7] Although some belong to new rows, they mainly fill in gaps in Table 1. Hepburn Romanization, despite its English bias, thus has the merit of providing a ready means for transcribing innovative moras.

On the other hand, innovative moras, by their very nature, are statistically infrequent. Moras like *chi* and *hi* occur thousands of times in ordinary running text before *ti* or *fi* is encountered even once. In certain practical situations, such as transmitting written messages, this can be wasteful. A better choice in these cases is the scheme shown in Table 3, which takes advantage of the fact that it is the phonemes

Table 2. Hepburn Romanization with Innovative Moras

a	e	i	o	u	mya			myo	myu
ba	be	bi	bo	bu	na	ne	ni	no	nu
bya			byo	byu	nya			nyo	nyu
cha	*che*	chi	cho	chu	pa	pe	pi	po	pu
da	de	*di*	do	*du*	pya			pyo	pyu
				dyu	ra	re	ri	ro	ru
fa	*fe*	*fi*	*fo*	fu	rya			ryo	ryu
				fyu	sa	se	*si*	so	su
ga	ge	gi	go	gu	sha	*she*	shi	sho	shu
gwa	*gwe*	*gwi*	*gwo*		ta	te	*ti*	to	*tu*
gya			gyo	gyu	tsa	tse	tsi	tso	tsu
ha	he	hi	ho						*tyu*
hya			hyo	hyu	*va*	*ve*	*vi*	*vu*	*vo*
ja	*je*	ji	jo	ju	wa	*we*	*wi*	*wo*	
ka	ke	ki	ko	ku	ya	*ye*		yo	yu
kwa	*kwe*	*kwi*	*kwo*		za	ze	*zi*	zo	zu
kya			kyo	kyu					
ma	me	mi	mo	mu					

(sounds) of the language that count, not the letters used to represent them.

A comparison of Tables 1 and 3 (the revised moras are italicized in Table 3) shows that the words *fuji* 'wisteria' and *chashitsu* 'tearoom' in Hepburn Romanization will become *huzi* and *tyasitu* in the new system. This may seem odd to a person who knows only English or

Table 3. Japanese Moras Revised: Cabinet Romanization

a	e	i	o	u	mya			myo	myu
ba	be	bi	bo	bu	na	ne	ni	no	nu
bya			byo	byu	nya			nyo	nyu
tya		*ti*	tyo	*tyu*	pa	pe	pi	po	pu
da	de		do		pya			pyo	pyu
				hu	ra	re	ri	ro	ru
ga	ge	gi	go	gu	rya			ryo	ryu
gya			gyo	gyu	sa	se		so	su
ha	he	hi	ho		*sya*		*si*	*syo*	*syu*
hya			hyo	hyu	ta	te		to	
{ *dya*		*di*	*dyo*	*dyu* }					*tu*
{ *zya*		*zi*	*zyo*	*zyu* }	wa				
ka	ke	ki	ko	ku	ya			yo	yu
kya			kyo	kyu					{ *du*
ma	me	mi	mo	mu	za	ze		zo	zu }

believes that the English values of the consonants are somehow innate. All that really matters, however, is that the phonetic values of the moras can be unambiguously read off from their phonemic representations, and that the letters used to represent phonemes are reasonably easy to remember. The system in Table 3 meets both these conditions for native and Chinese-derived words, the two high-frequency strata of the vocabulary.[8]

The system shown in Table 3 is, strictly speaking, the *Nippon-shiki* or 'Japanese-style' system devised by the physicist Tanakadate Aikitsu in 1885 (the same year as Hepburn). It is the forerunner of the *kunrei-shiki* system, so called because it was declared the official Japanese standard by Cabinet Order *(kunrei)* on 21 September 1937, and again on 9 December 1954; it was scheduled for adoption by the International Standards Organization (ISO) in 1986. The only major difference between the system shown in Table 3 and Cabinet Romanization is that Table 3 has both *di* and *zi* for Cabinet *zi* (Hepburn *ji*), *du* and *zu* for Cabinet (and Hepburn) *zu*, etc. These represent phonemic distinctions that have been lost in modern standard Japanese, but are sometimes maintained in kana spellings.

Besides requiring fewer letters to write Japanese, Cabinet Romanization has other important advantages. For example, it simplifies the description of the structure of the verb and adjective conjugations and the rules governing the voicing of consonants (explained presently), which apply in the formation of many compound expressions. In addition, it makes it possible to rearrange the moras into the pattern shown in Table 4, which brings out the high degree of symmetry in the moras used to form both native Japanese words and kango. For our purposes, this is the key point.

Hiragana and Katakana

Table 4 is just a step away from the kana. All we need to do is rearrange the alphabetized rows (common initial consonants) and columns (common final vowels) of Table 4 to form Table 5.[9] Figure 1 shows the left half of Table 5 in hiragana and Figure 2 shows the same array of moras in the corresponding katakana.

Kana are simply kanji (Chinese characters) or parts of kanji that have been changed in shape in the course of the development of the Japanese writing system. Throughout this evolutionary process, kanji have served a multitude of functions; the representation of the sounds of Japanese, mora by mora, is one of these functions.

Table 4. Revised Moras Arranged Alphabetically

a	e	i	o	u	nya			nyo	nyu
ba	be	bi	bo	bu	pa	pe	pi	po	pu
bya			byo	byu	pya			pyo	pyu
da	de	di	do	du	ra	re	ri	ro	ru
dya			dyo	dyu	rya			ryo	ryu
ga	ge	gi	go	gu	sa	se	si	so	su
gya			gyo	gyu	sya			syo	syu
ha	he	hi	ho	hu	ta	te	ti	to	tu
hya			hyo	hyu	tya			tyo	tyu
ka	ke	ki	ko	ku	wa				
kya			kyo	kyu	ya			yo	yu
ma	me	mi	mo	mu	za	ze	zi	zo	zu
mya			myo	myu	zya			zyo	zyu
na	ne	ni	no	nu					

In the earliest period of Japanese writing, any kanji could in principle, if not in practice, be used in this way regardless of its other possible uses; as the writing system matured, it became customary to write kanji so used in a reduced form that set them off visually from other kanji in the same text. This visual differentiation of kana from kanji, a classic case of form following function, greatly facilitated the reading and writing of Japanese. Two styles developed, one cursive (hiragana), and the other angular (katakana). Within each set, several alternative

Table 5. Revised Moras Arranged in Customary Order

a	i	u	e	o			
ka	ki	ku	ke	ko	kya	kyu	kyo
ga	gi	gu	ge	go	gya	gyu	gyo
sa	si	su	se	so	sya	syu	syo
za	zi	zu	ze	zo	zya	zyu	zyo
ta	ti	tu	te	to	tya	tyu	tyo
da	di	du	de	do	dya	dyu	dyo
na	ni	nu	ne	no	nya	nyu	nyo
ha	hi	hu	he	ho	hya	hyu	hyo
ba	bi	bu	be	bo	bya	byu	byo
pa	pi	pu	pe	po	pya	pyu	pyo
ma	mi	mu	me	mo	mya	myu	myo
ya		yu		yo			
ra	ri	ru	re	ro	rya	ryu	ryo
wa							

あいうえお	アイウエオ
かきくけこ	カキクケコ
がぎぐげご	ガギグゲゴ
さしすせそ	サシスセソ
ざじずぜぞ	ザジズゼゾ
たちってと	タチツテト
だぢづでど	ダヂヅデド
なにぬねの	ナニヌネノ
はひふへほ	ハヒフへホ
ばびぶべぼ	バビブベボ
ぱぴぷぺぽ	パピプペポ
まみむめも	マミムメモ
や　ゆ　よ	ヤ　ユ　ヨ
らりるれろ	ラリルレロ
わ	ワ

Figure 1 Hiragana	**Figure 2** Katakana

forms coexisted for each mora; over time, many alternatives gradually fell into disuse, but the standardization of one hiragana and one kata-kana for each mora of the language did not occur until this century.

Katakana, the angular variety, were originally used in marginal notes and traditionally associated with men's writing. Now they serve as the italics of Japanese script, being used to set off foreign words (other than those from Chinese), for emphasis, for writing telegrams, and for other special purposes. Hiragana, the cursive kana in which most of the classics by Japanese women, such as *The Tale of Genji*, were written, are used in all other situations that call for kana.

Besides the basic kana shapes shown in Figures 1 and 2, there are four additional elements in each of the two syllabaries. They represent the mora *N*

(hiragana ん   katakana ン)

and the archaic moras *wi, we,* and *wo*

(hiragana ゐ, ゑ, を   katakana ヰ, ヱ, ヲ) .

The three moras *wi, we,* and *wo* have merged with *i, e,* and *o* in modern speech, but the symbols for *wo* have been retained to write the common postposition *o.* (English has *pre*positions, Japanese has *post*-positions.) Thus, there are altogether forty-eight basic hiragana and katakana shapes.

Notice the diacritic sign in Figures 1 and 2 that resembles a double quotation mark. This is called *dakuten* or *nigori* and is used to indicate that the initial consonant of a mora is voiced. In Hepburn Romanization:

Unmarked	*Marked*
k	g
s ⎫	
ts ⎭	z
t	d
ch ⎫	
sh ⎭	j
h	b[10]

(Observe, by the way, how using Cabinet Romanization would simplify this chart: *ts, ch, sh,* and *j* would not have to be treated as special cases.) As noted earlier, the voicing of consonants *(rendaku)* frequently accompanies the formation of compound expressions in the language. Another diacritic, a small circle called *handakuten* resembling a degree sign, changes an initial *h* into a *p.*

Twelve kana also have small-size versions used for special purposes. To write the moras with -*y*-, shown in the right half of Table 5, small versions of the kana for *ya, yu,* and *yo* are used. Thus, *kiya* (two moras) and *kya* (one mora) both require two kana and differ only in the size of the second one. Double consonants are handled with a similar device: a small version of the kana for *tsu* is placed before the following mora. In other words, "small *tsu*" stands for *Q.* Eight other "small kana" are used less often: three (*wa, ke,* and *ka*) for archaic spellings, and five (*a, i, u, e,* and *o*) for innovative moras.

In typography, kana with and without diacritics are usually treated as completely different characters. As a consequence, a complete hiragana or katakana font contains more than eighty distinct characters. One would expect the rules that govern the use of this vast array of symbols to be simple, and in the current orthography, they are. Older kana usage, however, involved a number of arbitrary rules, not unlike those of English spelling. Words were written not as they sounded in modern Japanese but as they had been pronounced roughly eight or nine centuries earlier. The official position on older kana usage *(kyû-kanazukai)* has recently changed—we will take this up in Chapter 3—but it is enough to note the few vestiges of it that survive in current writing practice:

1. In addition to the postposition *o* (written *wo*) already mentioned, the postpositions *wa* and *e* conventionally are written *ha* and *he*.

2. In modern standard Japanese, the vowel sequences *ei* and *ou* sound the same as the "long vowels" *ê* and *ô*. In all but a handful of cases, however, *ê* and *ô* are rendered *-ei* and *-ou* in hiragana, not *-ee* and *-oo* as one would expect. (With katakana, a dash-like symbol, often called *bô* 'a stick', is used to indicate prolongation of the vowel of the preceding mora for one beat.)

3. Finally, the *di ≠ zi* and *du ≠ zu* distinctions, abandoned in Cabinet Romanization but not in its precursor, Nippon-shiki, are often preserved in kana spellings.

What does all this have to do with computers? As we will see, the large number of kana, the constant intermixing of katakana and hiragana in the same texts, the differences in hiragana and katakana usage, the etymological conventions of kana spelling, and the complications created by new vocabulary—all these contribute to the complexity of Japanese word processing. All this even before we get to kanji! Furthermore, as we will see later, kana have, compared with rômaji, some technical disadvantages for data processing. It is therefore important to see that rômaji and kana orthography both adhere to the phonemic principle. The only difference is the level at which one defines the units of speech represented: distinct vowels and consonants, or moras. One can argue from tradition for the use of kana on computers, but any claim that they provide a better or more accurate representation of Japanese speech is completely without merit.

Page Layout

In practice, kana are rarely used by themselves; usually they are mixed with kanji. Writing that uses this prescribed blend of kanji and kana is called *kanji kanamajiribun* in Japanese. In this style, as already remarked, katakana are used for emphasized words and words borrowed from foreign languages (unless customarily written with kanji in those languages). A vast number of words borrowed from Chinese or made up in Japan on the Chinese model (kango), as well as Chinese and Korean proper names, are written with kanji. Kanji are also used frequently to write all or part of many native words: proper and common nouns, and the first few syllables of many verbs, adjectives, and some adverbs. Hiragana take care of everything else: most adverbs, postpositions, verb and adjective endings, and those words or word-fragments for which the writer elects not to use the prescribed kanji—in many cases, it is a free choice. Before looking at the function of kanji in detail, we should consider some of the major characteristics of kanji kanamajiribun that have an impact on computer applications.

Virtually all government, commercial, and school writing submitted for publication or formal evaluation is prepared on manuscript sheets called *genkô yôshi*, which look something like pieces of wide-ruled graph paper. Plain blank paper is used too, but writing on genkô yôshi sets the standard of neatness in Japan. Writing is done within a large central grid marked off in alternating wide and narrow strips, with perpendicular lines dividing the wide strips into square cells of equal size. The typical sheet contains twenty strips of twenty cells: a total of four hundred cells. When setting a target length for a document, one asks for a certain number of 400-character pages; where an American might specify five hundred words, a Japanese would ask for, say, twelve hundred characters. Each kana, punctuation mark, and kanji (with a few exceptions) occupies one cell; spaces are not used except for paragraph indenting and in tabular formats. The absence of visible boundaries between words is tolerable because of the visual contrast between kanji and kana and the different roles they play in the orthography. As we will see later, this nonuse of spaces has had some interesting effects on the development of Japanese word-processing software. (There are rules for using spaces in braille texts, international telegrams, and other documents, but most Japanese are ignorant of them.)

Although spaces are not used as word delimiters, high-quality printing does use variable spacing to justify lines of type containing unequal numbers of characters. Such lines are sometimes necessary in order to avoid unattractive or confusing breaks between paragraphs and pages, to accommodate marginal notations (explained hereafter), to format lists (e.g., Chapter 3, p. 54), and so forth. The basic principle, however, is that strings of Japanese characters can be broken whenever the end of a line is reached. Since most Japanese word processors treat strings of alphanumerics the same way as strings of kanji and kana, the user must take special care to make sure that foreign words and phrases embedded in a Japanese text are properly hypenated and do not result in short lines. Especially when working with business and technical documents, in which Japanese and Western scripts must frequently be mixed, this can be a considerable annoyance.

Direction of Writing

Perhaps the best-known characteristic of Japanese script is that it can be written either like English, left to right in rows spanning the page from top to bottom, or in the traditional Chinese manner, top to bottom in columns spanning the page from right to left.[11] Figures 3 and 4 show ten sample sentences handwritten in horizontal and vertical format respectively. As the number of documents referring to interna-

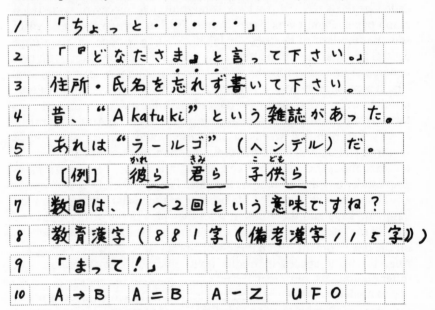

Figure 3 Horizontal Writing on Genkô Yôshi

tional and scientific matters increases, the Western format is gaining acceptance. Just imagine reading a report chock full of mathematical formulas or a textbook of English and being forced to cock your head to the right (or turn the page to the left) every time you hit an example! And the switch from vertical writing *(tategaki)* to horizontal *(yoko-gaki)* is not simply a matter of stringing out characters in a different direction. The "small kana" mentioned earlier are written in the right-hand half of their cells in vertical style but in the lower half in horizontal, often with a bit less space than usual after the preceding char-

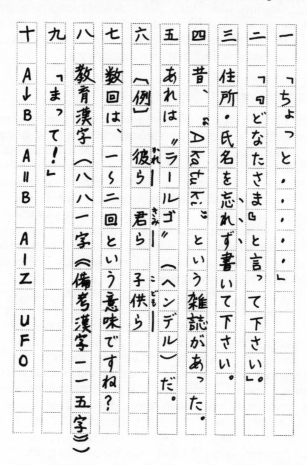

Figure 4 Vertical Writing on Genkô Yôshi

acter. (See lines 1, 2, 4, and 9 in Figures 3 and 4 for examples.) The bô (long-vowel marker) of katakana (cell 8, line 5) is rotated ninety degrees. Punctuation marks are particularly troublesome, as we will see presently, and there is even one nonpunctuation symbol (a repetition mark for a pair of hiragana) that can be used only in tategaki.

Switching from one style to the other is trivial for people working with pen and paper, but high-quality output by machine is another matter. In commercial printing, for example, tategaki and yokogaki type fonts are not generally interchangeable: tategaki fonts are purposely made slightly wider than high, yokogaki fonts, slightly higher than wide, to compensate for the optical illusion created by the bar-like lines of text on the page. Such typographical niceties have considerable cost implications for computer applications.

Punctuation, Numerals, Foreign Letters

Traditional Chinese writing does not use punctuation. Punctuation in Japanese is a relatively recent development (Twine 1984) and tends to be rather inconsistent. As one recent text for foreign students frankly admits, "There are no compulsory and uniform rules for usage and nomenclature of the various punctuation marks" (Hadamitzky & Spahn 1981: 40). "Western marks in yokogaki, Japanese marks in tategaki" is, at best, a crude rule of thumb. Especially in scientific and technical writing, which must often include alphanumeric and mathematical symbols, the variations in usage seem endless. There are basically four sources of possible confusion. (All examples are in Figures 3 and 4; line references refer to both figures.)

Competing Forms. There are both Japanese and Western versions of periods and commas, but one system sometimes lacks a counterpart in the other. Even when there is a counterpart, it is not always used. As the headings in Figures 3 and 4 show, in horizontal writing, arabic numerals are the norm; commas and decimal points within them are always Western-style even if other commas and periods in the main text are not. In vertical writing, it is more common to use Chinese numerals; however, in many cases, proper Sino-Japanese forms, which use kanji to indicate powers of 10, are not employed. Instead, one finds only the kanji for 1 through 9 and a special character (a plain circle) for 0, with Japanese-style commas marking off every third digit. The decimal point in this method is the Japanese *nakaten* (a centered dot), otherwise used as a separator like the Western slash (Figure 4, line 3, counting from the right) or to form ellipsis marks (line 1). All this violates normal Sino-Japanese counting practice, which has no zero, marks off every *fourth* place of large numbers, and uses explicit expressions for tenths, hundredths, and so on.

Repositioning. Periods, commas, and Western-style quotation marks, like the small kana, are positioned within their cells depending on whether the text runs vertically or horizontally (e.g., lines 4 and 5). Most interlinear notations appear to the right of the main line of characters in vertical format and above it in horizontal; this includes *furigana* (described later) and *wakiten*, dot-like marks placed next to each character in an emphasized passage (line 3). On the other hand, *wakisen*, a continuous line down the right edge of a column of characters, becomes underscoring in horizontal format (line 6).

Rotation. Japanese primary and secondary quotation marks (lines 1, 2, and 9) must be rotated ninety degrees to the left for horizontal text, like the long-vowel marker in katakana; parentheses and brackets (lines 4, 6, and 8) are also given a quarter turn to the right in tategaki, but the treatment of other non-Japanese characters varies widely: whole words and numbers are generally rotated to the right (lines 4 and 8), but isolated characters and acronyms are often left "upright" even if accompanying marks are rotated (line 10).

Different Shapes. Under repositioning and rotation, some punctuation marks also change in form. This is the case with wakiten and the *namigata*, a wavy mark roughly shaped like an N in horizontal style and like an S in vertical—notice the difference in orientation (cell 8, line 7). Western-style quotation marks for vertical text are often different in design from their standard forms (cf. lines 4 and 5).

It goes without saying that any computer system that accommodates all these intricacies, let alone a couple of thousand Chinese characters, can be tricky to operate. To give just one example, many word processors on the market today produce Japanese-style commas and periods by default in tategaki, Western-style in yokogaki; if you want to override the default, you must shift the period and comma keys. For the many people who prefer Japanese-style commas and periods in all kinds of text, this constant shifting significantly impairs input speed. Those who are willing to go along with the defaults, however, are not home free: some systems have a feature for reformatting yokogaki text as tategaki, and vice versa, but since both Japanese- and Western-style periods and commas can legitimately occur in both styles, they typically do not adjust the periods and commas.

Furigana

As we will see shortly, readers of Japanese may not always know exactly what words or word-fragments a writer intended to represent with a particular kanji. To eliminate doubt, the writer can use the narrow bands that separate the main lines of genkô yôshi for notations in small-sized kana (e.g., Figures 3 and 4, line 6). To a foreigner, these "side kana," known collectively as furigana, look a bit like the super- and subscripts of mathematical notation and, just like mathematical copy (often called penalty copy by printers), they can be troublesome. Only a few Japanese word processors provide a means for handling them.

In days gone by, furigana were used so extensively that some authorities regarded them as an integral part of kanji kanamajiribun. In 1922, for example, the newspaper *Tôkyô Nichinichi Shinbun* used 8,011 kanji-plus-furigana combinations, more than half of its total inventory of 14,531 kanji characters (Scharschmidt 1924: 189).[12] As late as 1947, some newspapers were still using furigana (Yamagiwa 1948), but today they no longer leave interlinear margins for furigana—when a clarifying note is needed, it is inserted in parentheses following the problematic kanji. In other types of publications, furigana survive. In fact, fanciful extensions of the furigana concept can even be found. Some recent authors throw in foreign expressions in roman letters and supply furigana giving the translation in Japanese. Then there is the complete inversion of the traditional relationship between notes and text: a foreign phrase, in katakana or roman, with a notation in undersized *kanji* on the side! Such conceits, easily executed on manuscript paper, must give Japanese printers nightmares. They are completely beyond the power of today's popular Japanese word processors, only the most advanced of which can handle ordinary furigana.

Besides complicating Japanese typography, the use of furigana has many important sociolinguistic implications. As we will see later, advocates of script reform have often *opposed* the free use of furigana; it may seem perverse for people concerned with improving mass literacy to want to ban reading aids that reduce the need to memorize kanji and their many usages, but from a Japanese perspective, it's quite logical. (Without furigana, authors who use obscure kanji have nothing to fall back on.) For now, it is enough to meditate on Sir George Sansom's observation concerning the explication of kanji by means of furigana:

One hesitates for an epithet to describe a system of writing which is so complex that it needs the aid of another system to explain it. There is no doubt that it provides for some a fascinating field of study, but as a practical instrument it is surely without inferiors. (Sansom 1928: 44)

Kanji

Sansom's words are excellent food for thought, but unfortunately, they also suggest, by contrasting two "systems," that Japanese can be written exclusively with kanji as easily as with kana. This is false, at least as far as the contemporary language is concerned. Previously, it is true, much official and educated writing in Japan took the overt form of classical Chinese—that is, kanji with no intervening kana. The reader was expected to know the rules for permuting kanji, glossing them with the appropriate readings, and supplying the necessary grammatical endings so that the whole text could be construed as Japanese. Special punctuation to guide the reader was sometimes supplied, but even with these aids, the ability to read such pseudo-Chinese, called *kanbun,* was a skill attained only by those who received a superior education.[13]

Although some fossilized kanbun phrases can be found in modern literary Japanese, kanji do not constitute an autonomous system for writing the language. There are stretches of Japanese that happen not to include kana, but in general kana cannot be avoided. In fact, all Japanese sentences can in principle be written entirely in kana.[14] The use of kanji is strictly conventional: they are customary substitutes for certain strings of kana under certain conditions. The string of kana replaced by a kanji in a particular instance is called its *reading.* Kanji readings may but do not necessarily correspond to actual words of Japanese. From a strictly logical, nonhistorical standpoint, such as a computer programmer might take, kanji are just a burdensome collection of visual abbreviations.

Regrettably, most people are not so logical. They think that kana are "phonetic" characters, while kanji are "ideographs," or to put it a bit more dramatically, that kana stand for meaningless sounds, while kanji stand for soundless meanings. Nothing could be further from the truth.

The concept of the ideograph has a long but far from venerable history. It "took hold as part of the chinoiserie fad among Western intellectuals that was stimulated by the generally highly laudatory writings of Catholic missionaries from the sixteenth to the eighteenth centuries" (DeFrancis 1984b: 133). The word "ideographic" itself originated with Champollion, who ironically was able to decipher Egyptian hieroglyphics only when he gave up the hypothesis that they were ideographs and started looking at them as phonetic letters (DeFrancis 1984b: 135–136). The key fault in the concept of "ideograph" is that it fails to distinguish between form and function. True writing is, by definition, the representation of speech. The use of pictures as mere tokens for real things does not deserve to be called writing any more than the communicative behavior of animals deserves to be called language: "A frightened goose suddenly aware of danger and rousing the whole flock with its cries does not tell the others what it has seen but rather contaminates them with its fear" (Vygotsky 1962: 6). It is only when specific linguistic forms are associated with pictures, as in the game of rebuses, that the leap to writing occurs.

This is the essence of DeFrancis's account of what he calls the Ideographic Myth. He bases his argument on data from Chinese, but it applies with equal force to Japanese, although in terms of form and particularly function Japanese kanji and Chinese characters are quite different. DeFrancis does not, however, deal with a third aspect of Chinese characters that is of great importance for computer work and for understanding the persistence of the Ideographic Myth. Kanji have not only *formal* and *functional* properties but also *nominal* values that are used to distinguish them as objects in their own right. It is this derived set of nominal properties, perhaps more than anything else, that confuses the discussion of kanji usage and creates the illusion that kanji possess meanings independently of language. In fact, language (speech) is the source of all meaning; the so-called meaning of a Chinese character is merely a by-product of its use in the writing system of a particular language, such as Mandarin, Japanese, or Korean.[15]

As written symbols, kanji obviously have form. This includes not only the visible form of the character but also, for certain computer input systems, the order and direction in which the strokes that make it up are written. As characters in a writing system, kanji have representational functions—in Japanese, each kanji typically has two or more. For this reason, Japanese script is more difficult to handle computationally than Chinese, in which all but a handful of characters have only a single reading, and Korean, in which Chinese characters are not used to represent native words. Finally, just as we give names to letters and symbols (H "aitch," & "ampersand"), kanji can be tagged or named for identification as objects irrespective of what they look like or how they are used. Such names may be mnemonically related to differences among the forms and functions of the kanji in a given set, but they can be, and in computer work often are, wholly arbitrary.

Form

The visible shapes of kanji used in everyday writing vary from simple forms such as

一 二 七 小 丁 十 八 三 人 入

to complex patterns like

機 識 難 護 潔 謝 穀 織 燃 議 . [16]

Each kanji, however "crowded," is supposed to occupy a roughly square area the same size as that filled by its neighbors in the text. "Crowded" characters are generally made up of two or more simpler component elements, which are sometimes kanji in their own right. In fact, the shapes of most kanji can be broken down into combinations of a relatively small number of constituent parts; often, several different analyses are possible. Imagine stretching or compressing these "building blocks," vertically or horizontally, and positioning them within the writing square. Virtually every imaginable combination is utilized: in the simple case of two elements, one of them can stand below (above), to the left (right) of, or within (around) the other.

Kanji shapes can be readily analyzed in this way because historically most of them were created by a reverse process of synthesis. A few kanji originated as simple pictures of things like mountains, flowing water, and so forth; their descendants are called *shôkei moji* in Japanese. Others (called *shiji moji*) were more iconic; for example,

一 二 三

for 'one', 'two', 'three'. A third group *(kaii moji)* combined characters of the first two kinds; for example, the 'sun' and 'moon' pictographs side by side form a logograph that stands for the word meaning 'bright'. But the overwhelming majority of kanji are of another composite variety called form-and-sound characters *(keisei moji)*.[17] Keisei moji were created by adding an extra element, called a radical *(bushu),* to an existing character: the Chinese syllable represented by the new character rhymed with the one represented by the original character, the radical giving a broad hint of the meaning of the word in which the new character was used. This trick of embellishing a character with a radical to warn the reader that it was being used, not in its original function, but rather to suggest a rhyming syllable, dates from at least the end of the second millennium B.C., if not earlier. It remains the principal means for expanding the inventory of characters in Chinese today (DeFrancis 1984b: 78–88).

Because the inventory of elemental shapes is relatively small and the percentage of composite kanji large, a great many kanji differ from each other in only one or two details of form; even kanji of some complexity can resemble each other closely. For example,

弧 狐   廷 延   慨 概

栽 裁   微 徴   逐 遂

There are even a few instances in which the same elements arranged in different relative positions form distinct kanji

e.g., 員 ≠ 唄 .

Different printed and handwritten styles further complicate the situation: careful "square-style" *(kaisho)* handwriting is easy to read, but slow to write, much like printing English letter by letter; the faster "running-hand" *(gyôsho)* style, like longhand with its various ligatures, is faster to write but harder to read. Figure 5, a page from a handbook produced in England during World War II to aid in the translation of intercepted Japanese messages, shows examples of the even more cursive "grass-script" *(sôsho)* style of handwriting. Three sôsho forms are given for each of the twenty kanji listed on this particular page.[19]

Handwriting styles are only one source of variant kanji shapes that now exist side by side with carefully written forms. Some are traditional; other variants are simplifications that have been legislated into existence by the Japanese government. China has instituted different and more far-reaching simplifications of character shapes. Only Taiwan, Korea, Hong Kong, and some overseas Chinese communities retain Chinese characters in their full complexity, but even in China and Japan, older forms are found in all materials published before the simplifications took effect. Variants include correct forms of similar but distinct kanji, vulgar "abbreviations" with strange ligatures and omitted strokes, archaic forms, once standard forms now abandoned, and even outright mistakes that are too common to be ignored.

Needless to say, working out methods to output kanji on computers is a major undertaking. In the next chapter, we will look at some of the problems involved.

Figure 5 Running-Hand and Grass-Script Kanji (*Source:* Daniels 1947: 119)

39

Function

As already remarked, kanji can be thought of simply as substitutes for kana. For example, the adjective *utsukushii* 'beautiful' can be (and often is) written with five kana, which stand for the moras *u, tsu, ku, shi,* and *i,* respectively:

うつくしい

There is, however, a kanji which may be used to represent (among other things) the *utsuku* portion of this string:

美しい

In this case, three kana are replaced by a single kanji; in others, one kanji is substituted for a single kana. In every case, however, one thing is constant: the replacement of kana with kanji means that the reader must know in advance what the kanji is supposed to stand for.

In this sense, kanji constitute a kind of code. In cryptography, a *code* is an arbitrary substitution of one word or phrase for another. There is no rhyme or reason to it, and *only* those words or phrases in a message for which there is a prearranged substitution can be encoded or decoded. A *cipher,* on the other hand, is a procedure for changing or scrambling the letters of a message. Once you know the rules of the procedure, you can encipher or decipher *any* message whatsoever. (For this reason, it is standard practice to inject a certain element of code, such as a keyword, into cipher systems to enhance their security.) The only real difference between learning kanji and learning a secret code is that the assignments of readings to kanji were not made *with the intent* of causing confusion.

Nevertheless, they often do cause confusion. Even in the simple example just discussed, there is room for confusion. In modern Japanese, *utsuku* is not, linguistically speaking, the stem of the adjective *utsukushii.* One says

utsukushii	'[it] is beautiful'
utsukushikereba	'provided [it] is beautiful'
utsukushikatta	'[it] was beautiful'
utsukushisô da	'[it] seems (like it ought to be) beautiful'
utsukushiku nai	'[it] is not beautiful'

and so forth, building on the stem *utsukushi,* not *utsuku.* There are historical reasons for the current rule that dictates that the kana for *shi* must follow the kanji in this case. But in general, whenever kana are used to write the inflectional endings of verbs and adjectives, one simply must know how much of the word is represented by the kanji and how much must be written with kana. Kana used in this way, called *okurigana,* are a major headache for word-processor manufacturers.

Okurigana usage reflects just one aspect of the essentially arbitrary way in which kanji are assigned functions in the writing system. Readings of kanji in personal and place names are notoriously troublesome because they are often not associated with the kanji in any other context. Ordinary vocabulary offers its share of difficulties too. Studies of journalistic writing practices cast considerable light on these problems. A 1971 analysis found, for example, that kanji accounted for 2,258 (86.8%) of the 2,601 different types of characters used to write Kyôdô News Agency dispatches but only 462,209 (46.1%) of the 1,001,554 total characters transmitted (Hayashi et al. 1982: 206). An earlier study (Hayashi et al. 1982: 244–245) showed that the 200 most frequently used kanji accounted for more than half of all those appearing in newspapers and magazines. Clearly, using kanji as arbitrary replacements for kana strings is, in terms of the work one gets out of each individual kanji in the inventory, an extravagant indulgence.

The world of journalism provides other illuminating data on kanji usage. In a handbook on style published by the *Asahi Shinbun,* Japan's second largest newspaper, hundreds of individual words and phrases are dealt with (Katayama 1981: 240–412). A study of the nine categories into which these are divided provides a good introduction to some of the basic problems Japanese writers have to contend with on a daily basis.

1. The Japanese government has promulgated a list of 1,945 kanji for everyday use, called *jôyô kanji.* If a word includes a kanji not on this list, a synonym should be used instead. For example, one should use

$$\textit{taimen} \text{ 体面 'honor, reputation'}$$

instead of

$$\textit{koken} \text{ 沽券 'dignity, credit'}$$

because the first character of *koken* is not a jôyô kanji.

2. As we have already seen, kanji can be used to write native as well as Sino-Japanese words. In the former case, one says that the kanji "takes a *kun* reading" or gloss; the kanji stands for all or part of a native Japanese word with a meaning similar to that of the Chinese

word associated with the kanji. In the past, it was common for well-educated writers to apply different kanji in different contexts to the same Japanese words, using the meaning of the Chinese word associated with the kanji to guide their selection; the "nuances" of Japanese this pedantry was supposed to bring out were, as often as not, entirely specious. Modern practice discourages the gratuitous use of such kun assignments. Thus, for example, the verb *shigeru* 'flourish' should now be written

$$茂る \text{ , not } 繁る \text{ ,}$$

even though both forms make use of jôyô kanji.

3. Many native words of Japanese do not correspond closely to words of Chinese, and, in earlier times, attempts were made to write them using kanji in a rebus-like way. The idea is similar to English "spellings" like E-Z for "easy," Xing for "crossing," and so forth, in which letters and numerals stand for their names. Kanji used "out of context" in this way are called *ateji*; their use is discouraged. Thus

$$medetai \quad 目 出 度 い \quad \text{'auspicious'}$$

is to be written

$$めでたい$$

instead, since the readings of the kanji *(me, de, ta)* are etymologically false (*medetai* is not a compound of *me* 'eye', *de* 'go out', and *ta*, which is just the first mora of one of the proper readings of the third kanji).

4. Whether or not it has a kun reading, a kanji almost always has one or more *on* readings; these are simply the Japanese approximations of the Chinese syllable associated with the kanji. Because the phonemic structure of Japanese is so much simpler than that of Chinese, many different Chinese syllables come out sounding alike in Japanese. Homonyms therefore arise: for example,

$$itaku\ suru 委託する\text{'be dependent on (someone)'}$$

and

$$itaku\ suru 依託する\text{'entrust (someone with something)'.}$$

These are distinct words, but so often confused in writing that *Asahi* recommends using only the latter.

5. In the previous case, we had true homonyms. In other cases, there

is really no difference in word meaning at all: for example, for *uki*
written

雨期 or 雨季 'rainy season',

the choice of kanji is purely stylistic. Here *Asahi* recommends using
the more common writing, which in this case is the former.

6. The multiplicity of kanji readings has led to numerous incorrect
usages that survive despite the best efforts of pedagogues to stamp
them out. Naturally, these must be avoided. For example, some people
write the native adjective *akudoi* 'vicious, gaudy'

悪どい

with a kanji for *aku* and two kana for *doi*. This kanji can stand for
Sino-Japanese *aku* 'evil', but that *aku* is not etymologically a part of
akudoi.

7. A large class of exceptions are known as *dôkun iji* 'different characters, same kun' or *dôon igi* 'different characters (literally, meanings),
same on'. Categories 2 and 4 are of this kind, but there one alternative
is judged unacceptable. Here, both alternatives are allowed, and one
must decide when to use one or the other. For example, *kawa* 'river'
can be written either

川 or 河 ;

that is, *kawa* is a kun of both these kanji. But one is supposed to use
the second kanji only in certain fixed phrases, names, and so forth.
Similarly, the verb *sagasu* 'search, hunt for' can be written either

探す or 捜す.

The first form is to be used except when this word is in phrases like
"hunt for the criminal."

8. Some kanji not on the jôyô kanji list are nonetheless approved for
use by the Japanese Newspaper Association: thus,

nagauta 長唄 '(singing used in Kabuki performance)'

is acceptable, even though the second kanji is not on the government
list.

9. Finally, some two- and three-character compounds that stand for
single native words are even more aberrant than those included in Category 3. In the example of *medetai* above, at least *me, de,* and *ta* are
legitimate readings or parts of readings of the three kanji involved.

Words like

小豆 *azuki* 'red beans'

and

白粉 *oshiroi* 'face powder',

however, require a false reading of at least one of the kanji. Spellings of this type are technically called *jukujikun* (Hayashi 1977: 109, Paradis et al. 1985: xiii), but for convenience we can lump them together with ateji.

Although we have looked at only one or two examples in each of the foregoing categories, it should be kept in mind that they are just representatives of hundreds of such anomalies that must be dealt with in everyday writing. Not surprisingly, it is the functional role of kanji in the writing system that is mostly responsible for the complications of Japanese computing.

Identification

Neither shapes nor functions provide a method for naming or identifying kanji uniquely. For computers, any numbering scheme is in principle just as good as any other, but human beings usually need something more mnemonic. For centuries, people have been trying to break down the myriad kanji into small, relatively manageable groups on the basis of shape or function. To find a specific kanji or to file it away in its proper location, one first determines to which group it belongs, and then searches the kanji already there, which may be subordered according to some other criterion.

Shape is the most common starting point. Most Sino-Japanese dictionaries are organized on the basis of shape because most kanji are keisei moji (form-and-sound characters): it is natural to group them together by radical and use the number of strokes left over after the radical is counted to sort within each group. To handle other kinds of kanji, one invents nonhistorical "radicals" so that every kanji can be treated either as a radical or a radical plus a "remainder." Although simple in conception, this method is by no means easy to apply. The traditional list of 214 radicals, which goes back to the early eigthteenth century, does a poor job of reflecting the actual distribution of component shapes in kanji: some categories contain hundreds of kanji, some hardly any; moreover, in the recent simplifications, many kanji lost their traditional radicals. Even in unaltered kanji, there may be several candidates for dictionary radical: the principles underlying the traditional classification (which were not always applied consistently anyway) are often unclear to the modern reader, who must therefore rely on intelligent guesswork and accumulated experience to look up characters quickly. Variant forms of the same kanji require cross-references; the number of strokes is often obscured by differences between printed and handwritten forms; and so forth.

On occasion, one needs to refer to kanji shapes in the absence of actual writing. Since many place and personal names sound alike but are written with different kanji, it is frequently necessary (on the telephone, for example) to speak of a particular kanji without being able to write or show it. To do so, you might say that you are thinking of 'three-stroke *kawa*' *(sanbongawa),* to distinguish it from all other kanji that can be read *kawa,* or that the correct kanji for *ichi* in this case is the one written with a single horizontal stroke *(yoko-ichi).* Because kanji shapes vary over such a wide range of possibilities and cover that range so uniformly, naming kanji in this way is of only limited usefulness. Indeed, when Japanese talk face-to-face, the preferred technique for clearing up confusion about kanji, in the absence of pencil and paper, is pantomime: using the right index finger like a pencil to "write" the character in the air or on the palm of the left hand.

Often this is impossible, and one uses instead a common word, for all or part of which the kanji may stand, as a label for the kanji. There are dozens of kanji that can read *tô,* but only one which can also represent the noun *higashi* 'east'; this character is easily identified as *higashi to iu ji* 'the character *higashi*'. This doesn't work when the kanji in question has only one reading. For example, in identifying the kanji that stands for *tô* in the word *satô* 'sugar', one can do little more than say something like, "It's the one you use to write the last syllable of the word for sugar." If that fails, one must go back to shape: "It's the kanji with the 'rice' radical on the left, and the Tang of 'Tang Dynasty' on the right."

The Ideographic Myth

The necessity of improvising names for kanji is of interest not only because it is common in daily life, but also because it reveals an important—perhaps the most important—reason for the survival of the Ideographic Myth. We say that red traffic lights "mean stop" and green ones "mean go," but no one believes that "reading" a traffic light is anything like reading the directions on a can of soup or reading *From*

Here to Eternity.[20] Yet people do seem to think that reading a Chinese character is somehow like reacting to a red light. Chinese characters, like anything else, can be employed as mere signals, or as tokens of a code (recall the code/cipher distinction), but they are then no longer part of a writing system. To qualify as a writing system, one must not only be able to use a collection of symbols to express *some* meanings; one must be able to use them to express *any* meaning that can be expressed in a given language. It is therefore hardly remarkable that Chinese characters can serve as mere signs or code symbols. It is very remarkable, however, that anybody should think that that is all they ever are.

One nineteenth-century scholar wrote that the Ideographic Myth "may justly be ascribed to the vanity of the Chinese literati" (DeFrancis 1984b: 145)—and, he might have added, of some of their foreign students—but personal or class vanity is hardly a convincing sociolinguistic explanation. A more promising approach is to begin with the observation that most Chinese characters are keisei moji— that is, of the radical-plus-remainder type. This means that it is often possible for readers to guess at words written with unfamiliar characters by using the semantic and phonetic hints provided by the characters' structure. In particular, despite centuries of sound changes, the remainders (characters less their radicals) still provide an excellent guide to rhymes:

> If a reader of Chinese knew only a hundred characters, almost every other character in a piece of writing would be familiar to him. With a knowledge of 1,100 characters, only every tenth character would be unfamiliar, and in two-thirds of the remaining 90 percent of the characters there would be a useful phonetic clue to help the reader recall the pronunciation of the character. Indeed, this two-thirds figure of useful phonetic clues also applies to the 10 percent of the characters with a lower rank frequency than 1,100. Thus a reader with a knowledge of the phonetic component in Chinese writing has two chances out of three of guessing correctly the pronunciation of any given character he is likely to encounter in reading. (DeFrancis 1984b: 108)

The same considerations apply to Sino-Japanese vocabulary as well. Because many kanji are used to represent native Japanese words, the phonetic clues provided are not always of help; but the fact that many kanji take multiple readings more than makes up for this, since a kanji learned in one context may be recognized in another even when its reading is in doubt. In both Japanese and Chinese, moreover, seldomly seen characters are more likely to occur in compounds than in isolation. It is therefore often possible to guess at a whole two- or three-character expression instead of an individual character. This is usually a much easier task, especially when the reader has some knowledge of the subject matter. And, of course, silent reading allows opportunities for glossing over hard-to-read characters, looking ahead, reviewing earlier passages, and so forth.

All these tricks for dealing with kanji at the periphery of one's reading ability work because the connections between the shapes and functions of kanji provide such a rich multiplicity of pathways between writing and language. Indeed, scientific research on the process of reading suggests that, even when words are written in Chinese characters, the phonological recoding of the characters is a crucial step in the overall process (see DeFrancis 1984b: 167–176 and Yamada 1980b for reviews of the literature). Why, then, do the techniques that Chinese and Japanese use for coping with hundreds of kanji create the illusion that language plays no role in the comprehension of kanji?

In Japanese reading, one scans the text rapidly, taking in patterns of characters that correspond to whole grammatical structures. Since there are no spaces between words, this process alone is no doubt quite demanding psychologically. Uninterrupted reading continues unless and until one or more kanji do not immediately suggest precise words; at that point, special strategies for "decoding" individual kanji may come into play. Significantly, those who read Japanese, native and non-native speakers alike, can almost always tell instantly whether a kanji they do not recognize is one that they have or have not encountered previously. One has the uncanny feeling that one understands the whole *before* knowing all of the parts. This is no paradox: one really does recognize whole patterns of writing all at once, just as, when looking at the well-known optical illusion, one sees a wine cup one moment and, suddenly, two kissing silhouettes the next. It is only because we begin to learn how to read by consciously applying explicit rules that we assume that fluent reading is simply the rapid, subconscious application of more rules of the same kind. In the case of kanji, the early rules link up individual characters with one or more meaningful words of the language; as reading becomes easier, the temptation is strong to attribute this development to the establishment of a direct linkage betwen kanji and meaning that bypasses language. After all, the meaning of the whole passage is understood even when there is conscious doubt as to the precise function of some of the kanji. A computer would have to know what the parts are in order to figure out the value of the whole; illogically, we apply the same logic to ourselves.

Introspective reflection on the process of reading reinforces our misguided intuitions. By way of analogy, consider the difference between numbers and numerals. Novice programmers have to be taught to distinguish carefully between numbers, like ten, and numerals, like 10. The numeral 10 can be the hexadecimal representation of sixteen or the binary representation of two as well as the decimal representation of ten; and as a string of numeric characters, "10," stored in computer memory, its arithmetic value is almost certainly none of these. Yet in everyday speech and writing, ten and 10 are interchangeable. For similar reasons, one ought to say that this or that kanji is used in the writing of *a word that means* "east," "sugar," or whatever. But this is an awkward way of talking, and even foreign students of Japanese quickly pick up the habit of saying "That's the kanji for 'east'" or "That *tô* is 'east'." When speaking and thinking in Japanese, things get even worse because self-referentiality comes into play: the readings of kanji are themselves Japanese utterances. Thus, for example, the innocuous Japanese sentence

Sore wa satô no tô desu.

can be interpreted either as

That's the [kanji read] *tô* in the word *satô*.

or as

That's the [kanji read] *tô* which means 'sugar'.

The problem with sentences like this is what philosophers call use/reference ambiguity: the word in question (here *satô*) can be taken either as a token of itself (as in English, "Sugar is easy to misspell") or as a word in normal usage (referring to that sweet, white stuff in the jar on the kitchen shelf). More generally, when one starts talking about a symbol system (arabic numerals, Chinese characters, or whatever) in the language to which the system refers, a peculiar inversion takes place. The symbols seem to take on a life of their own as the fundamental dependency of symbol on speech is internalized.

It bears repeating that this is by no mans a uniquely East Asian phenomenon; as the number/numeral analogy suggests, it is probably a universal response to use/reference entanglements in all literate cultures. What makes the Japanese experience different is its sheer magnitude. Mastering kanji is something like trying to memorize the answers to thousands of "trivia" questions, but it is hardly a game; to fail to learn this multitude of isolated facts so well that they become automatic reflexes is to cut oneself off from literate Japanese society. No wonder Japanese are convinced that kanji are wordless molecules of meaning!

The psychological strength of this conviction notwithstanding, it is an illusion. Any illiterate can say exactly what he thinks, although the language in which he thinks consists only of what he has learned through his ears, but no one can write in a language he does not understand.

2

Practical Consequences
of a Large Character Set

The structure of the Japanese writing system has important practical
as well as psychological effects. Because written communication is the
essence of most computer applications, we must know what these
practical effects are and how they are related to other aspects of Japanese culture. For this purpose, a mere catalog of the customs and practices of Japanese literacy would be both too limited and too broad: too
limited because assimilated Western technology tends to overshadow
important aspects of the Japanese way of doing things, and too broad
because even "uniquely" Japanese reading and writing habits that
have a wide-ranging impact on daily life are often only tangentially
related to the structure of the writing system.

Consider, for example, the use of seals. Instead of signing one's
name, the standard procedure in Japan is to use vermilion (*shu*, cin-
nabar paste) and a stamp-like seal engraved with the characters of
one's name. Almost every adult has at least two seals: a registered one
called *jitsuin*, for legal documents, usually carved in ivory or stone and
kept in a safe place; and one or more cheaper seals, often mass-pro-
duced wooden or plastic affairs with surname only, for use at the bank,
and so forth. Unlike signatures, seals are physically transferrable.
Sometimes it is convenient to be able to entrust a seal to someone else,
but losing one can be a major catastrophe. For that reason alone, the
use of seals affects how the Japanese conduct their personal and business affairs.[21] But can this influence be traced back to the use of kanji
itself? It is true that the traditional approach to calligraphy, which
emphasizes copying of master models, is at odds with the idea of distinguishing individuals by their handwriting, but the history of seals
(Hiraga 1983) shows that they came into use rather recently, and pri-

marily in response to practical needs, not deep cultural preferences. Seals were not adopted by the general populace until the middle of the seventeenth century and were not consistently used by the ruling classes before that time. The use of kanji in names did not make them necessary; indeed, had it not been for the system of official registration introduced in 1694 to stamp out counterfeiting, they might not have become a permanent part of Japanese life. In fact, one of the original *raisons d'être* for seals was illiteracy. Both seals and kanji were imported from China, but clearly the use of the former was not caused by the use of the latter.

There are some aspects of Japanese life, however, that are both economically significant and linked to the structure of the writing system. We will focus our attention on some of the more important of these practices, which lie at the border between culture and technology.

Alphabetization

Alphabetized lists are so ubiquitous in modern life that it may come as a shock to learn that the technique of putting words in order by comparing them letter by letter from beginning to end is a relatively recent innovation. Yet the first explicit statement of this now familiar rule is found in the *Catholicon* of 1286 compiled by Giovanni di Genoa, who seems to have believed that it was original with him![22] In Japan, analogues to alphabetization are based on kana, for which there are two kinds of ordering. One makes use of the *Iroha uta*, a poem of unknown authorship (though often attributed to the Buddhist priest Kûkai) dating from the eleventh century.[23] The other is the phonemically oriented *gojûon* or *a-i-u-e-o* arrangement of kana shown in Figure 1. The first attempt at grouping words by kana is found in the dictionary *Iroha jirui shô* compiled by the courtier Tachibana no Tadakane in the late twelfth century. As in early Western works, the grouping is by initial character only; subgrouping is by meaning. In modern dictionaries, the gojûon sequence is used almost exclusively, and the principle of absolute ordering is applied. Nonetheless, many difficulties remain. The basic problem is that "[i]n determining dictionary order, no distinction is made between whether a kana is written with a diacritical mark or not, whether a kana is written large or small, or whether it is hiragana or katakana, except when one of these distinctions must be used to differentiate between two otherwise identical words" (Hadamitzky & Spahn 1981: 23). Japanese authorities do not agree on the order in which to apply these criteria when an arbitrary choice must be made. One possibility, outlined by Hadamitzky and Spahn, goes like this:

1. Longer words follow shorter.
2. a. Kana with diacritics follow those without.
   b. Syllables with initial *p-* follow those with *b-*.
3. Small kana follow large.
4. Katakana follow hiragana.

The order of the rules is crucial as the following examples show (Hadamitzky & Spahn 1981: 24):

bariki	ばりき	before *harikitte*	はりきって	(1 over 2)
cho	ちょ	before *chiyogami*	ちよがみ	(1 over 3)
kappa	カッパ	before *kappatsu*	かっぱつ	(1 over 4)
hakki	はっき	before *hatsugi*	はつぎ	(2 over 3)
kisu	キス	before *kizu*	きず	(2 over 4)
atsushi	アツシ	before *asshi*	あっし	(3 over 4)

A further wrinkle is introduced by the vowel-lengthening bô mark. "Some dictionaries simply ignore it, as a hyphen would be ignored in English-language alphabetization. Others take it to represent the katakana for the preceding vowel sound" (Hadamitzky & Spahn 1981: 24).

Other complications are created by the practical necessity of interfiling alphabetic and Japanese-script data. Where should one put *flexible shaft* in a dictionary of automotive terms? An obvious expedient is to have a separate alphabetic listing; but this means that a Japanese who wants to look up a foreign word must know how to spell it. In fact, he or she may only know it in its katakana rendition, that is, in its Japanized pronunciation (in this case, *furekishiburu shafuto*), which is sometimes not much of a clue. If a separate listing is not possible, then a standard Japanese pronunciation for each foreign term must be agreed upon. This is easier said than done: for example, the name Richard can become Japanese *richâdo, rishâru,* or *rihyaruto* depending on whether the source is English, French, or German; "violin" can be pronounced as either *vaiorin* (with an innovative initial mora) or *baiorin* (the conservative variant); and so forth.[24]

Of course, analogous problems arise when working with alphabets; for example, in alphabetizing bibliographical entries, special rules are needed to deal with multiword titles, proper names, abbreviations, numerals, foreign orthographies, and so on. These extra rules sometimes conflict with one another, and one ends up having to make arbitrary decisions, as with kana; Knuth (1973: 7–9) offers an excellent illustration of the problems involved in his book on computer sorting. In Japanese, however, things are worse: when words are written in kanji, one must know how to read them (that is, reduce them to kana) before one can apply any rules at all. Surrounding context is often of no help, especially when the kanji in question represent a proper name.

Telephone directories (Davidson 1980) and other large name lists are an obvious case in point. For them, a special system is used in which each of the individual characters that make up names (kana, kanji, or rômaji) is treated like a separate word. The general principle is this: if the initial "words" of two names are pronounced differently, the names are put in gojûon order; if the "words" sound alike but are written with different characters, the name with the "simpler" character goes first; if both the readings and characters are the same, the next "words" of the two names are compared, and so forth. Of course, there are other rules, such as those required for deciding which of two characters is the "simpler," what counts as the "reading" for the purposes of this ordering procedure, and so on. Just to give a hint of the kinds of questions that must be resolved: What does one do when two kanji of the same number of strokes have the same reading? If a one-character name is derived from a verb or adjective, is the inflectional ending included in its "reading"? What is the correct "reading" of something like "A-1" in the name of a shop?

Lists sorted in this way almost always violate strict gojûon ordering but have the convenient property that names beginning with the same one or more kanji are clustered together locally. (The clustering is localized because many kanji can take multiple readings; therefore, words beginning with the same kanji may be scattered throughout the list.) The following list of surnames (culled from the membership list of a Japanese academic society) illustrates the discrepancies:

Telephone Book Order		*Dictionary Order*	
Tsuda	津 田	Tsukamoto	塚 本
Tsunokuma	津野熊	Tsuzi	辻
Tsumura	津 村	Tsuzome	都 染
Tsuzome	都 染	Tsuda	津 田
Tsu(d)zuki	都 築	Tsuchida	土 田
Tsukamoto	塚 本	Tsu(d)zuki	都 築
Tsuji	辻	Tsunogaya	角ヶ谷
Tsuchida	土 田	Tsunokuma	津野熊
Tsunogaya	角ヶ谷	Tsunoda	角 田
Tsunoda	角 田	Tsumura	津 村
Tsuruga	敦 賀	Tsuru	鶴
Tsuru	鶴	Tsuruga	敦 賀

Clearly, if one knows both how to write and pronounce a name, it is easier to find it on a telephone-book-order list than a dictionary-order list. If only the kanji are known, the kind of list does not matter much since one must guess at the correct reading, and many kanji have more than one. For instance, as a man's name,

$$正$$

can stand for Tadashi or Masashi; in multi-character names, it can take on the readings *tada, masa, shô* and so on. If only the reading is known, dictionary order is easier because it groups all homophones together. Compiling a dictionary-order list also requires less information (stroke counts rarely need to be taken into consideration). Compilation of either type of list, however, is a burdensome task if kanji entries are not accompanied by glosses in kana or romanized form, since then the compiler must memorize all this information.

Indexing is perhaps the most common and economically important example of large-scale list making. Without indexes to serial publications, abstracts of reports, and other synoptic aids, especially in the hard sciences, a modern researcher simply cannot cope with the flood of information in his or her field. And, of course,

> [e]very serious book of nonfiction should have an index if it is to achieve its maximum usefulness. A good index records every pertinent statement made within the body of the text. The key word here is *pertinent*. The subject matter and purpose of the book determine which statements are pertinent and which peripheral. An index should be considerably more than an expanded table of contents and considerably less than a concordance of words and phrases. (*The Chicago Manual of Style* 1982: 512)

The last quoted sentence is particularly important for two reasons: Japanese in fact rely on tables of contents far more than indexes; and many people wrongly believe that computers have automated this sort of work.

> There are, of course, indexes that are mechanically—or better, electronically—produced. One is called a KWIC (for "key word in context") index. A computer is given a list of key words and terms and ordered to search a data file (such as a whole book on magnetic tape) for each instance of them, record every occurrence in a context of a few words on either side of the term, note its location (such as page and line number), record the terms in alphabetic order (and, for multiple occurrences, in order of occurrence), and print out the whole listing. A KWIC index is thus a kind of concordance of preselected terms—names, words, sequences of words, anything the computer is programmed to search for.

> KWIC indexes have many uses, but there is no way they can substitute
> for a real index compiled by a real human being. . . .Indexing requires
> decision making of a far higher order than computers are yet capable of.
> (*The Chicago Manual of Style* 1982: 519)[25]

Since indexes are relatively short and often contain headings other
than names, the Japanese practice is to use dictionary order; however,
the heavy use of kanji makes it hard to see the pattern of this ordering.
The kanji at the beginning of consecutive entries are usually different
unless the entries begin with the same word. Hence, when hunting for
a particular word, one must keep switching between pronunciations (to
decide whether to move forward or backward in the list for the next
comparison) and written forms (to spot the item sought, if it is there).
Alphabetic indexes are forgiving by comparison: misspelling the word
sought ("does it have one *l* or two?") or encountering an unfamiliar
word in an entry will usually not create much delay because the visual
appearance of words is in relatively close accord with their pronunciation, even in English, which is notorious for nonphonemic spellings.
Finally, kanji are intimately tied to the Sino-Japanese intellectual tradition, with its emphasis on classification rather than generalization.
Although many Japanese books now have indexes, there is still a
noticeable tendency to make elaborate tables of contents the main
guide to a book's contents; separate name indexes are common, and
subject indexes, when supplied, are often short and lack subheadings.

Filing is like indexing except that one is working with several documents instead of just one. In both cases, the goal is to make it possible
for someone to locate information without hunting through the actual
documents in which it is contained. The problems of kanji filing are
the same as those of kanji indexing, but the scale of the task is larger.

Because it is so difficult to retrieve documents by key words written
in kanji, and because producing documents by hand is such a chore,
virtually every company and governmental bureau has developed its
own idiosyncratic methods for keeping track of its paperwork. Classified multicopy filing systems have become more common since the
introduction of inexpensive copying processes, but when something
must be found, the memory of the individual employee still plays a
greater role in Japan than in the West.[26] Much work is handled face-
to-face or on the telephone and so goes undocumented. Manuals
detailing operating procedures, common in Europe and the United
States, are rare, and such standard business practices as taking minutes
at meetings are almost unheard of. This is not to say that Japan has

avoided the ills of modern bureaucracy—quite the contrary—but that it is a country where using human brains for filing cabinets is accepted as normal.

Surely the library catalog is the king of files. It is noteworthy that Japan has, for a country of its economic stature, very few public libraries. Some statistics cited by Welch (1976: 32) vividly illustrate this point. In 1970 there were 881 public libraries in Japan, including branches, of which 81 were in Tôkyô. Since Tôkyô then had a population of about 11 million, that is about one facility for every 155,000 residents; the U.S. ratio is one to 25,000. Furthermore, the average public library in Japan at that time had holdings of only 33,000 volumes and acquired only about 2,200 per year, although Japan was publishing more than 30,000 new trade books annually. The administrative attitude toward public libraries in Japan has been one of "benign neglect." Computerized automation of library tasks in Japan began in 1968, but as late as 1975 was still largely confined to the management of circulation and acquisitions, and similar housekeeping routines (Tanabe 1977: 103); according to a letter in the *Tôkyô Shinbun* of 2 May 1986 from the director of the National Diet Library (which, incidentally, keeps its nearly three and a half million catalog cards in alphabetical order), the library had not yet put into operation the computerized catalog system that it began developing in 1977. All this is particularly disappointing because, as Roszak (1986: 173) observes, "if computerized information services have any natural place in society, it is in the public library. There, the power and efficiency of the technology can be maximized along with its democratic access."

Although the present situation has roots in Japanese cultural history,[27] the continued use of kanji definitely hampers major improvements in it. The traditional system of cataloging books by titles, not by author or subject, is now in conflict with the recommendations of the International Standards Organization (ISO), which specify main headings by author's name (see Oda 1977). But even if every librarian in Japan suddenly decided to cooperate with the ISO overnight, the switchover would be a monumental undertaking even with the help of computers. Everything already said in regard to dictionaries applies equally to libarary catalogs, which in addition must cope with archaic language. Names are especially problematic. They frequently include rare kanji that are seen nowhere else as well as kanji that take on seldom-used and hard-to-remember readings (ateji). The same name may have more than one representation in kanji, and the same kanji string may stand for more than one name. If all this were not bad enough, because of the linguistic function of names, their context is of virtually no use at all in figuring them out.

The Book Trade

Japan's relative lack of library services is compensated for by its numerous bookstores, many of which handle second-hand books, sometimes exclusively. This phenomenon can be seen as a response to the problem of keeping tabs on the wide variety of books and periodicals written in traditional script. Just as office workers function as living files for their organizations, so the network of bookstores serves as a kind of giant library catalog. In the Kanda Jinbô-chô area of Tôkyô, near many of the city's colleges and universities, a few hundred such bookstores, some quite small, line the streets for blocks. Different stores specialize in art, history, law, medicine, foreign publications, and so forth. There is at least one large general-purpose bookstore near almost every major urban railway station.

The heavy reliance on bookstores rather than libraries is linked to the writing system in another way: it is one of the chief reasons that Japan is said to be the world's most literate nation. Since Japan is such a book-loving society, the argument goes, the current writing system has to be judged a success in pragmatic terms, no matter how incommodious it may be theoretically. But when we look at what Japanese buy to read and why they buy so much of it, a different picture begins to emerge.

The Japanese are great consumers of the printed word, but high sales figures can be deceptive. When books must be bought rather than borrowed, there will necessarily be a lot of redundant investment. Most university faculty have large personal collections, including scores of infrequently consulted works that their Western counterparts would typically expect their institution's library to provide. Some faculty actually rent warehouse space to store their books. The bookstore system, moreover, is hampered by oligopoly control of national book distribution by two companies (Nippan and Tôhan), taxes on book inventories, and the inability of older publishers to deal with competition from the increasing number of smaller firms.[28]

There has been a noticeable decline in the quality of what is being published and read in Japan. As a prominent American journalist recently noted, "The dedicated literacy of Japan is yet another cause for admiration, but the content of the reading matter—especially on the trains, where no one knows his neighbor and in principle everyone is unobserved—is not. Some of the men are reading books, but more are reading either 'sports papers' or thick volumes of comics, the size of telephone books" (Fallows 1986: 36). Authors, translators, and editors in serious publishing interviewed during 1985 agreed that the industry was due for a major shake-up. They pointed out that well-established houses such as Iwanami, accustomed to a steady income produced by anthologies of Japanese literature, multivolume histories, encyclopedias, dictionaries, and other classics, were being deserted by the reading public. Among the larger houses, only those that, like Shô-gakukan, have a major stake in the burgeoning educational market, are solidly in the black. Serious monthlies like *Chûô kôron* and *Bungei shunjû*, the flagships of their respective publishers, are rumored to be in trouble. *Focus,* a new and extraordinarily successful weekly, contains (besides advertising) little more than extended captions on sensational photographs. It is said to be purposely designed so that any "article" can be read in the time it takes a commuter train to get from one station to the next. Paperbacks increasingly cater to this market as well. Of the three leading national newspapers, *Asahi,* which does not shy away from the kind of serious writing Americans would associate with, say, the *New York Times,* has been steadily losing ground to the less demanding *Yomiuri* for the past ten years or so; number-three *Mainichi* almost went bankrupt in 1979 (Sorita 1985), and the once popular Japanese edition of *Reader's Digest* has recently ceased publication.

The most spectacular change in contemporary Japanese reading habits is the boom in comics. As Frederik Schodt points out in his recent study of this genre,

> [o]ver 4.3 billion books and magazines were produced in Japan in 1980, making it one of the world's most print-saturated nations. But 27 percent of this total, or roughly 1.18 billion, were comics—*manga*—in magazine and book form. As some enterprising reporters have discovered, Japan now uses more paper for comics that it does for its toilet paper. (Schodt 1983: 12)

Japanese comic weeklies sell in the millions of copies: they are avidly devoured by adults (both men and women) as well as children, and one is as likely to see them in the hands of office workers and university students as of delivery boys and taxi drivers.

One can hardly describe this heavy consumption as reading in the usual sense:

> According to an editor of Kôdansha's *Shônen Magazine*, who must know about such things, on the average it takes the reader twenty minutes to finish a 320-page comic magazine. A quick calculation yields a breakdown of 16 pages a minute, or 3.75 seconds spent on each page. (Schodt 1983: 18)

As Schodt explains (18–23), this rapid pace is possible because of the heavy use of purely visual, often cinematic effects and illustrations sometimes covering several pages. Captions are used sparingly and often can be skipped. The choice of letters (hiragana, katakana, kanji, or roman) and direction of writing are often varied to create different moods. A large percentage of captions are just "sound effects" of the *POW* and ZAP! variety—the Japanese repertoire is far richer than the English and, if anything, plays a more dominant role. When the linguistic meaning of a caption really matters, furigana are frequently supplied, as well illustrated by the sampling of both pre- and postwar comics reproduced in Schodt's book. In short, Japanese comics provide a respite from the rigors of kanji culture.

Schodt is ambivalent on this point. He sees comics as a vehicle for escape from the oppressiveness of a crowded, conformist society, but he is also eager to deny the charge that they "contribute to illiteracy" (152). He casually accepts Vogel's 1979 assertion that illiteracy does not exceed one percent in Japan and confines his comments on furigana to a brief marginal note. A photo caption (144) says that "except for gag and newspaper strips, word balloons in most Japanese comics are not hand-lettered but typeset." This is technically true, but a "cute" style of lettering has developed in many comics. This style is typified by hiragana with uncompleted crossings, "fat" circular loops, misplaced strokes, and oversized tops. Ordinarily, kanji are written slightly larger than kana; in this childish style, however, they are the same size, and often exhibit peculiar stroke order as well. A Japan Broadcasting Corporation (NHK) program first broadcast on 22 July 1985 reported that, in a national survey of 3,400 junior high school students, 72 percent of the girls and 20 percent of the boys habitually imitated this comic-book writing, much to the grief of their parents and teachers, who often could not read what their children wrote. Perhaps comics do not "contribute to illiteracy" in Japan, but it is hard to believe that they contribute anything positive to the quality of Japanese literacy either.

There are those who would argue that comics are the epitome of kanji culture, rather than an escape from it.

> Sergei Eisenstein, the Russian filmmaker, perceived a link between the ideogram and what he called the inherently "cinematic" nature of much of Japanese culture. . . . [A]rtist Osamu Tezuka has said of the drawings in his comics: "I don't consider them pictures—I think of them as a type of hieroglyphics." (Schodt 1983: 25)

Schodt favors a more practical theory that places the audience rather than the artist at the center of things.

> Comics, however, could not have become an integral part of Japanese culture unless there was a genuine need for them. To be sure, the small child in Japan reads comics for the same reason children everywhere do—they are immediately accessible when still learning to read, and fun. But for older children, teenagers, and adults, comics are faster and easier to read than a novel, more portable than a television set, and provide an important source of entertainment and relaxation in a highly disciplined society. (Schodt 1983: 25)

There are undoubtedly many other reasons for the decline in the quality demanded by today's Japanese readers, including the influence of televison and more discretionary income. Nonetheless, it is hard to escape the conclusion that the cumbersome nature of reading and writing in traditional script is partly responsible for this trend.

The perennial strength in the sales of dictionaries and other reference works may seem to contradict this line of reasoning, but on closer examination, it merely serves to reinforce it. The fully armed Japanese reader or writer needs two basic dictionaries: a *kokugo jiten,* in which words are listed in kana order, and a *kanwa jiten,* which lists Sino-Japanese words according to their initial kanji. Because it is often hard to find a particular kanji in a kanwa jiten even if it has indexes of kanji by reading and/or stroke-count, most people try to get by with just a kokugo jiten. When they come across an unknown kanji, especially if it isn't the first one in a compound, they usually take a guess at its reading and try to find the word in which it occurs in their well-thumbed kokugo jiten rather than haul out the kanwa jiten, which they may not have used since high school.

In 1980, NHK conducted a survey that assessed, among other things, frequency of kokugo jiten usage (Hayashi 1982: 488). Respondents varied in age from under 20 to over 70 and came from a wide variety of occupations. They were asked whether they used kokugo jiten regularly. Homework was excluded in the case of students; still, 61 percent of the youngest age group said they used kokugo jiten often or occasionally. Remarkably, the percentage actually *increases,* hitting a peak among Japanese in their late thirties, of whom only 26 percent said they never or seldom used kokugo jiten. The usage rate then falls off, perhaps because many white-collar workers are promoted around this age and do less business writing, and because the children of most mothers above this age are old enough to start looking up words for themselves. Nonetheless, the rate does not fall to the 50 percent "crossover" point until age 60, when many people are starting to experience a deterioration in vision.

Specialized dictionaries abound. Some have analogues in the West: bilingual dictionaries, technical glossaries, collections or proverbs and quotations, word lists for children at different levels of reading ability, and so on. Others exist only because of kanji. For names, ordinary kanwa jiten usually don't suffice, and one needs a *jinmei* (personal name) or *chimei* (place name) dictionary. There are also *nankun jiten* for finding difficult kun readings in words other than names. For deciphering handwriting, calligraphic dictionaries of different kinds are available. Handbooks for writing formal letters of all kinds are far more common than in the West. Only thesauruses and other works that rely heavily on subject indexing are rare.

Typing and Computer Input

As already remarked in regard to filing, writing letters and other business documents in Japanese is a tedious chore. A software developer who designed a Japanese word-processing system for a major U.S. manufacturer put it this way:

> As a result of its curious history the Japanese language has the most complex script in the world: . . . the Japanese have had no reasonable way to type their own language; more than 90 percent of all documents in Japan are handwritten, or rather handcrafted. A slip of the writer's hand, and a page must be torn up. Moreover, most documents are hard to read unless the writer happens to be an accomplished calligrapher. To be sure,

there does exist a *kanji* typewriter, rather like a small typesetting machine, but the device is slow and tiring to use. Professional typists are comparatively rare, and their productivity is about 20 characters per minute, or only 10 pages per day. (Becker 1984: 99)

Arthur Koestler, although primarily interested in quite different aspects of Japanese culture, couldn't help being struck by the same thing:

An American editor has described his incredulous astonishment when [in 1953] he visited the building of one of Japan's mammoth daily newspapers, with a circulation of four to five million. He saw its scientific wonders, from the rotation presses in the basement, through the telephotographic and speed-graphic equipment, to the helicopter park and the carrier-pigeons on the roof; he saw every trick and gadget of mass-communication, except—typewriters. To our minds, a journalist without a typewriter is like a samurai without a sword; in Japan not only newspaper offices, but business offices and government departments must do without them. Fantastic as it seems, business in one of the great commercial empires of our time is almost universally transacted by handwriting—and without keeping carbons for the record. (Koestler 1961: 180–181)

Typing is crucial because blind touch typing is so much faster than handwriting. A practiced typist can reproduce a letter, for example, in a fraction of the time it would take to copy it by hand. This is obviously due in part to the fact that the eyes never have to shift away from the text, but just why touch typing is so efficient is still something of a scientific mystery.

Consider a typical secretarial task, the retyping of a document. ... [I]t closely resembles a series of choice-reaction-time tasks, in which a subject is presented with a single visual stimulus from a set of two or more stimuli after being instructed to rapidly press a particular button for each of the possible stimuli. Under optimal conditions ... the average latency, or delay between the presentation of the stimulus and the pressing of a button, is approximately 250 milliseconds. The paradox of typing is that a latency of 250 milliseconds yields a typing rate of 48 words per minute. ... Yet speeds of twice that rate are fairly common. (Salthouse 1984: 128)

Moreover, touch typing is a skill almost anyone can learn. It is much easier to become a proficient typist than a proficient pianist, for example, although both activities superficially seem to make the same demands on coordination and dexterity. On properly designed keyboards, many typists can outperform Salthouse's "fairly common" rate of ninety-six words per minute. And of course, typing is ideal for computer input: it is easy for computers to deal with strings composed of a few dozen distinct characters, and easy for humans to learn how to reduce natural language to such strings with little or no conscious effort.

Kanji upset this happy relationship. There are basically just three ways to input kanji, as shown in Figure 6 (from Unger 1984a: 241). These three methods can be called duplication, dictation, and indication, or alternatively inscription, transcription, and description, or even simply writing, spelling, and coding, though this last triad can be misleading. There are only three input techniques because kanji are completely characterized by their formal, functional, and nominal values (i.e., shapes, readings, and identifying names). Duplicating or inscribing a kanji is just that: writing it down or in some other way presenting the machine with its graphic form. In dictating, the operator

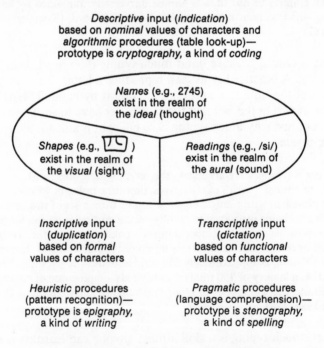

Descriptive input (*indication*)
based on *nominal* values of characters and
algorithmic procedures (table look-up)—
prototype is *cryptography,* a kind of *coding*

Names (e.g., 2745)
exist in the realm of
the *ideal* (thought)

Shapes (e.g., 𝍶)
exist in the realm of
the *visual* (sight)

Readings (e.g., /si/)
exist in the realm of
the *aural* (sound)

Inscriptive input
(*duplication*)
based on *formal*
values of characters

Transcriptive input
(*dictation*)
based on *functional*
values of characters

Heuristic procedures
(pattern recognition)—
prototype is *epigraphy,*
a kind of *writing*

Pragmatic procedures
(language comprehension)—
prototype is *stenography,*
a kind of *spelling*

Figure 6   The Three Modes of Kanji Input

uses a microphone or a typewriter keyset to input speech data; the program in the machine attempts to transcribe (convert) these data into the desired symbols. Indicating and describing kanji are the same thing from the machine's viewpoint though slightly different from the user's. The operation of a mechanical Japanese typewriter is an example of indication: one literally points to a different slug of type (or pushes a separate button) for each distinct symbol. The use of more abstract codes, such as numbers, for the same purpose is more appropriately termed description.

There are many different combinations and implementations of these three basic Japanese input methods, but, with one important exception, none allows for fast, accurate, relaxed touch typing of the kind we take for granted as a cornerstone of modern business and technology in the West. As a result, Japan has been "very slow at phasing out the traditional business practice of keeping on staff too many over-qualified college graduates to do mostly routine document preparation by longhand" (Yamada 1983a: 315).[29]

Data Processing

Input is unquestionably the key issue in Japanese data processing. The difficulty of kanji input literally begins and ends at the user's fingertips, and no amount of fancy software or hardware can alleviate it. On the other hand, the use of kanji also has a significant impact on output and computation (i.e., the machine-internal manipulation of symbolic data). These are problems you can "throw money at" with some hope of success. Nevertheless, they lack what engineers call "elegant" solutions and contribute significantly to the underutilization of computers in Japan.

Output

As we have seen, some kanji can be written with only a few strokes of the pen, but many are highly intricate. These become even more complicated when they are printed in a typeface, such as the Ming style used extensively in Japanese printing, that makes use of serifs and lines of varying thickness. In the typical Japanese book one finds only seven or eight characters per inch; compare this with English typescript (ten or twelve per inch) or standard newspaper advertising copy (fourteen per inch). The various inked and blank regions that make up a kanji are generally smaller than those that form alphanumeric characters drawn to the same scale. A dot-matrix, ink-jet, or similar kind of computer printer designed for English, which uses clusters of dots to form characters, usually does not have the resolution to produce kanji at the same scale as ordinary letters and numerals.

Similar considerations apply to video display screens, on which characters are made up of clusters of off and on picture elements, or pixels. A matrix 8 pixels wide and 16 pixels high provides plenty of space for standard alphanumeric characters, including ascenders and descenders like k and g, diacritic marks, with leeway for sub- and superscripts, and suitable intercharacter spacing. In fact, many American VDTs allow for even fewer pixels per character. Kanji, however, require a matrix of at least 24-by-24 pixels. Much Japanese equipment makes do with 16-by-16, but this requires some intentional distortion of basic kanji shapes (illustrated in Figure 7). The more pixels per char-

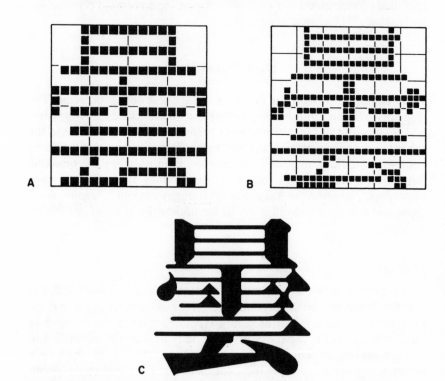

Figure 7   Dot-matrix Patterns of a Troublesome Kanji: (A) 16-by-16 Grid; (B) 24-by-24 Grid; (C) Ordinary Typeface

acter, the fewer characters can be fit onto the screen at the same time. American personal computers typically allow for 24 lines of 80 characters each, or 1,920 per screen. By contrast, the extremely popular NEC 9801 personal computer, which has a capacious 640-by-480 (307,200-pixel) display, cannot show more than about 530 Japanese characters per screen—and then only because it uses 16-by-16 characters. To obtain the better-looking 24-by-24 characters found, for example, on the IBM 5550, more than a million pixels are required to handle roughly the same number of characters. Some manufacturers, not satisfied with the visual appearance of 24-by-24 characters on their hardware, use a 32-by-32 standard.

Resolution is only part of the problem. The matrix pattern of every character the hardware displays has to be stored somewhere in the system. The sheer number of kanji required for Japanese makes this a formidable requirement. The Japanese Industrial Standard (JIS-C6226 [1983]) specifies a two-tier kanji inventory. Level 1 (high-frequency) characters alone number 2,965, and there are a further 3,388 Level 2 (low-frequency) kanji, for a grand total of 6,353; many large systems (e.g., Fujitsu JEF) include more, and even small word processors often allow the user to add extra kanji on an ad hoc basis.

The sheer magnitude of the kanji inventory is perhaps the main reason the Japanese, who are usually fastidious about such things, are willing to put up with the often unsightly 16-by-16 characters.[30] Most computer hardware stores data in multiples of 8 binary digits, or bits: 8 bits make 1 byte. With 32 bytes, the "on/off" status of every one of the 256 pixels in a 16-by-16 matrix can be specified simply by assigning one bit to each pixel. When the same technique is applied to a 24-by-24 matrix, 4 times as many bytes are required even though only 2.25 times as many (viz. 576) pixels need to be represented. This is because there is no direct way to access half a byte.

The word direct here is important. Every computer provides ways to access specific bits within a single byte. The computations needed to keep track of which strings of bits begin in the middle of a byte and which do not are not particularly complicated; they do, however, take time to execute. This is an example of the kind of trade-off that must be considered constantly in computer system design: the cost of a smaller storage requirement is often slower processing time, and vice versa. Several more subtle mathematical techniques can be used to squeeze the same information into fewer bits; but such data compression inevitably entails extra computing time to reconstruct the original matrix before it is passed along to output hardware for display. Sixteen-by-sixteen characters are ugly, but there is no other way to keep memory costs down and plotting speed high without resorting to even more expensive output hardware.

Besides this kind of computational overhead, there are other sources of delay to worry about. Kanji patterns can be retrieved fastest from read-only memory, but it is relatively expensive; for the sake of keeping total system costs down, it is often necessary to store some (or all) kanji on slower media such as disks. In this case, since two kinds of memory are being used, a new kind of computational overhead enters the picture: the computer has to "know" which kanji it has already brought into active memory so that it won't search the disk unless absolutely necessary. Finally, kanji take longer to produce on plotters and other devices that actually "draw" characters line by line. Any one of these operations—retrieval from memory, memory management, and physical output—may require only a few milliseconds in any one particular instance, but their cumulative effect can be substantial.

All these factors conspire to make the cost of outputting kanji relatively high. The Japanese have made great strides in improving the resolution of displays, making cheaper, more compact memories, and speeding up the output of complex graphics; as a result, kanji output is now within an affordable range for many users. But the cost of hardware is falling for *all* systems, not just those that use kanji. The difference in price between hardware that can output kanji and that which cannot will likely continue to shrink, but the use of kanji on computer systems will always require the devotion of a greater percentage of total system cost to output than if kanji were not used at all.

Coding Kanji

In order for a computer to use kanji, they must be assigned code numbers. The Japan Industrial Standard (JIS) provides one basis for doing this, but it has many defects.

Inevitably, it is an arbitrary code. The order of the letters in the alphabet is also arbitrary, but there is a difference of three orders of magnitude between the number of letters in the alphabet and the number of kanji in general use. The JIS Level 1 kanji are grouped roughly in dictionary order according to their most common or distinctive readings. Level 2 kanji are arranged by radical, more or less in the traditional way. Subgroupings are generally by total stroke count, but there are exceptions, as, for example, when the simplified version of a character is immediately followed by the older, more complex version.

Given a kanji at random, there is no way to reconstruct its JIS code without resorting to one or more complete indexes of all JIS values.

Furthermore, the code is incomplete. Various computer manufacturers have tacked on whatever extra symbols they please in whatever order they wish. New kanji can only be added on an ad hoc basis since there is no way to derive code numbers logically. In addition, some machines are designed to use an internal coding scheme different from JIS, making conversions to (or from) JIS codes through software only when the machine transmits (or receives) data through its communications port. For all these reasons, a user may not always be able to move data generated on one system to another.

Finally, because the number of kanji is large, any coding scheme that accommodates them complicates other data-processing operations. One byte (8 bits) can encode up to 256 distinct characters; this is more than enough for alphanumeric operations, and in the United States and elsewhere, the rule is generally "one byte to the character." Two bytes (16 bits) can encode 65,536 characters, more than the number of kanji in the largest lexicon; hence, the JIS codes for kanji are based on a "two bytes to the character" rule. Unfortunately, most Japanese computer applications require mixing alphanumerics with Japanese script. This means either that all symbols besides kanji must also be encoded with two bytes, or else that special "escape codes" must be used to signal the computer when there is a change from one- to two-byte data, or vice versa. (The computer has to be told when to switch because the single-byte codes are also legal parts of the two-byte codes.)

All these factors add to the cost of the system by imposing heavier memory requirements. Because many expressions can legitimately be written in two or more ways, involving different combinations of kanji and kana, interrogating a Japanese database can involve a considerable amount of extra computing time as well. Internationally used software must be substantially modified to allow for kanji codes, and, since spaces are not ordinarily used to separate Japanese words, special algorithms for the morphological analysis of Japanese words and phrases are also needed.[31]

Optimists like to think that the coding problem will largely disappear if international standards for Chinese characters are formulated. They reason that the explicitness of a single, public standard will more than make up for any defects in its design. Unfortunately, there is no practical hope of such a standard being agreed to. Japan, Korea, China, and Taiwan, each have their own, largely incompatible standards. China, at least, would surely not want to commit itself to a plan that would hamper further script reforms. (Each "simplification" of character shapes increases the total number of characters that must be differentiated.) The CJK (Chinese-Japanese-Korean) codes of the bibliographic system used in the Library of Congress and many university libraries throughout the United States are simply a grand amalgam that attempts to make room for every variant character shape and every major national standard. Some large manufacturers are going their own way with proprietary machine-internal coding schemes. The time is approaching, if it is not already past, when so much information will have been encoded in these arbitrary schemes that the sheer cost of re-entering data (even with computer assistance) will make it impossible for a genuine international standard to be established.

Software

Only with costly hardware is it possible to output, compute with, and input kanji; software costs are even stiffer. One expert conservatively estimates that "the cost of software in the United States in 1980 was roughly 84 percent of the combined cost of software and hardware" (Boehm 1983: 79), and although there is some argument over where to draw the line between software and other nonhardware expenses (Cragon 1982, Graham 1983), there can be little doubt that the worldwide trend is upward. In Japan software is, if anything, even costlier because almost all computer programming must be done in English-based programming languages. Even with the advent of passable kanji word processing, the level of documentation is poor, and it is generally agreed that Japan lags behind the United States and Europe in software.

> There is no dispute among industry participants that Japan lacks the software capability needed to fuel its computer sales. . . . The reason for this lag stems from two interrelated sources: (1) the lack of emphasis on national projects that needed high-level software capabilities, and (2) the low esteem of software engineers/programmers as a profession. For example, 20 years ago the United States launched its National Aeronautics and Space Administration (NASA) space programs, which acted as a catalyst for developing software systems. Conversely . . . Japan had no comparable government-sponsored program and did not establish software priorities until the late 1970's. In part a reflection of the national focus (or the lack of it) and in part a reflection of cultural values, the Japanese educational system, as a result, did not prepare the talent it needed to develop software. Although Japan has some 50 scientists and

engineers per 10,000 in the labor force, less than 6 percent of them become software engineers or programmers. In actual numbers, Japan has only 7 percent of the number of software professionals in the United States. (Ohmae 1983: 70–71)

A dissenting opinion, to the effect that the software gap is just an illusion, was put forward by Sophia University professor Gene Gregory in 1982 and recently reiterated by him in a book on the Japanese electronics industry. According to Gregory,

[t]o say that Japanese industry lags in software engineering but leads the world in production efficiency, robotics and quality control is a bald contradiction where bold perspicacity is most important. The reality is that, far from suffering any inherent cultural or social handicap in software engineering, as is often suggested by those who hold to the gap theory, Japanese industry has a proven record of innovation in the design and application of complex software systems. What *is* different about the software industry in Japan is its organizational structure, which tends to obscure the visibility of software production and renders it more difficult to define and to measure. (Gregory 1985: 258)

The problem with Gregory's argument is that it does not take into account either the substance of Japanese programs or the quality of the Japanese software production environment. Much of the software on which Japanese industry runs is in fact imported or closely modelled on (more bluntly, copied from) foreign sources. Software development often proceeds on an ad hoc, special-purpose basis; because almost all detailed documentation is in English, the Japanese have a hard time keeping up with the ideas and practices of programmers overseas. Consider, for example, the following report on the software for Hitachi's S-810 supercomputer:

Other than assembly language, the only language available at the laboratory is FORTRAN. Now, I don't want to put down FORTRAN; it was the second computer language I ever learned (back in the days of FORTRAN II), and it is still one of the best tools around for handling complex numbers and other kinds of heavy-duty number crunching. And there are some fine optimizing compilers for FORTRAN (largely because of some of the main weaknesses of the language, like its lack of structure). But since the supercomputer group is supposed to be on the leading edge of the push for improvement in software productivity, I asked the Hitachi researchers what kinds of software tools were used to speed up program development and improve maintainability. I got blank stares. I then asked if they used something like a RATFOR (Rational FORTRAN) preprocessor. I got more blank stares. I was obviously talking about something completely unknown to them. RATFOR is a preprocessor whose use is essentially free: the source code appears, for example, in the book *Software Tools* by Brian K. Kernighan and P. J. Plauger, and the actual preprocessing is very fast, even on personal computers. The benefits, in terms of development speed and program maintainability and readability, are enormous. Even more to the point, such programs have been available and widely known in the U.S. and elsewhere for more than 10 years. (Raike 1985: 406)

The author has heard any number of similar firsthand experiences like this from professional translators in Tôkyô who deal with Japanese software documentation, and others involved in the computer business there.

As for the "organizational structure" of the Japanese software industry, it is indeed different, but Gregory's interpretation of this difference is questionable. A more plausible view is suggested by H. J. Welke's study of Japanese data processing, based on his research at MITI from January 1979 through June 1980. Welke notes that, although Japan has been "very successful in developing its information industry," it suffers from "a weak and under-capitalised computer service industry which is dependent on the assignments of the computer manufacturers and general companies" and "a software market which is still 'under-developed'" (Welke 1982: 1). On the supply side,

[t]he main reason for the poor situation of the software industry is the attitude of the users towards software. They regard it as part of hardware and are not willing to pay for it separately. Even the Ministry of Finance grants financial support for the acquisition of hardware in government departments more readily than for software, although the Japanese government is making a great effort to promote the development of the software industry. However, since computer manufacturers have decided to unbundle their software costs, the situation of the software industry is supposed to improve.

Another reason for this situation is the fact that ordinary users are not very willing to use general-purpose software. Most companies, organisations, ministries, agencies and municipal bodies have large data processing divisions which are developing the software for their own use and are sceptic towards the use of software packages which are "black boxes" and which they do not understand as much as their own programs. A further impediment against the use of software packages is the absence of standardisation of business in Japanese companies. For example, Fujitsu tried to develop an accounting system, but since every customer wanted to make major modifications, it discontinued this development. After the oil crisis, however, financial considerations have become more important to Japanese companies and they are becoming much more willing to purchase software packages. (Welke 1982: 83)

Welke goes on to cite five additional problem areas, all related to fundamental economic and social conditions of the software development business in Japan. The overall situation was clearly not good at the end of 1980, and the hopeful notes on which Welke concluded his paragraphs have not been justified. According to a more recent report from the Japan Information Processing Development Center, as late as the end of 1982 "80% of all systems software sold in Japan" was still supplied by the mainframe manufacturers themselves, who were "still bundling software to the sale of hardware" (JIPDEC 1984: 40). The same report notes that an increasing percentage of applications software was being produced by independent software developers, but that users were still creating the majority of application programs. The advent of personal computers has not altered the situation very much: according to Raike (1986: 352), except for Japanese word-processing packages, some of the most popular application programs are Japanese versions of U.S.-made spreadsheets and database managers. Raike believes that "a large part of the reason for the low circulation [of Japanese software] is simply the low volume of mutually compatible computers like those found in the IBM PC family," but considering that the lack of meaningful standards for Japanese-script handling is the major reason why no one company has been able to achieve a dominant position in personal computers in Japan like that of IBM in the United States, one must question the adequacy of this explanation. It seems instead that the development of general-purpose software in Japan is being stymied by the script problem, which remains effectively unresolved despite the boom in sales of word-processing hardware and software.

On the demand side, Welke finds four reasons for the limited use of general-purpose software:

[1] the business structure of Japanese companies is as yet less standardised than that of American or European firms;

[2] text processing is more difficult for the Japanese language than for Western languages;
[3] Japanese users are not yet aware of the value of software, therefore they are not willing to pay separately for software;
[4] the experts of d[ata] p[rocessing] divisions want to develop their own software systems. (Welke 1982: 122)

Conditions 1, 3, and 4, already mentioned in connection with the problems of the service industry, to a great extent are products of condition 2. Even today, almost all written documentation in Japan originates in handwritten form. This is why there are so few standards of business practice. Now that computers have arrived, none of the competing manufacturers is eager to agree on any but the most urgently needed standards, each hoping to impose its standards on the others and attain a near-monopoly position à la IBM. Meanwhile, end-users cannot wait and must spend hundreds of man-hours "reinventing the wheel." The result is that sophisticated, high-quality software is rarely encountered outside the organizations that write their own. As a consequence, Japanese computer users have nothing against which to judge the quality of the software available to them unless they travel overseas or tap into international data networks.

The JIPDEC report quoted earlier provides other evidence of the negative effect of kanji on the Japanese software market. Japanese software makers have registered more language processors than any other kind of program (Table 6); and, as the report notes, "there would be no sense in registering software that wasn't being marketed" (JIPDEC 1984: 42). Since fiscal 1979, the language (i.e., Japanese script) processing share of total software production has been shrinking; but, on the consumption side, a 1982 survey by the Nippon Data Processing Association found "[t]he highest usage rate was for language processors (78%), followed by utilities (26.3%) and computer operation management systems (11.8%)" (JIPDEC 1984: 45). Since there was no lack of demand, the drop in language-processing software development can only be attributed to market saturation and the inability of software developers to come up with fundamentally better approaches to the problem rather than to user satisfaction.

Indeed, although 60.5 percent of the 368 companies that were using software products at the time of the NDPA survey "indicated that they were satisfied with their packages when it came to meeting processing needs," only 39.0 percent "were satisfied with the results achieved using ready-made software to improve work performance," and 42

Table 6. General Purpose-Software Registrations in Japan by Type of Program (Cumulative)

Program	Fiscal Year				Net Change
	1979	*1980*	*1981*	*1982*	
Language processors	218	400	557	691	473
Software development/support	127	252	398	510	383
Process control	65	167	316	404	339
Financial planning/management	75	207	274	369	294
Communications control	64	140	234	332	268
Scientific/engineering	44	143	236	274	230
Distribution service	14	50	123	145	131
Data processing/retrieval	7	54	88	113	106
Production	23	32	40	49	26
Social development	10	18	31	51	41
All programs registered	647	1,463	2,297	2,938	2,291
Annual Percentages (%)					
Language processors	33.7	27.3	24.2	23.5	−10.2
Software development/support	19.6	17.2	17.3	17.4	−2.3
Process control	10.0	11.4	13.8	13.8	3.7
Financial planning/management	11.6	14.1	11.9	12.6	1.0
Communications control	9.9	9.6	10.2	11.3	1.4
Scientific/engineering	6.8	9.8	10.3	9.3	2.5
Distribution service	2.2	3.4	5.4	4.9	2.8
Data processing/retrieval	1.1	3.7	3.8	3.8	2.8
Production	3.6	2.2	1.7	1.7	−1.9
Social development	1.5	1.2	1.3	1.7	0.2

Source: JIPDEC 1983/1984 Computer White Paper.

percent complained about "the abundance of packages available that could only be used on specific machines or for specific purposes" (JIPDEC 1984: 45–46). Equally telling was the finding that imported software was selling well: The three packages that had cumulative sales of more than ¥2 billion as of August 1983 were all imports, as were 10 of the 17 that had sales volumes between ¥200 million and ¥1 billion, and 9 of the 17 with volumes between ¥50 million and ¥200 million (JIPDEC 1984: 50–51).

Thus, despite Welke's optimism (Welke 1982: 124–127, 138), the lack of adequate kanji text processing remains a major impediment to software development and utilization.[32] Sales of Japanese word processors and other office automation equipment are booming, but fundamental breakthroughs, particularly in input, have yet to be made.

While new computerized bulletin boards and data retrieval services flourish in the United States, and the French government contemplates putting a computer terminal in every home, "[t]oday only two percent of the Japanese people can operate computers" (Karatsu 1985: 119). The ancient technology of writing with kanji and the future technologies of communicating through computers are in fundamental conflict. Hardware engineering can help keep this conflict within tolerable limits—provided always that computer users are willing to foot the bill—but it cannot offer an ultimate remedy. Computers do not raise productivity unless people restructure the way they do their work to take advantage of the new opportunities the computers afford (Bowen 1986), but this process of adaptation is impossible without well-written, flexible, general-purpose software. In the case of Japan, that means making some changes in the writing system, or at least in the customary ways of doing things that have evolved to accommodate it.

It's either that or inventing a completely new kind of computer.

II

POLITICS
AND
CULTURE

3

The Price of Tradition

Clearly, some computer tasks that would be very easy and cheap to do using a phonemic representation of Japanese data are difficult and expensive to do using kanji. But difficult does not mean impossible, and judging whether or not a particular price is fair is a notoriously subjective matter. Current trends in computer usage in Japan suggest that the Japanese are willing to pay anything for the dubious privilege of being able to use kanji on computers. In countless everyday applications, output involving kanji is not needed, yet Japan seems prepared to foot the bill for lavish output devices and all the extra costs associated with maintaining kanji databases. When it comes to input, things are even worse. Why not use standard alphanumerics? This simple bit of decidedly low-tech engineering would cost next to nothing in terms of hardware, resolve all the problems touched on in Part I, and be extremely easy to implement, since any native speaker of Japanese can learn how to transcribe the language in roman letters quickly and accurately in a few hours. Why cling to kanji under these circumstances?

At one level, the answer is obvious: kanji are part of Japanese culture; Japanese don't want to give them up just because of computers. But this is inadequate: there are many areas of Japanese life in which people seem quite happy to let kanji usage fall into decline. The use of kana and rômaji where kanji were once *de rigueur* is now accepted practice in Japanese typography. The mass media are using ever greater numbers of gairaigo (Passin 1980: 48). Chinese-style word formation is fast losing its position as the principal means of making up new words for new things and ideas (Passin 1980: 49–61, Kabashima 1981). In most situations, Japanese have abandoned Chinese methods of writing numbers and calculations. No one seems to feel that these things are detrimental to Japanese culture. But the suggestion that it might be wise to use standard alphanumerics in those computer applications that do not specifically require kanji output leaves most Japanese bewildered. Almost everyone seems willing and able to recite a whole litany of reasons for retaining kanji: the language contains too many homonyms to be written phonetically; the native vocabulary, after centuries of erosion by Chinese, is too impoverished to meet the needs of a modern society; Japanese ways of thinking depend on schooling in kanji. All such statements (these are but a sampling) are simply false. Why do the Japanese keep repeating them?

One line of thought, put forward forcefully by linguist Roy Andrew Miller, holds that "[t]o the Japanese today, the Japanese language is not simply the way they talk and write. For them, it has assumed the dimensions of a national myth of vast proportions" (Miller 1982: 5). The essence of this myth is that the Japanese language is different from all other languages to a superlative degree: all languages differ from one another, but Japanese is unique "to a higher order" than all the rest. From this idea flow

> claims to the effect that the Japanese language is exceptionally difficult in comparison with all other languages; or that the Japanese language possesses a kind of spirit or soul that sets it apart from all other languages, which do not possess such a spiritual entity; or that the Japanese language is somehow purer, and has been less involved in the course of its history with the normal process of language change and language mixture that has been the common fate of all other known human languages; or that the Japanese language is endowed with a distinctive character or special inner nature that makes it possible for Japanese society to use it for a variety of supralinguistic or nonverbal communications not enjoyed by any other society—a variety of communication not possible in societies that can only employ other, ordinary languages. (Miller 1982: 10–11)

There is a sizable grain of truth in this. Like residents of any smallish country with a long history, the people of Japan tend to run very hot or very cold about their native tongue. Either it is the most refined, most subtle, and most aesthetically perfect language in all the world, or else it is the most difficult, most illogical, and most mysterious. Either way, the point is that one's own language is "unique" in a sense very close to "superior," though the hubris of the sentiment is masked by the choice of words. All this is not particularly Japanese and Miller is not the first to observe it.

Miller's account of the causes of these ethnocentric language attitudes, however, is new. We must digress to examine his interpretation in some detail, for two reasons. The first is that Miller, who enjoys considerable academic stature in the United States (he is currently president of the American Oriental Society), has chosen to make his case in bitterly sarcastic terms, often embroidering the facts for the sake of heightened rhetorical effect.[1] Indeed, his tone in *Japan's Modern Myth* is so caustic that, as of 1985, it was rumored that no less than three Japanese publishers interested in bringing out a translation backed down once they had had a chance to read the original carefully. As one sympathetic but critical reviewer notes, the "bellicose and exaggerated style" of the book "makes Miller look like a grumpy old man" (Chew 1984: 479).[2] Because we will be making many critical observations about contemporary Japanese attitudes toward kanji, we must take care to distinguish our interpretation of these observations from Miller's.

Miller's explanation of Japanese views on language is one calculated to appeal to Americans, especially if they lived through World War II. Unfortunately, it is also the explanation least in consonance with the historical facts. This is the second reason it deserves special attention. According to Miller, "[t]he nationalist-fascist dictatorship that led Japan into its ill-advised military adventures" made use of "an elaborate sustaining myth" that "may be broken down into three equal parts."

> One comprised selected elements drawn out of indigenous Japanese religious beliefs; the second embraced a selection of nineteenth-century nationalistic fantasies borrowed from Western Europe, particularly from Prussia; and the third was rooted in a number of Japanese elaborations and perversions of the already quite sufficiently perverted "master race" or "superman" ideas that had by then begun to become popular in the Third Reich. (Miller 1982: 35)

This ideology, according to Miller, did not perish in the cataclysm of 1945. Instead, it underwent a metamorphosis in which its focus shifted to the Japanese language.

> The desolation of the bombed-out cities of postwar Japan was at once both the most eloquent and the most painful metaphor for the spiritual and intellectual desolation of the Japanese themselves. In city after city, nothing of all that had seemed so very substantial was left standing. What little had survived the nightly fire raids had immediately to be

pulled down before it collapsed of its own damaged weight. The day the war ended, nothing of Japanese life seemed to have endured—except the language. (Miller 1982: 36)

Daily encounters with Occupation troops heightened Japanese awareness of their linguistic isolation and encouraged "the emergence of the Japanese language as the fetish focus for a new national sustaining myth," but "[t]he old myth had been rich in elements relating to the language," which provided the seeds for the new (Miller 1982: 38–39). Thus, Miller's theory is essentially one of transference and continuity—and this is why it ultimately fails as an account of contemporary Japanese attitudes toward language.

In the first place, it oversimplifies and distorts the history of the pre-1945 myth, which Carol Gluck has painstakingly traced through its formative years in the Late Meiji Period (1867–1912). Although she devotes a chapter to "the language of ideology" in the metaphorical sense of "language," nowhere does she uncover the kind of ideas about language, in the strict sense, that Miller alleges were there all along.[3] Concepts such as "national essence" *(kokusui)*, "distinctive national character" *(kokuminsei)*, and "Japanism" *(Nihonshugi)* were not tied to language, and were in fact first articulated by intellectuals opposed to either Shintô or Confucian national doctrine (Gluck 1985: 112–113). These concepts changed in meaning over time and became part of the vocabulary of Miller's "old myth," but prejudices specifically about language are simply not "among the dependent clauses of the Meiji ideological utterance" (Gluck 1985: 286) that managed to survive 1945.

The second problem with Miller's surrender-trauma theory is that it doesn't jibe with chronology. Some of the strongest believers in linguistic nativism today are Japanese who have no adult experience of the war or Occupation, while many otherwise conventional Japanese of the prewar period held views about language more liberal than those of their postwar counterparts. Certainly, the Occupation was a turning point, but as far as attitudes toward language are concerned, it was a transition from a period of intellectual diversity and boldness to one of uniformity and complacency. Miller's theory gets the order backwards. Today's linguistic nativism is not a remnant of ultranationalism clung to by defeated Japanese who lost everything else, but a distinctively postwar conservatism that appeals to affluent Japanese who never learned (or have chosen to forget) the lessons of the past.

Finally, Miller's argument fails to discriminate among the different kinds of nativist thinking he identifies. Japanese attitudes toward the writing system, foreigners, literature, education, and so on, are for him just different aspects of a single phenomenon. In fact, belief in the indispensability of kanji cuts across the spectrum of Japanese public opinion in a way that most if not all the other ideas Miller attacks do not. There are plenty of liberal-minded Japanese who are dissatisfied with the way English is presently taught in Japanese schools, who laugh at the suggestion that foreigners can never really learn Japanese, who are opposed to the government's discriminatory policies toward resident Koreans, and who scoff at the theories of Tsunoda Tadanobu.[4] In short, plenty of Japanese reject one or more of the attitudes that Miller imputes to the nation as a whole. Yet these same people, when asked about kanji, will repeat, as if rehearsed, the whole host of stock explanations for the use of kanji mentioned earlier.

What, then, lies behind the Japanese attachment to kanji? The answer, as we shall see, is to be found in the combined effects of the educational and script reforms introduced under the Occupation. These reforms have greatly increased the ability of the school system to inculcate the population with what might be called the folklore of kanji, not only by increasing the number of students in school and the years they spend there, but also by demanding more of the individual student while cheapening the social value of being literate.

Kanji and Literacy

Today's Japanese writing system is a remarkably complex and unwieldy thing, but it must be kept in mind that it is a simplified version of the system that existed prior to 1945. Following World War II, the Japanese government took several major steps toward script reform, culminating a long period of both public and official discussion of the many forms and styles of Japanese writing that stood in the way of full economic and social development (Twine 1983, Seeley 1984). Without those decades of preparation, it is unlikely that the government would have been able to respond to Occupation recommendations for reform as promptly and effectively as it did. Between 1946 and 1959 it moved to limit the number of kanji in daily use, eliminate almost all archaic kana spellings, simplify hard-to-write kanji shapes, place restrictions on kanji readings, and standardize okurigana usage. Seeley calls these the TK Reforms because the 1,850 approved characters were known as the *tôyô kanji*.

Many scholars who have written about Japanese literacy are of the opinion that the TK Reforms were rather superfluous, something that was done to appease Occupation personnel who were advocating much more radical kinds of reform, such as romanization by edict. In this view, Japan was a relatively literate nation even at the end of the Tokugawa Period (1600–1867); if there were any problems with kanji before 1945, the TK Reforms eliminated them. There is, however, an important distinction to be made between literacy as usually defined in technical studies (minimum ability to read and write) and literacy as a vehicle for full and free participation in society. The use of kanji makes this distinction crucial: one might be able to write and read kana and know the principles underlying the use of kanji yet be unable to read texts without furigana or write an acceptable petition to the authorities. Before 1945, this discrepancy was greatly intensified by the heavy influence of written Chinese on Japanese style. Although writing in colloquial Japanese certainly existed, formal writing demanded familiarity with kanbun, and although the kanbun tradition gradually waned in the twentieth century, traces of it can still be found in ordinary kanamajiribun writing. Chinese literary studies were a major part of the prewar higher school curriculum (Roden 1980), and ability to use kanbun expressions is still regarded as a sign of erudition.

In Western countries, there is a similar gap between mere literacy and the level of education at which the doors to social equality and remunerated creative accomplishment are opened; but the Western gap is negligible compared with the one that existed and continues to exist in Japan, where all literacy, and hence all education, is grounded in kanji. Claims of literacy rates in excess of 99 percent (e.g., Sakamoto & Makita 1973: 444) are grossly misleading if not downright false. As Miller notes (1982: 186), this figure must be wrong simply because the percentage of handicapped persons physically unable to read must exceed one percent in any normal population. More to the point, however, the reason Sakamoto, Makita, and other Japanese claim super-high rates of literacy is that they accept a definition of literacy that totally ignores its social significance.

Prewar Literacy

Some historians of the "modernizaton" school, which has dominated postwar scholarship in the United States, have also missed this point. In Black et al. 1975, a comparative study of Japanese and Russian modernizaton, Russia fares poorly whenever literacy is mentioned, yet virtually no hard evidence is offered for the sanguine view of early Japanese literacy. For example,

> The difficulty of the Japanese writing system seems not to have been an overwhelming obstacle in the spread of literacy. Japan in the first place shared with the rest of the East Asian cultural zone a boundless respect for the written word and for scholarship. One may further surmise that the very difficulty of the Japanese writing system made it a great challenge, and hence desirable, while at the same time it provided a level of discipline and patience in the acquisition of literacy that doubtless had positive effects in the realm of social stability. Writing in particular was a highly refined artistic tradition, so much so that all artistic production in premodern times was intimately associated with the written word. In Japan literacy received an aura of prestige far greater than it did in Russia. (Black et al. 1975: 108)

The difficulty of the writing system certainly was, and remains, a force for "social stability," but what does that, or "artistic production," have to do with literacy? The key question is *how many* Japanese were able to read and write, and *at what level*. The evidence presented is too impressionistic to allow for any meaningful conclusions. One cannot, for example, infer from the use of "signboards to communicate the will of the shogunal and domain authorities" (Black et al. 1975: 109) that there was "an increasing reliance on the written language in the political system of Tokugawa Japan"; more likely than not, the ordinary citizen learned what a signboard said because some educated person read it out loud to the anxious crowd that had gathered to see it posted. Again, the fact that "Fukuzawa Yukichi's *Conditions in the West* . . . is reported to have sold 150,000 copies in its first edition in 1867" (109) is meaningless in isolation and must be interpreted in relation to the extraordinary novelty and timeliness of Fukuzawa's subject and the number of potential readers.[5]

A more revealing use of publication statistics is found in Kinmonth's study of the self-help literature of the Meiji Period, where the question of literacy is mentioned in connection with the influential pamphlet *Gakumon no susume* (The Advancement of Learning) by Fukuzawa Yukichi. This was actually the title of a series of seventeen pamphlets published between December 1871 and November 1876. But the first outsold the rest: by 1880, Fukuzawa estimated that 200,000 legitimate and 20,000 unauthorized copies were in circulation. On this basis he concluded that one out of every 160 Japanese had read it. Kinmonth goes further, claiming that "perhaps as many as 1 out of

10 or even 1 out of 5 *who could read it* had done so" (Kinmonth 1981: 45; emphasis added). Particular attention should be paid to the way in which Kinmonth arrived at these figures.

> For a rough calculation of potential audience, I assumed, as did Fuku-zawa, a total population of 35 million. From this I deducted one third for infants and nonliterate juveniles, one-half of the remainder for females, and assumed that 20 percent of the remaining population (2.3 million) could read *Gakumon no susume* in its original form. Ronald Dore has placed late Tokugawa literacy at 40–50 percent for males, a figure that has been criticized by Japanese scholars as being somewhat overly optimistic. See Fukaya [1969] p. 55, n. 127. Considering that in the late 1890s conscription tests were turning up total illiteracy rates of 25 percent (see Fukaya [1969] pp. 285–286) and that *Gakumon no susume* was fairly difficult in its original form (so much so that some illicit versions were simplified), 20 or even 10 percent seems a more reasonable rate. (Kinmonth 1981: 45–46)

Even with "total literacy rates of 25 percent," nineteenth-century Japan may very well have been more literate than Russia. But the significance of this purely quantitative observation pales in the light of the enormous qualitative difference between the Japanese and alphabetic writing systems.

This is hardly a new or radical insight, although views such as those of Black et al. are all too common. Other scholars have been more sensitive to the problems inherent in the definition of literacy. For example, in his 1965 *Society and Education in Japan,* Herbert Passin stresses the growth of education during the Tokugawa period, the diversity of its intellectual life, and the role of its educational institutions as precursors of later educational reforms (Passin 1982: 13–61). He concludes that "[w]hen feudal Japan first blinked her eyes open on the modern world," roughly four of every ten Japanese adults were literate (Passin 1982: 56–57; see Table 7); however, he is quick to note that "[m]uch of it was certainly of a very low order—perhaps the bare ability to write one's name or to read simple materials with effort" (Passin 1982: 58). Taira (1971: 375–376), working with Ronald Dore's (1965: 321) optimistic though qualified estimate of school attendance by the end of the Tokugawa Period and later school-attendance statistics, puts the male and female literacy rates in 1868 at about 35 and 8 percent, respectively. Although he notes a rise to about 75 and 68 percent, respectively, over the next forty-five years, he emphasizes the need to analyze "Meiji Japan's progress in education and literacy without the glow of 'rapid' economic development in the background."

Table 7. Estimates of Japanese Literacy at the Beginning of the Meiji Period

Social Group	Estimated Literacy (%)	Proportion of Total Population (%)	Calculated Rate of Literacy (%) (min)	(max)
Samurai		"7"		
Men	95–99[a]	3.5	3.3	3.5
Women	"50"	3.5	1.8	1.8
Merchants		"3"		
Cities		0.6[b]		
Men	"70–80"	0.3	0.2	0.2
Women	60[c]	0.3	0.2	0.2
Smaller towns/rural	"50–60"	2.4	1.2	1.4
Artisans		"2"		
Cities	"50–60"	0.4[b]	0.2	0.2
Smaller towns/rural	"40–50"	1.6	0.6	0.8
Farmers		"87"		
Villages				
Notables	95–99[a]	4.4[d]	4.2	4.4
Middle layers	"50–60"	13.0[d]	6.5	7.8
Lower peasants	"30–40"	60.9[d]	18.3	24.4
Peasants in the more				
isolated areas	"20"	8.7[d]	1.7	1.7
Others	50	1[e]	0.5	0.5
TOTAL			38.8	47.0

Note: Figures in quotation marks are from Passin 1982: 57; other figures are estimated or calculated.
[a]"Almost 100%."
[b]In a footnote, Passin says that "towns and cities may have run as high as 15 to 20 per cent" of the total population; for the purposes of calculation, the high estimate (20%) was used.
[c]"Their women folk—perhaps somewhat higher than samurai women."
[d]That is, 5%, 15%, 70%, and 10%, respectively, of Passin's "87%."
[e]Passin's population breakdown sums to 99%.

Quantitatively, the spread of literacy in Meiji Japan was credible enough. Qualitatively, however, the "compulsory" education imposed on the unwilling populace without a full commitment of public resources ("compulsory" but not "free") was painful as well as wasteful. (Taira 1971: 372)

Taira specifically identifies the use of kanji as a factor contributing to the questionable qualitative results of the prewar educational system (390–391) and takes pains to explain the attitudes that made kanji and kanbun sacrosanct:

Spoken Japanese was only a tool of oral communicaton, and even lowly beings like beggars and thieves were capable of speaking it. Writing, therefore, had to show the mark of accomplishment with rules of its own sharply distinguished from the ordinary manner of speech. Often, written Japanese placed style, grammar and aesthetic value above the requirements of clear communication. Written Japanese was, therefore, grossly inadequate as a means of conveying precise technical information, though enormously effective as a tool of moral exhortation or of emotional appeal. But to be influenced by written Japanese, the ordinary souls had to have the text read to them by a person with the appropriate level of literacy. For the same reason, those who were literate considered themselves many flights above the ordinary people. *The standards of literacy for written communication were so high that many, despite good elementary education, gave up their efforts to rise to that level of literacy and consequently allowed their elementary knowledge of written Japanese to atrophy.* (Taira 1971: 392; emphasis added)

Although Gluck paints a somewhat brighter picture of the same period, emphasizing the growth of the press as a factor in social change, she notes that "[t]he establishment of the written colloquial language *(genbun itchi)* and the widespread use of *furigana* glosses increased the accessibility of newspaper and popular works" (Gluck 1985: 172–173). This is something of an understatement: accessibility could not have increased otherwise. As Twine remarks in her study of pre-twentieth-century script reform movements,

Years of arduous study were required to master the literary forms and script of officialdom, and only the upper classes had the leisure to devote to it. The degree of literacy attained by the commoners was usually just sufficient for the small concerns of everyday life and the perusal of popular fiction. (Twine 1983: 116)

As always, we must not forget that the use of both kana and kanji makes the definition of literacy in the case of Japanese unusually broad.

Lower-class education extended to little more than the *kana* scripts; even upper-class children, ostensibly receiving a thorough Confucian education, often merely learned to recite passages by heart rather than actually read and understand them. Hours of concentrated study were required to memorize characters before the contents of books could be absorbed. (Twine 1983: 117–118)

Despite Japan's rapid economic development during and after the turn of the century, reliable figures on literacy are hard to find. Government reports were—and still are (Booth et al. 1984: 7)—little more than estimates based on school attendance. Writing in 1947, the only statistics that John DeFrancis found worthy of quoting were from the German study cited in Chapter 1 (Scharschmidt 1924):

> Before the war the requirements for graduation from lower primary school, which is all the education received by most Japanese, included the ability to read and write 1360 Sino-Japanese ideographs and to recognize another 1020, or a total of 2380 in all. Tests conducted when male youths were called up for military service years later showed that twenty-year old youths with public school education remembered how to write an average only 500 or 600 and to recognize only 1000 of the 2380 ideographs which they had once learned. (DeFrancis 1947: 220)

Figures on the rate of "practically illiterate" young men turned up by conscription tests, such as those cited in 1931 by Nitobe Inazô, also suggest that the educational system was not meeting its stated goals (see Table 8). In a 1929 work, Nitobe refers to "an illuminating study made of the language instruction as given in Japanese and European, especially Bavarian, schools," which showed that "Japanese children spend 44% of their school days in learning their mother tongue as against 31% by Europeans" (Nitobe 1972: 4.433). He continues,

> The result of investigaton seems to show that the vocabulary and the reading capacity of an ordinary Japanese youth at the age of fifteen is about on a level with the average German child of eight.
>
> A curious corroboration of this statement is furnished by observations of the blind, who learn to read by the Braille system only the 47 characters of the Kana and who are not taught Chinese ideographs. It has been repeatedly proved that the blind acquire, in the same length of time, more solid knowledge than ordinary children—be it of history, geography or literature. (Nitobe 1972: 4.433–434)

Table 8.   Rate of Illiteracy among Military Conscripts

Year	Number Tested	Number Illiterate	
1927	514,364	54,000	10.50%
1928	572,012	53,780	9.40%
1929	465,809	39,073	8.39%

Note: Figures for 1929 do not include Tôkyô and Ôsaka Prefectures; all figures are based on Nitobe 1972: 3.245.

Unfortunately, neither Scharschmidt nor Nitobe cite sources for their information.

Other evidence of the period just before and during World War II is frankly anecdotal. The following example comes from the writings of the late Tôdô Akiyasu, one of Japan's foremost Chinese linguists:

Postwar Japan was able to rebuild rapidly. Could it have done so had it not cut military expenditures to the bone under the protection of the [new] Constitution? Across the country, young and old alike came to be able to read newspapers and magazines and to write letters and diaries. Would this have happened without the revolution in Japanese orthography? When those of us who know the past think back to before the war, surely these are the facts which make the deepest impression on us. I was drafted into the 36th Regiment of the Mie Prefectural Infantry; among the 150 men in my company, some from the Shima seacoast and the mountainous areas of Iga couldn't read a whole sentence. I was ordered to teach ten or so, who could not even write kana properly, every evening. The company commander made them learn the Imperial Rescript to Soldiers and Sailors *(Gunjin chokuyu)* by rote, and they would bark it out with their eyes fixed on the ceiling: "Military men should set their mind on nitrogen [*chisso*] (which should have been 'frugality' [*shisso*])." Whenever I went back to the country for the weekend, old couples in the neighborhood would bring me letters from their sons and ask, "Please read this for us." (Tôdô 1982: 173–174; trans. JMU)

Personal reminiscences—even accurate ones—are certainly not the best sort of evidence, but when a scholar who has devoted his entire life to the study of the Chinese language and writing system comes down squarely on the side of script reform, one must pause to reflect. Moreover, illiteracy and the poor technical education of the average conscript figure in other wartime reports. In one case, a soldier sent to fetch a replacement part for a damaged artillery piece returned with a completely different part; he had forgotten the official kango name he had been told—to him, it was just a meaningless string of syllables (Hoshina 1949: 209). Incidents like this often led to disaster (Hirai 1948: 330), and by 1940, the army had limited the number of kanji for weapon parts to 1,235 and was studying the possibility of cutting that number in half (Hoshina 1949: 210, 215). Ironically, the military continued to pepper its reports in civilian newspapers and magazines with obscure, hard-to-read kanji in the belief that this would impress and cow the general public (Hirai 1948: 327–328).

The first full-fledged attempt to measure literacy was carried out in

1948. This survey, conducted by the Civil Information and Education (CI&E) Section of the Occupation, involved the testing of about 17,000 Japanese men and women between the ages of fifteen and sixty-four throughout the country. According to Ishiguro Yoshimi, who chaired the survey's Central Planning and Analysis committee, it was a first not only by Japanese but also by world standards (Ishiguro 1951: 181). It is of particular interest not only because of its statistical thoroughness but also because some Japanese (e.g., Ishii 1983: 22) cite it as proof that the level of literacy of the majority of prewar Japanese was actually quite high. Certainly that is the interpretation that Joseph C. Trainor, who worked in the Education Division of CI&E from 1945 to 1952, chose to give it in his memoirs:

> The results showed conclusively that with the exception of one group, those who had had no formal education, Japanese of all ages, degrees of schooling, occupation, or whatever other characteristic, possessed the ability to read, write and comprehend materials of the type which regularly appeared in their newspapers. The performances on the tests varied in relation to the amount of schooling and the age level; but to the extent that ability to read newspaper material was a measure, the Japanese could without hesitation be described as literate. Results of measurements in the other skills were similar and it seemed possible to put forward as a tentative conclusion the contention that the Japanese people possess the ability to use their language effectively in their social lives. (Trainor 1983: 323)

Trainor's views obviously support the usual appraisal of prewar Japanese literacy. It must be remembered, however, that he was a civilian employee of the Occupation and strongly believed in the official policy of not interfering in Japanese affairs unless absolutely necessary for the fulfillment of specific Occupation aims such as fostering democratic institutions, eradicating the effects of ultranationalist propaganda, and so on. Trainor himself was not surprised by the results of the survey; they "were startling and disturbing *to many who had preconceptions regarding the reading ability of the Japanese people*" (323, emphasis added). By this he clearly meant reform-minded officers of the Language Simplification Branch, for whom he had little respect (300–308), and the various Japanese proponents of romanization, whom he considered "extremists" (57, 315, 325). Even if his opinions did not bias his judgment of the survey results, there are three other reasons for discounting his assessment. He was not involved with the survey itself (Yomikaki Nôryoku Chôsa Iinkai 1951: 32); his understanding of the

Japanese writing system and general linguistics was deficient (e.g., Trainor 1983: 214, 313, 315, 318, etc.); and some of his statements (written in 1952–1953, immediately upon his return from Japan, though published later) are contradicted by documents of the time that have recently come to light (cf. Nishi 1982: 199–205).

Most important, the conclusions of the literacy survey itself (Yomikaki Nôryoku Chôsa Iinkai 1951: 425–430) do not agree with Trainor's. The survey found that the rate of illiteracy (*monmôritsu*, complete inability to read or write) was indeed very low; *but it also concluded that only 6.2 percent of the population were literate in terms of the survey definition, which was liberal.* Full literacy was defined as answering all questions correctly; illiteracy was defined as scoring zero. By today's standards, all the questions were very simple. The ability to write kanji from dictation *(kanji no kakitori),* which was identified as the single most important skill tested, was found to be "remarkably low" in *all* groups surveyed. Performance was closely correlated with levels of formal education; subjects whose education had been disrupted by the war did significantly poorer in all areas. This showed that mastery of the basics, without years of supplementary instruction in kanji, was inadequate for full literacy. Finally, the claim, long made by script reform advocates, that the average Japanese experienced trouble dealing with mass communication media was deemed proven.

After 1945

Clearly, although the *rate* (quantity) of complete illiteracy before World War II was low, so was the *level* (quality) of literacy achieved by the average Japanese. It might be thought that, thanks to the postwar reforms of the schools and the writing system and the general improvement in the Japanese standard of living, disparities in levels of literacy have been eliminated. The truth, however, seems to be quite the opposite: even today, despite the thoroughness of Japanese secondary education, the quality of literacy it imparts is not uniformly high.

Sixty years after Scharschmidt, and thirty-seven years after his own research on the subject, DeFrancis could report no change in the level of individual student accomplishment.

Sato Hideo, head of the Research Section for Historical Documents, National Institute for Education Research in the Japanese Ministry of Education, has estimated that public school graduates, who now receive nine years of compulsory schooling, retain a recognition knowledge of the 1,945 kanji but soon forget how to write all but 500 or so (1980: personal communication). (DeFrancis 1984b: 217)

What has changed is not average student performance but the number of students involved, or, to put it another way, what is expected of the average Japanese youngster. Compulsory education was extended from six to nine years soon after the war. The Report of the U.S. Education Mission, submitted to General MacArthur on 30 March 1946, noted that "approximately 85% of Japanese children terminated their formal education after leaving elementary school" (U.S. State Department 1946: 21); by 1974, more than 90 percent of all students were graduating from high school (twelfth grade), a higher percentage than in the United States (Rohlen 1983: 3). As a result of this change, the burden of learning thousands of kanji, once shouldered by only a small, virtually all-male fraction of the school-age population, must now be borne by nearly all Japanese children. Students who cannot make the grade, once a minority within a small minority, now constitute, in absolute numbers, a substantial group. What is more, the level of literacy that these students are having a hard time reaching no longer commands the kind of respect it once did.

Postwar Japanese education has been very effective in many ways. It is a mistake, however, to suppose that cultural homogeneity carries over into uniform academic achievement.[6] While cram schools *(juku)* flourish and competition among diligent students remains keen, the willingness of young Japanese to read material written at a high level, apart from schoolwork, has clearly declined over the past twenty years. Comic books, sports newspapers, and sensational weeklies are crowding out serious books and magazines, and many of the larger, older publishing houses are said to be ailing financially. In one of the Kôbe high schools Rohlen studied between 1974 and 1975, an extreme but not necessarily extraordinary case, the level of student literacy was appalling.

> The "discussion" comes to an end. Everyone opens his book to the appropriate page, and the teacher appoints a student to read aloud. His progress is slow as he stumbles over three or four characters per sentence. I am shocked to find that I know some characters the students are regularly missing. And so it goes for the remaining class time: seven lines of text covered in thirty minutes. The almost constant corrections of pronunciation make the lesson unbearably tiresome and boring. There is no time to discuss the meaning of the essay, its style, or its charm. The fact is that the students simply cannot read it. (Rohlen 1983: 29)

Sakura is a night-school, the least prestigious of the five studied by Rohlen. "Rarely are there more applications than openings to Sakura, and to fill its official quota of eighty freshmen the school has a late application period and has been willing to accept students clearly incapable of high school work" (Rohlen 1983: 32). But these very qualifications only go to show that the stock claims of 99 percent literacy cannot be taken seriously.

One indicator of extreme stress is suicide. Student suicides in Japan are often ascribed to the intense pressures of "examination hell,"[7] but as Rohlen (330–331) points out, police officials classified only 26.6 percent of the suicides committed during the first half of 1977 by persons under twenty-one as "school-related." And according to an earlier national study, "although 90 percent of the fifteen- to nineteen-year-old group were in school in 1974, 24 percent of the suicides in this group were committed by people not in school" (Rohlen 1983: 333). The greater concentration of cases among those few who had already dropped out of high school or left school after ninth grade (the last year of compulsory education) suggests that the rate of Japanese juvenile suicide is not as directly tied to the mad rush to pass entrance exams to elite high schools and universities as is usually thought. If the exams are not the immediate problem, what is? Rohlen (1983: 334) mentions "the custom of not keeping slow students back and the relatively undeveloped use of screening techniques to discover (and perhaps treat separately) students with learning disabilities." Another, simpler explanation is possible, however: If students don't keep pace in the learning of kanji, they gradually and inevitably fall behind in all areas of study. Unless they are obviously handicapped, society makes no allowance for them because the writing system has become a sacred cow.

An examination of postwar juvenile suicide rates implicates the writing system in another, more subtle way. The peak years for juvenile suicides were 1955 through 1958 (Rohlen 1983: 329). There was a marked drop after 1958, which as Rohlen points out contradicts the hypothesis that exam pressures are the prime cause of youth suicides: "[a]s the percentage of young Japanese involved in the pressures of the exam system increased, the suicide rate for their age group declined" (328). But what about the dramatic rise up to 1955–1958? It was during this period that the first wholly postwar educated students were leaving school. For them and their successors, the TK list of 1,850 kanji, though intended as a maximum limit on the number of kanji, was actually a minimum standard of literacy. They were, in this sense, the first generation in Japanese history to carry the full weight of kanji in a society that all too often equates knowledge of many kanji with real intelligence. There were undoubtedly other factors that contributed to the cresting of the juvenile suicide rate around this time, but it is hard to believe that the stress and anxiety of this unprecedented situation did not have something to do with it. A mere twenty years before, it was "common sense" that only the handful of young men who went on to higher schools and universities could read and write thousands of kanji or needed to; now, in the middle of hard times and scarce jobs, that was the yardstick by which everyone was to be measured.

Significantly, the first postwar surge of popular interest in the Japanese language occurred at just this time. The press called it a Japanese language boom *(Nihongo bûmu)*, and it was marked by bestsellers such as *Nihongo (The Japanese Language,* 1957) by Kindaichi Haruhiko, *Nihongo no kigen (Origins of the Japanese Language,* 1957) by Ôno Susumu, and a host of similar books. The Ministry of Education carried out a second literacy survey (1955–1956), but the findings turned out to be rather similar to those of 1948. "The results of [both] the surveys well illustrate the phenomenon of 'restricted literacy.' Between 20% and 50% of Japanese language users were described as experiencing intense or noticeable problems in the use of the written language" (Neustupný 1984: 118). But there was much more interest in the uniqueness of the Japanese language than in these mundane and rather unpleasant statistics. As uncertainties about the new educational system were rendered moot by more and larger graduating classes, Japan settled down to the happy myth of 99 percent literacy. "No new survey of literacy has been conducted since 1956" (Neustupný 1984: 120).

Political Maneuvering

This period also marked the beginning of a political backlash against the limited script reforms that had begun with the tôyô kanji list of 1946 and culminated with the okurigana rules of 1959. Some of the Ministry of Education officials, such as Shiraishi Daiji (interviewed 8 January 1986), and others who were responsible for the TK reforms had mistakenly believed that they must accept a restriction in the number of kanji in order to forestall an Occupation romanization edict (never a serious threat). In fact, however, there had been years of preparation for limited script reform; only Japanese decided exactly what steps would be taken. Recommendations were made by a fairly representative and independent Japanese Language Council (Kokugo Shingikai) in a relatively apolitical atmosphere.

All this changed toward the end of the fifth term of the JLC, which lasted from 30 March 1959 to 22 March 1961 (Ôkubo 1978: 105–133).

In early 1961, four conservative JLC members, with the acquiescence and probably the cooperation of responsible government officials, used filibuster tactics to prevent the JLC from electing a nominating committee. This gave the Minister of Education a free hand in appointing new JLC members for the sixth term, which began in October. In March 1962, the new council chairman announced that he, the vice-chairman, and six other members whom he had selected, would serve on a newly created Executive Committee. This new committee would initiate all matters to be considered by the council as a whole. At the third Executive Committee meeting, it was announced that the ministry was going to change the regulations governing the JLC. The Executive Committee consented. The new order gave the Minister the exclusive right to make JLC appointments. It took effect on 27 April 1962, without approval of the full Council. Chigusa Tatsuo, a justice of the Tôkyô Supreme Court and a member of the Executive Committee, pointed out the consequence of this action at the third Executive Committee meeting: "If the Minister [of Education] is to make the appointments, there is reason to fear that only those whose opinions are identical with those of the current Minister will be appointed" (Ôkubo 1978: 117; trans. JMU). He elaborated:

How shall we formulate a national language policy that is consistent not just with the language of the past but with the present and future [needs] of the people? This is the weighty charge of the Japanese Language Council. If national language policy swings to the left or right with every change of Minister, it is obvious that consistency will be lost, and that major educational problems will result as well. . . . I would like to point out that if Council members are selected by the Minister alone, then, whenever there is any complaint in the Diet about this Council, the *Minister of Education* will have to bear the *entire* responsibility. (Ôkubo 1978: 118–119; trans. JMU)

Chigusa's words were prophetic. In less than ten years, the tôyô kanji (TK) would be superseded by the jôyô kanji (JK). Superficially, this made little difference; the JK list is the TK list plus an additional 95 kanji. The preamble to the new list, however, effectively repudiated the spirit if not the substance of the previous reforms. Describing the JK list merely as "a guide" *(meyasu)*, not a definite recommendation to eschew unlisted kanji, the preamble is laced with vague language that undermines the ostensible purpose of selecting kanji for general use in the first place. Thus, "it is expected that kanji use will conform to this List as far as possible," "there is suitable scope for reflection in its application, according to the circumstances at the time," "there is no objection to deviation in certain areas from the way kanji are treated in this List," and so on (Seeley's translations [1984: 284]). The TK reformers, implementing an idea proposed in the 1930s by the author Yamamoto Yûzô, had recommended that furigana be avoided lest writers rely on them to justify the use of obscure kanji. The JK preamble, by contrast, first damns with faint praise the concept of limiting the number of kanji, and then superciliously remarks, "In cases where kanji seem difficult to read, one method might be to consider using furigana where necessary."

As already observed, the TK list had been intended to set a cap on the number of kanji for general use. Instead, it ended up establishing a floor under the number of kanji, a plateau which one had to reach in order to be in the running for admission to top universities and top-level jobs. The JK preamble carries this subversion of the TK principles a step further. It addresses itself to "usage by persons who have to some extent experienced life in actual society or educational institutions after finishing study in the period of compulsory education," implying that, if anything, formal schooling should aim *beyond* the limits set by the JK list.

Small wonder that, when an Ad Hoc Education Council (Rinji Kyôiku Shingikai) was convened in 1985, the fundamental issues of script and literacy were not even on the agenda. This Council was commissioned mainly because the government faced declining school enrollments and the prospect of an oversupply of teachers in the years ahead, and wanted expert sanction for a major overhaul of the educational system. That was, however, not the only reason for the creation of the Council. There is also the increasing incidence of school-related violence (including assaults on teachers, unwarranted corporal punishment, so-called bullying [*ijime*] among students, etc.); outright refusal to attend school (*tôkô kyohi*—different from simple truancy); steadily growing dependence of cram schools (*juku*); and the frequent re-entry problems of Japanese children who have attended schools overseas. The possibility of a connection between kanji-based literacy and at least some of these problem areas is not hard to see, and it is remarkable that the council, although it has recommended greater emphasis on creativity and less on rote learning, has chosen not to examine it.

Perhaps even more telling is the most recent JLC pronouncement on kana spellings. On 7 March 1986, the JLC issued relaxed guidelines on kana usage. Just as the JK list seems to be only a slightly expanded TK list, the new recommendations on kana usage appear to entail only trivial changes. Indeed, the only major change is to permit the use of hiragana *zi* and *zu* for etymologically correct *di* and *du* in certain words; however, this minor adjustment is accompanied by a general statement that effectively opens the door to reintroduction of the prewar kana spellings done away with during the TK reforms. Interestingly, the constituency most pleased by the JLC's action is the word-processor manufacturers. They do not want their machines to disappoint customers; the relaxation of the official rules means that they can now, in good conscience, program input routines that accept grammatically incorrect strings. For anyone who takes the problems that motivated the TK reforms seriously, however, the new JLC announcement is just one more regrettable step backwards.

Thus, the anti-TK backlash, which began just after the first "Nihongo boom," has won the day. Although the writing system remains simplified in one sense, it has become a greater burden than ever before. The attitudes of Japanese toward language and writing reflect this change. Before the war, even ultranationalists thought nothing of forcing Chinese and Koreans to learn Japanese and abandon their native languages; today, the man in the street is genuinely amazed at foreigners who speak and read Japanese. Before the war, some of Japan's best minds were among the supporters of script reform; today, only a few show any interest in the subject at all. Before the war, a thorough knowledge of kanji was a ticket to first-class citizenship, but no one ever suggested that illiterates and semiliterates formed a culturally distinct group; today, it seems that internalization of kanji is a necessary (though by no means sufficient) condition for being Japanese.

Confusing Language with Writing

An important ingredient of this postwar shift in attitude is a systematic, often deliberate confounding of language with writing. Although versions of the Ideographic Myth can be found scattered throughout the prewar literature, Japanese scholars have built theories upon it in earnest only since the first postwar "Nihongo boom." Their articles and papers all follow a pattern: At the outset, it is assumed that kanji possess innate prelinguistic meaning. Various data are then "explained" on the basis of this false assumption, showing (circularly) that using kanji is quite different from (indeed, superior to) all other methods of writing the Japanese language.

Of the linguists who give this position its veneer of authority, Suzuki Takao of Keiô University is perhaps the best known. Certainly, he is one of the most prolific (see Suzuki 1963, 1969, 1975a, 1975b, 1977, etc.). He also played an important role in the JK affair (Ôkubo 1978: 181–182) and has recently claimed that word processors have "clinched it for the survival of Chinese characters" (Chin & Martin 1986). According to Suzuki, the use of kanji confers a special advantage on the Japanese writing system by lending Sino-Japanese compounds a "semantic transparency" that comparable words of English allegedly lack.

> [T]he *on* and *kun* readings of Chinese logograms have become so internalized in the mind of the Japanese that they believe that almost all characters have two variant readings without thinking much about the historical development.... [E]ach logogram evokes in our mind a meaning, an idea, and a concept. And to say that the Chinese characters in Japanese (though not in Chinese) have a twofold phonetic realization is tantamount to saying that the Japanese conceptual system which exists *in potentia* is put into the state of actualization *(in actu)* through the instrumentality of two different phonetic media. (Suzuki 1975b: 180–182)

What Suzuki is trying to say is that, because most kanji have both an on and a kun reading, they are endowed with special cognitive properties when used to write Japanese. Even someone familiar with Japanese linguistics, however, is likely to get lost somewhere around "*in potentia*." The following illustration, makes clearer what Suzuki has in mind:

> In Japanese, the Aegean Sea is written
>
> 多島海 ,
>
> and pronounced as ta-tô-kai. Even those who have never set an eye on this term before, to say nothing of knowing where it is, can easily *explain* the meaning of it, for they can automatically paraphrase the term with the *kun* reading of the characters as shima-ôii-umi [*sic*], meaning "sea of many island(s)." The ease with which the Japanese associate a phrase or a word with its literal meaning is made possible by the dual phonetic

renderings of the Chinese characters in the Japanese writing. (Suzuki 1975b: 189)

Because the kun readings of kanji are more or less just Japanese words, and since learning how to "spell" Japanese entails memorizing kun readings, Suzuki thinks that Sino-Japanese compounds are more "transparent" than English compounds that make use of Latin and Greek roots. This, however, confuses meaning with etymology. If etymology were meaning, we would have no need of textbooks, only dictionaries! As Miller explains in his comments on Suzuki 1975a, "Etymology tells where a word came from, not what it means. To know what it means, you have to know the language, and moreover, you have to know the word" (Miller 1982: 190). Indeed, he could have gone farther: etymology can be misleading. To take an English example, consider "anti-Semitic." Arabic is a Semitic language, but this word definitely has no connotation of "anti-Arab." It goes far beyond "anti-Jewish"—the Spanish Inquisition was anti-Jewish, but spared converts to Catholicism. To know what "anti-Semitic" really means, one must know something about Nazi ideology, its historical background, the Holocaust, and so on. Knowing the roots involved is not enough. In the same way, the fixed readings of kanji often give only a hint—sometimes a wrong hint—of the meanings of the words they are combined to represent.[8]

Developers of Japanese and Chinese word processors are another source of misinformation. Engineers, whose knowledge of linguistics is typically confined to what they have picked up from writers like Suzuki, have little awareness of the great care that must be taken in the design, execution, and evaluation of psycholinguistic experiments. For example, in one study (Doi & Yoneda 1982), twenty members of the authors' own research organization were timed as they read Japanese selections written in different styles (customary, kana-only, rômaji, and so on). There was no attempt to assess comprehension, no pretest training in the unfamiliar modes of reading, and no experimental control. The authors seemed to believe that the use of sophisticated statistical techniques would somehow compensate for these obvious procedural errors. All they really succeeded in showing was that their subjects could read texts written in a familiar manner much faster than texts written in an unfamiliar manner. Since it takes hundreds of hours for a native speaker of any language to learn how to read it fluently in even one script, this is just what one would expect. Yet there are Japanese computer scientists who unabashedly cite studies like this as proof that Japanese simply cannot read their own language in rômaji.[9]

Reading theorists are perhaps best represented by Sakamoto and Makita, whose 1973 survey article is a classic in the genre of supposedly scientific defenses of kanji. They simply assert, without delay, that "each Kanji has its own meaning" (1973: 441). They go on to make a great deal of photographs taken by Sakamoto of the eye movements of college students reading identical sentences written alternatively all in hiragana and in a normal mixture of hiragana and kanji. From this "experiment"—presumably the use of different transcriptions of identical sentences was supposed to serve as a control—they conclude that the use of kanji makes reading quicker and more accurate. In explanation of this result, they note that the use of kanji reduces the total number of symbols that must be read and provides visual contrast that compensates for the nonuse of spaces. At the top of their list (443), however, is the unfounded assumption that kanji possess innate meaning; missing entirely is any discussion of the obvious fact that no educated Japanese reads all-hiragana texts. In short, Sakamoto and Makita fail to see that it is the Ideographic Myth itself that must be subjected to empirical testing, not the "superiority" of using kanji.

This is further illustrated by their discussion of dyslexia in Japan, which they claim is virtually nonexistent because of the nature of the Japanese writing system. Their own account of how they reached this conclusion, however, puts it in doubt. For example, Makita specifically instructed the schoolteachers he surveyed in 1966 to disregard "those with intellectual retardation or visual impairments" (1973: 459) instead of collecting as many cases as possible and analyzing the data himself. This was a methodologically questionable step to take in a society where schoolchildren are never kept back a grade for academic failure and teachers are held fully responsible for their charges' progress. Negative survey results from "child guidance clinics, educational counseling services, and other child study institutions" (460) are probably also misleading because their clientele is self-selecting. In the United States, dyslexia is often diagnosed in children referred to a specialist because of behavioral problems; it is entirely possible that dyslexic children in Japan exist but are better at compensating for their disability socially—because Japanese writing involves both kana and kanji, it may be possible to have trouble with one kind of character but not the other.

Even if the clinical incidence of dyslexia in Japan is actually lower than elsewhere, it is not evident what features of the Japanese writing system, if any, might be responsible. There is little unanimity among experts on the relationship between social factors and Japanese reading ability (e.g., cf. Duke 1977 and Overly 1977). Experiments comparing kana and kanji have produced some evidence that it is easier to learn to recognize symbols when they are identified with whole words rather than with meaningless subword syllables, and also that graphic complexity does not in itself make symbols harder to learn (Steinberg et al. 1977, Steinberg & Oka 1978, Steinberg & Yamada 1979a).[10] But as DeFrancis (1984b: 171) notes in his criticism of similar Chinese/English tests, results based on a sample of only a few characters may have little or no bearing on the real-life task of learning hundreds of characters. In any case, such results certainly do not demonstrate that Chinese characters facilitate the reading of Japanese or Chinese, nor do they imply that kanji express meaning "directly." Indeed, what reliable experimental evidence exists suggests that, at some level of cognition, speech recoding is essential for the interpretation even of allegedly ideographic characters. Although numerous experimental studies purport to show that kana and kanji are processed differently in the brain, each and every one is flawed with unjustified assumptions and methodological oversights (Paradis et al. 1985: 57–58); none comes close to demonstrating hemispheric lateralization (dominance of one hemisphere of the brain over the other) or any other consistent difference between kanji and other kinds of writing. Nor do any of the sixty-nine clinical cases of acquired dyslexia in Japanese patients dating as far back as 1901 provide the slightest evidence that kanji reading bypasses speech recoding (Paradis et al. 1985: 196–199); on the contrary, taken together, they show that reading of kanji and kana, like that of other scripts, is a predominantly left-hemisphere activity.

The shortcomings of the work to date analyzed by Paradis and his colleagues do not deter Kaiho Hiroyuki, the psychologist at Tsukuba University who recently coined the phrase "sciencing kanji." In his contribution to a collection of essays, which he edited and issued under this unusual title, Kaiho begins by citing an experiment that he claims proves what Suzuki would call the semantic transparency of kanji. In this experiment, a variation on a classic technique first reported by J. R. Stroop in 1935, subjects are timed as they attempt to identify colors as quickly as possible. The colors are presented in three forms: as kanji, as hiragana, and as meaningless X's. The kanji and hiragana are purposely selected to spell the name of a color different from that of the ink used to write the word itself; the subjects subconsciously read these distracting words, and this interferes with their attempts to name the colors. According to Kaiho, a hundred trials took 80.6 seconds with kanji, 72.1 seconds with hiragana, and 56.9 seconds with the X's (Kaiho 1983: 36). He then gives these data a most bizarre interpretation: the greater interference caused by kanji versus hiragana shows that the brain processes kanji *more quickly*. This follows from Kaiho's unexamined assumption that kanji communicate linguistic meaning without the aid of language, and that a semantic conflict *must be* the cause of the slowdown in the color-naming task. Actually, however, the delay is better explained by the observation that shape and color recogniton compete for the same cognitive resources in the brain's right hemisphere (Yamada 1985: 257–273): kanji are processed more slowly than kana and X's simply because they are the more complicated patterns. In addition, as noted by Paradis et al. (1985: 22), "the color terms used in these studies are those that are usually written in kanji, and hence the kana Stroop stimuli are less familiar than their kanji counterparts." This alone might well account for the greater delay with kanji.

One contributor to Kaiho's book deserves special attention because he unwittingly shines such a bright light on the sociolinguistic motives of the "kanji scientizers." This is Sasaki Masato, a lecturer at Tsukuba; his chapter is entitled "Kanji for the Blind." There are, in fact, two competing kanji braille systems: Hasegawa's, based on readings, and Kawakami's, based on graphic components (radicals). The differences between them, however, pale into insignificance when one considers the common aim shared by proponents of both systems. Evidently, they agree with the twelfth-century Chinese encyclopedist Zheng Qiao, who wrote, "The world is of the opinion that those who know Chinese characters are wise and worthy, whereas those who do not know characters are simple and stupid" (DeFrancis 1984b: 1).[11] Why else would anyone expect the sightless to give up a perfectly adequate kana-based braille system? (For a brief account of Japanese braille, see Unger 1984b.) One wonders what prewar Japanese intellectuals would have thought of such a condescending attitude. Nitobe Inazô, for one, would have been shocked. As if to underscore his comments of 1929 cited earlier, he later wrote:

> To a foreign observer, the number of years devoted to secondary education must seem strangely out of proportion to the results obtained. To the Japanese, the explanation is easy. . . . [T]he blind man can be better educated than his more fortunate brethren who are endowed with good

sight; for the former, by acquiring the forty-seven letters of the *I-ro-ha* syllabary, through the Braille system, can read history, geography or anything written in that system; whereas he who has eyesight cannot read the daily papers unless he has mastered at least 2000 characters. (Nitobe 1972: 3.274–275; cf. 1972: 4.248–249)[12]

The very idea of using patterns of a few embossed dots to represent kanji belies many of the stock arguments given for maintaining their use: their aesthetic mystique; the ways in which they save space on paper; the alleged ease with which they are learned; their "semantic transparency"; the wholesome effects of practicing calligraphy; and so on. It shows that the Japanese attachment to kanji is intimately tied to the shared experience of mastering a complex body of knowledge that defines group membership. Whether kanji facilitate communication or not is a secondary consideration.[13] What really matters, as kanji braille so clearly shows, is the sociolinguistic function of the Ideographic Myth: to sanctify the status quo.

Cultural Independence

Of course, the defense of kanji culture through allegedly scientific methods is a relatively esoteric business. More common is the time-honored practice of twisting historical and linguistic facts to meet the demands of the Ideographic Myth. Such slanting of the linguistic history of East Asia is certainly not a postwar phenomenon; however, postwar education in Japan has elevated what was once a collection of harmless fables, of interest to only a few, into a set of clichés that every Japanese schoolchild is taught as the justification for hours of copying and rote memorization of Chinese characters.

At its most moderate, the historical rationalization for kanji holds that Japanese aesthetic sensibilities, intellectual perspectives, and national characteristics are so wedded to the age-old use of Chinese characters that, without them, Japanese culture as we know it would be threatened. At its most extreme, it is the impossible prediction that the Japanese language itself would perish without kanji. The comments of Dr. Uenohara Michiyuki, senior vice-president of Nippon Electric Company (NEC), one of Japan's leading computer manufacturers, are typical.

People using European languages can engage in data-exchange and dialogue with machinery through typing with almost the speed of conversation. But this is impossible in the Japanese language. If oral input becomes possible, th[is] handicap will be totally eliminated. Because of the phonetic simplicity of the Japanese language relative to European languages, oral input will give the Japanese an advantage, reversing the present situation. The world is made in such a way that advantages and disadvantages are always offsetting relationships.

The ultimate mission of technology is to make up for disadvantages of human beings and society and bring them progress. If it ruins advantages that human beings have, it does not deserve to be called technology.

A local culture is something that has been developed through the long history of the region and human life itself. It should not be altered because of technology. Rather technology must be altered to fit the local culture. If the Japanese language is abolished for the sake of convenience of usage of computers, the Japanese will be deprived of their identity. (Gregory & Etori 1981: J40)

Even those who see the merits of script reform are not immune from the temptation to read deep historical significance into the continued use of kanji:

A reform of the written language would not only do away with a major hindrance which clogs the wheels of the nation's affairs; it would also save years of heavy intellectual grind in the life of every successive generation. It would have even more far-reaching consequences, because the confusions and ambiguities of the Japanese script are reflected in the structure of Japanese thinking. And that, perhaps, is the cause of their instinctive resistance against reform of the script. They refuse to part with the comforts of ambiguity, and prefer the printed page, like the streets of the capital, to remain a labyrinth, where only the initiate, guided by his intuition, can find his way—or lose it in agreeable detours. (Koestler 1961: 182–183)

Uenohara, Koestler, and others who have written about the psychosocial aspects of Japanese script exaggerate the connection between kanji and culture. Some psychological factors (notably use/reference ambiguity) make the Ideographic Myth attractive, but they are not linked specifically to Japanese culture. When we hunt for the alleged connections beween the use of kanji and the Japanese mind, there turn out to be few if indeed any at all.

We discover, for example, that although the Japanese writing system has undergone a gradual process of evolution over the centuries, it has been relatively stable compared with changes in Japanese thought and life. Japanese of the sixteenth century, for example, behaved in ways that today's proponents of "Japanese uniqueness" would have us believe were never part of Japanese culture.

> They were ardent party-goers, sophisticated hosts, eloquent discussants, and even internationally open-minded. Hideyoshi, the famous military ruler of the sixteenth century, hosted an enormous open-air tea party in 1587, to which he invited all kinds of people from the emperor down to commoners, and even foreigners. A Jesuit missionary, Francis Xavier, testified that the Japanese of his time were far from being shy and that they visited him so often to ask questions that he could hardly get any sleep. Another missionary, Organtino, reported that the two vices Japanese hated most were an impatient attitude toward other people and irrationality in discussion. (Yamazaki 1981: 65)

If the use of kanji is even remotely responsible for the alleged inability of modern Japanese to cope with plain-talking foreigners and straightforward logic, it is hard to understand how these "uniquely Japanese" deficiencies could have escaped the attention of sixteenth-century observers. Historical continuity does not preclude change, and for this reason alone, we ought to be suspicious of any claims of a direct, psychological connection between script and culture.[14]

We also discover that there is only a small grain of truth in the well-known tale that Chinese characters have made it possible for Japanese, Chinese, and Koreans to communicate through writing despite their mutually unintelligible languages, a state of affairs that allegedly could not have arisen had Chinese script been alphabetical. The historical and linguistic evidence flatly contradicts these claims (DeFrancis 1984b: 149–160). Although a common inventory of characters is a necessary condition for interlinguistic written communication, whether in East Asia (classical Chinese), the Islamic world (classical Arabic), or some other multilingual "culture zone," it is by no means a sufficient condition. The Japanese did not merely receive kanji from China: they imported the entire apparatus of Chinese literature, historiography, science, philosophy, religion, government, and art. Classical Chinese was able to serve as a channel of communication for the Japanese elite, in the final analysis, not because of their mastery of the writing system per se, but because of their assimilation of the ideas Chinese letters brought to them. Indeed, once planted on Japanese soil, the seeds of these ideas often grew into living traditions quite different from their continental counterparts.

Lexicography is a pertinent example. The compilation of dictionaries has a history of more than a thousand years in Japan and although inspired by Chinese models, shows a remarkably original development. Of course, the Japanese couldn't help being innovative in the treatment of their own language, but even in the case of classical Chinese, they were not mere copyists. Indeed, there is today no Chinese dictionary that can rival the thirteen-volume character dictionary of Morohashi Tetsuji (1883–1982), the pinnacle of Japanese sinology. Where the Japanese did slavishly follow the Chinese was in their uncritical acceptance of the idea that the Chinese language consists entirely of monosyllabic words. Modern linguistics shows that this idea is categorically false (Kennedy 1964: 274–322)[15]—yet another reason for rejecting the Ideographic Myth—but to this day, despite the internationalization of Japanese scholarship, it continues to color Japanese thinking about the nature of language and meaning.

The same pattern can be seen more generally in the Sino-Japanese tradition of teaching and study, which eschews reasoned disputation (Mizutani 1979, 1981) and ranks historical precedent ahead of empirical observation as a source of authority (Nakayama 1974, 1984). It sanctioned the withholding of information as a tool of power; thus, for example, it made perfect sense for an advocate of education for the samurai elite, Ogyû Sorai (1666–1728), to write:

> It is not necessary that the common people should be taught anything apart from the virtues of filial piety, brotherly submission, loyalty, and trustworthiness. Their reading should not extend beyond the *Classic of Filial Piety (Hsiao Ching),* the *Lives of Famous Women (Lieh Nü Chuan),* and other improving biographical collections which deal with the relations between sovereign and subject, father and child, man and wife. The study of other works will merely increase their cunning and will lead to disruption. (McEwan 1962: 132; also in Passin 1982: 190–191)

Today, the tradition lingers on in the way Japanese newspapers and television dote on the views of academic and literary celebrities, regardless of their specialties, while giving scant coverage to better-informed experts who lack the traditional scholarly credentials. And we see it in the obsessive cramming and rote memorization of purely factual information that takes up so much of Japanese primary and secondary education—an obsession, incidentally, also characteristic of the current American infatuation with data processing (Roszak 1986: 156–160).

If these and other traditions were ever, in any sense, caused by the

Japanese adoption of Chinese characters, they are now so thoroughly entrenched in Japanese life that a radical change in the writing system would probably not affect them in the slightest. More than a hundred years ago, this was already clear to the statesman Mori Arinori. In the early 1870s, he concluded that mere romanization of the script would not be enough to cut Japan loose from the entangling web of Chinese words and ideas that he believed had to be abandoned if Japan were to become a competitive, modern trading nation (Sakakura 1985: 66–70). Mori suggested adopting a simplified form of English as a new national language! Although he wisely dropped this idea as unworkable, his reasoning was, and still is, impeccable: to believe that the grip of Chinese tradition on modern Japanese life would suddenly loosen if the script were altered is to trivialize centuries of Japanese history.[16]

Ironically, although the continued use of kanji serves to keep Japan linguistically isolated by holding down the number of foreigners who can read Japanese, this artificial "language barrier" has done nothing to prevent the steady erosion of both imported and genuinely native traditions. In his 1981 book *How Will the Japanese Language Change?*, Kabashima Tadao predicted that the influx of loanwords, particularly from English, into modern Japanese would eventually lead to the demise of kanji. Whether kanji are a boon or a nuisance makes no difference: the fact of the matter is that Japanese are adapting English to their word-making needs today with the same alacrity with which they adapted Chinese more than a thousand years ago; productive use of Sino-Japanese morphology is declining as traditional Chinese scholarship becomes less and less relevant to success at work and in society. Dr. Uenohara's concern that technology might "abolish" the Japanese language (i.e., traditional Japanese script) is therefore misplaced. If Japan is under some kind of sociolinguistic threat, the aggressor is not technology but English and the other languages that serve as international modes of communication in the computer age.

4

A Conflict of Technologies

The very idea of a "sociolinguistic threat" is questionable. The English language has certainly not suffered as a consequence of massive infusions of foreign vocabulary, and the Japanese propensity for word borrowing can only enrich their language and make it more resilient. The only thing "threatened" by technology is the Chinese-based writing system. There is a real problem—how to use the Japanese *language* on computers—but it can be solved without damaging the continuity of Japanese civilization. Its solution does not require artificial intelligence or any other costly, untried method. It is simply a matter of distinguishing between those computer applications that require output in traditional script and those that do not. To those that do not (the majority), one applies the cheap technique of writing Japanese phonemically.

It may be worthwhile to review at this point why kanji pose a dilemma for data processing just to make it clear that "unique Japanese ways of thinking" have nothing whatsoever to do with it. Table 9 (Unger 1984a: 241) summarizes nine key problem areas. The rows of this chart correspond to the nominal, functional, and formal properties of kanji. As already explained, practical inventories of kanji for data-processing use are inevitably large, must allow for ad hoc additions, and do not have well-defined, easily remembered collating sequences. The use of kanji in writing is redundant because kanji merely add a metalinguistic veneer to the content of what is written; moreover, only a few kanji are used frequently. Kanji usage is ambiguous because of multiple readings, and artificial in that kanji selection is often arbitrary or optional. Finally, we have seen that the complexity of kanji shapes requires high-resolution output hardware; that variations in kanji shape make it necessary to describe them in abstract terms; and that the graphic homogeneity of kanji makes it difficult to tell many of them apart.

Table 9.   Nine Incompatibilities of Kanji on Computers

When kanji are used to represent Japanese-language data on computers, they are:

	Wasteful	Imprecise	Unwieldy
because sets of kanji are	(1) Large	(2) Open	(3) Ill-ordered
because readings of kanji are	(4) Redundant	(5) Ambiguous	(6) Artificial
because kanji shapes are	(7) Complex	(8) Abstract	(9) Homogeneous

The practical consequences of these nine problem areas are shown in the columns of Table 9: kanji on computers waste system resources, impede software development, and unnecessarily complicate both computation and I/O functions. It is clearly wasteful to use thousands of intricate symbols when a few simple ones would suffice to convey the same information. The fuzzy definitions of the number, use, and form of kanji demand data-bound programs and guarantee that almost every program that does anything more with kanji than display them is a one-of-a-kind endeavor. Lack of a nonarbitrary collating sequence restricts the use of sorting, a fundamental step in countless applications; the artificiality of kanji usage slows down kanji input; and the homogeneity of kanji images hampers optical character recognition.

Even this analysis is probably an oversimplification, but there is no need to belabor the point. Kanji are a problem for computers because, by their very nature, they lack the properties that well-behaved computer data should have. Ironically, just those aspects of kanji that bedevil data processing have made possible or have resulted from their use by human beings over the centuries. To whatever extent one can legitimately call the historical use of kanji a success, it is because the vagaries and fluidity of kanji are well suited to the way people think and work. It is bad enough that would-be scientizers of kanji like Suzuki, Sakamoto, Makita, and Kaiho have taken the Ideographic Myth seriously. What is worse is that by imputing unreal powers to kanji, they belittle the remarkable capacities of the human beings who use them. In so doing, they misrepresent an important body of empirical evidence that calls into question the idea that the human mind is just a computer.

Kanji and AI

As previously remarked, there is a spectrum of AI theory ranging from weak to strong. Almost everyone is prepared to accept the idea that a machine that reproduced all the biological processes of the human brain would reproduce what the brain does. The goal of weak-AI research is to model such biological processes using computers. Strong-AI researchers, such as those connected with the Fifth Generation project, however, are striving to produce the same results the brain does (indeed, to outperform the human brain) without going to the trouble of emulating the chemistry and physics of the living organism. They operate under the unproven assumption that "[a] physical symbol system has the necessary and sufficient means for general intelligent action" (Newell & Simon 1976: 116). "Physical symbol system" here refers to anything that contains (1) physical patterns (symbols) that can form larger physical patterns (expressions), and (2) means for modifying expressions so as to produce other expressions. "A physical symbol system is a machine that produces through time an evolving collection of symbol structures" (116). As noted in one widely used AI textbook, the Physical Symbol System Hypothesis underlies all (strong) AI research but

> is only a hypothesis. There appears to be no way to prove or disprove it on logical grounds. So it must be subjected to empirical validation. We may find that it is false. We may find that the bulk of the evidence says that it is true. But the only way to determine its truth is by experimentation. (Rich 1983: 4)

Certainly, no one would object to an empirical quest for verification of the Physical Symbol System Hypothesis, but AI experimentation is not the only way to proceed. Dozens of reports in newspapers and magazines make it clear that governments and corporations are plowing big money into AI on the strength of assurances from experts like Feigenbaum and McCorduck that the hypothesis is, for all practical purposes, already proven. More to the point here, it is not true that the successful operation of a program written by AI researchers establishes their theories. AI programs such as DENDRAL (chemistry), CADUCEUS (medicine), EURISKO (engineering), and so on, work because they attack tightly circumscribed problems in specific disciplines and take advantage of the clearly defined boundary conditions of these problems. Whether the particular techniques used in these programs can be generalized and applied to more loosely defined problems (such as natural-language translation) is indeed an open question; the programs themselves do not constitute evidence that settles the issue of the Physical Symbol System Hypothesis one way or the other. On the other hand, logical arguments, such as those of Searle (1983: 262–272, 1984: 28–56), may very well help us resolve the issue, even though they are not narrowly empirical in the way AI programming is.

In the strong-AI view, all meaning is reducible to information in the narrow sense of mathematical information theory—that is, the off/on binary digits (bits) of the computer. Certainly, impressive feats can be achieved with digital computers, and it may well be that some sort of power of symbol manipulation is necessary for intelligence. It does not follow, however, that it is *sufficient* as well. Intelligence as we experience it also entails consciousness, creativity, the ability to make sense out of new experiences, and so on. The fact that feelings and thoughts are caused by neuron firings and other biochemical events going on in the brain does not mean they are unreal. As Searle notes, there is no paradox in the view that "brains cause minds and yet minds just are features of brains" provided that we clarify what we mean by "cause":

> A common distinction in physics is between micro- and macro-properties of systems—the small and large scales. Consider, for example, the desk at which I am now sitting, or the glass of water in front of me. Each object is composed of micro-particles. The micro-particles have features at the level of molecules and atoms as well as at the deeper level of subatomic particles. But each object also has certain properties such as the solidity of the table, the liquidity of the water, and the transparency of the glass, which are surface or global features of the physical systems. Many such surface or global properties can be causally explained by the behaviour of the elements at the micro-level. (Searle 1984: 20)

Thus, water is wet, but "I can't . . . reach into this glass of water, pull out a molecule and say: 'This one's wet.'"

> In exactly the same way, as far as we know anything at all about it, though we can say of a particular brain: "This brain is conscious," or: "This brain is experiencing thirst or pain," we can't say of any particular neuron in the brain: "This neuron is in pain, this neuron is experiencing thirst." (Searle 1984: 22)

The mental phenomena we experience and believe others to experience are therefore real even though they are, to use Searle's phrase, entirely "caused by and realized in" the brain. To separate out the "logic" and "knowledge" of intelligence from the rest of mental activity is a hopeless task. Intelligence is no more a separable essence of the brain than wetness is a separable essence of water. We are far from understanding how our brains work, but we already have enough evidence from gestalt psychology, linguistics, and other sciences of human behavior to see that intelligence is not a soul-like entity that can be distilled from the body.[17]

Can Intelligence Be Artificial?

Considerations like these prompted the title of Hubert Dreyfus's classic book *What Computers Can't Do* (1979). Dreyfus divides AI programs into four categories according to application: problem solving, game playing, natural-language processing, and pattern recognition. These categories also give us a rough idea of the extent and variety of the issues with which AI is concerned as an academic discipline. Within each category, four "areas" of intelligent behavior can be distinguished:

Area I is where the S-R [stimulus-response] psychologists are most at home. It includes all forms of elementary associationistic behavior where meaning and context are irrelevant to the activity concerned. Rote learning of nonsense syllables is the most perfect example of such behavior so far programmed, although any form of conditioned reflex would serve as well. Also some games, such as the game sometimes called Geography (which simply consists of finding a country whose name begins with the last letter of the previously named country), belong in this area. In language translating this is the level of the mechanical dictionary; in problem solving, that of pure trial-and-error search routines; in pattern recognition, matching pattern against fixed templates.

Area II is the domain of Pascal's *esprit de géométrie*—the terrain most favorable for artificial intelligence. It encompasses the conceptual rather than the perceptual world. Problems are completely formalized and completely calculable. For this reason, it might best be called the area of the simple-formal. Here artificial intelligence is possible in principle and in fact.

In Area II, natural language is replaced by a formal language, of which the best example is logic. Games have precise rules and can be calculated out completely, as in the case of nim or tic-tac-toe. Pattern recognition on this level takes place according to determinate types, which are defined by a list of traits characterizing the individuals which belong to the class in question. Problem solving takes the form of reducing the distance between means and ends by repeated application of formal rules. The formal systems in this area are simple enough to be manipulated by algorithms. . . . Heuristics are not only unnecessary here, they are a positive handicap. . . . In this area, artificial intelligence has had its only unqualified successes.

Area III, complex-formal systems, is the most difficult to define and has generated most of the misunderstandings and difficulties in the field. It contains behavior which is in principle formalizable but in fact intractable. As the number of elements increases, the number of transformations required grows exponentially. . . . As used here, "complex-formal" includes those systems which in practice cannot be dealt with by exhaustive enumeration algorithms (chess, go, etc.), and thus require heuristic programs.

Area IV might be called the area of nonformal behavior. This includes all those everyday activities in our human world which are regular but not rule governed. The most striking example of this controlled imprecision is our disambiguation of natural languages. This area also includes games in which the rules are not definite, such as guessing riddles. Pattern recognition in this domain is based on recognition of the generic, or of the typical, by means of a paradigm case. Problems on this level are open-structured, requiring a determination of what is relevant, and insight into which operations are essential. . . . We might adopt Pascal's terminology and call Area IV the home of the *esprit de finesse*. (Dreyfus 1979: 291–294)

Thus, there are game-playing, problem-solving, language-processing, and pattern-recognition tasks characteristic of each of the "areas" of intelligent activity. The four areas do not form a universal hierarchy of difficulty; on the contrary, as Dreyfus points out, Area IV demands the use of only the simplest, most fundamental processes of human cognition, processes without which even the computationally trivial tasks of Area I could not be carried out. The numbering of Areas I through IV rather reflects the relative difficulty of programming computers to simulate human performance. For human beings, different considerations come into play. To take just one case,

Human beings are able to recognize patterns under the following increasingly difficult conditions:

1. The pattern may be skewed, incomplete, deformed, and embedded in noise;
2. The traits required for recognition may be "so fine and so numerous" that, even if they could be formalized, a search through a branching list

of such traits would soon become unmanageable, as new patterns for discrimination were added;

3. The traits may depend upon external and internal context and are thus not amenable to context-free specification;

4. There may be no common traits but a "complicated network of overlapping similarities," capable of assimilating ever new variations.

Any system which can equal human performance must, therefore, be able to

1. Distinguish the essential from the inessential features of a particular instance of a pattern;

2. Use cues which remain on the fringes of consciousness;

3. Take account of the context;

4. Perceive the individual as typical, i.e. situate the individual with respect to a paradigm case. (Dreyfus 1979: 128)

Similar conclusions can be drawn from observations of the ways in which man and machine deal with natural languages, problem solving, and game playing. In Dreyfus's terminology, people use (1) essential/inessential discrimination rather than trial-and-error search techniques; (2) fringe consciousness rather than heuristic guidance; (3) ambiguity tolerance rather than context-free precision; and (4) perspicuous grouping rather than trait lists. The items on the computer side of this list are fairly obvious, but the human side may not be clear at first. Dreyfus (following the gestalt psychologist Wertheimer) uses *insight* to describe essential/inessential discrimination but does not provide handy labels for the other three human propensities. At the risk of some oversimplification, we will call them simply *concentration*, *perspective*, and *imagination*.

Kanji as Counterexample

We are now ready to explain why historical kanji usage constitutes empirical evidence against strong-AI claims.

Consider first the writing and recognition of individual characters in Japanese script. If we try to formulate an unambiguous set of instructions for writing a kanji, taking into account its typical variants and all the kanji that might be mistaken for it, we quickly discover that its shape, which intuitively seems to be a very obvious, concrete thing, is surprisingly abstract and hard to pin down. Writers may intentionally or unintentionally alter the length, curvature, and (when a writing brush is used) thickness of individual strokes as well as features pertaining to clusters of strokes, such as their number, relative placement, relative size, order, and interconnection. Similar variations occur with kana; moreover, ligatures (extra strokes joining characters) are often seen in the writing of certain common combinations. This freedom in writing is not just an expression of Japanese tastes; given the available writing tools, the writing of thousands of different characters for purposes of communication would have been unbearably difficult without such freedom. Leaving aside feedback from the spin-off of calligraphy as an art for art's sake, workaday writing practice evolved in practical directions that took advantage of the natural human ability to distinguish what is essential from what is inessential in a tangled skein of visual data.

This, of course, is Wertheimer's definition of insight. As Dreyfus stresses, it is not merely a human ability, but a necessary part of human perception. Recall the winecup/silhouettes illusion. If any preliminary computer-like searching of databases is required to see the winecup or the silhouettes, there is certainly no conscious awareness of it; yet a conscious act of will readily causes the figure to become the ground and the ground the figure. Clearly, whatever automatic processes beyond our control enable us to perceive the boundaries in the picture, something more is involved in seeing it as a picture of either a winecup or two kissing faces.

A programmer has no choice but to reproduce the results of insight by exploiting the computer's ability to search large databases rapidly. Optical character recognition (OCR) is a pertinent example. OCR of Chinese characters is an area of intensive research and development because special hardware capable of scanning conventionally printed documents and feeding them, code number by code number, into a computer would save a huge amount of tedious input. Many papers on OCR can be found in proceedings of international conferences devoted to handling Chinese script on computers (e.g., Hong Kong, 12–15 October 1980; Washington, D.C., 22–23 September 1982; Beijing, 12–14 October 1983; Tôkyô, 17–19 October 1983; San Francisco, 26–28 February 1985; see also Lackshewitz & Suchenwirth 1983). Most of these papers include comments to the effect that the authors have achieved 98 or 99 percent accuracy with a sample of a couple of thousand Chinese characters. To the extent that recalcitrant cases can be handled without too much trouble on an ad hoc basis, such claims are meaningful; however, we are interested here less in what can be done than in how it is done.

For OCR programs, just the tasks of telling where the individual characters are on the page is itself a major problem; usually it is handled by placing various constraints on the raw data. If machine capabilities are to be measured against human capabilities, this amounts to giving the machine a large handicap. Neat handwriting on genkô yôshi, for example, without ligatures between characters (let alone strokes), a fairly modest demand for a machine designer to make, is a lot to ask of human users. For the sake of argument, however, suppose the machine is given only neatly written text on preformatted paper. Determining the gross outlines of characters on the page is just its first step; it must now determine what each character is. Brute-force comparison of whole arrays of pixels against thousands of stored images is impractical not only because of the enormous memory it would demand, but also because it requires formal criteria that define what constitutes a match. To use the anthropomorphic language often encountered in computer science, how does the computer decide whether a deviation from its stored pattern is relevant or not?

OCR programs employ a variety of mathematical techniques to extract statistical information from the gross pixel array, and carry out their database searches using this more compact representation of the character. The idea is that much of the raw data can be thrown away without sacrificing essential detail. (This assumes, of course, that information in the real world can always be broken down into discrete quanta, like the memory bits in a computer.) Searching for matches with abstract data not only saves time and memory but also simplifies the matching criteria. Significantly, some of the most successful OCR programs look for variations in highly derivative entities (e.g., geometrical projections) and test abstract topological criteria (e.g., connectedness) far removed from the strokes and radicals so intuitively obvious to human beings. It is computationally more difficult to get the computer to look for strokes and radicals because it amounts to solving the problems associated with locating individual characters on the page all over again, only on a smaller scale.

Furthermore, the abstraction strategy is possible only because the programmer can take advantage of prior knowledge of the redundancies in the shapes of kana and kanji. Unfortunately these shapes are also homogeneous, and no formal set of features can entirely eliminate troublesome cases such as the kanji numeral

三

versus the katakana

ミ *mi.*

This is not a problem for human beings because they rely on imagination (perspicuous grouping) rather than abstract trait lists. In other words, while the computer must proceed by process of elimination, human beings, aware, consciously or unconsciously, of the pragmatic context of their reading as well as of the individual character shapes, see what the characters must be in order to make sense of the whole. This is why a human reader may fail to spot an incorrect kanji that looks nothing like the one intended if it is part of a homonym. Human writers generally don't commit such gross errors when writing by hand, but thanks to Japanese word processors, more and more of these literally unnatural mistakes are finding their way, past proofreaders' eyes, into neatly printed documents.

Consider next the writing and reading of Japanese script as a process of communication. Whether to use kanji or hiragana at a particular juncture depends on many factors. Some are highly principled considerations based on the content of the text (what it is talking about) and its communicative function (who will read it and why); some are personal judgments concerning the relative merits of consistency versus intentional variation, contemporary versus earlier style, or proper versus vulgar usage; some are just quirks of fate such as bad line and page breaks, momentary forgetfulness, not having a dictionary handy, distractions, or fatigue. Were it not possible to concentrate on the ideas and language to be written while all these things clamored for attention at the fringes of consciousness, no one could write coherently at all. And this is just the beginning: decisions also have to be made concerning which kanji to use when there is more than one possibility; whether or not to follow guidelines on permissible kanji, their shapes, kana spellings, and okurigana usage; whether to modify quotations from older writing and, if so, how; when to use furigana; when to use optional punctuation; whether to use innovative or conservative katakana spellings in gairaigo; whether to use standard alphanumerics or try to avoid them—in short, all the other editorial choices inherent in Japanese script.

This interplay of habit and caprice, experience and creativity can be simulated on computers only by means of heuristic procedures. These are often explained as "rules of thumb" akin to the hunches and knacks people use in problem solving, but it would be more honest to describe them simply as procedures knowingly invoked under certain untested assumptions. The idea is to avoid getting lost in interminable sequences of computations by building certain probabilistic biases into the structure of the program that give it a fair chance of making a lucky guess.

Heuristics can, of course, yield good results. As Dreyfus notes, however, heuristic procedures are useful only when dealing with the kind of if/then reasoning found in analyses of games like chess. This is often called reading ahead, but Dreyfus calls it "counting out" to set up a clear contrast with "zeroing in," the kind of holistic evaluation of the board that necessarily precedes counting out. You don't need to see the diagram or even know the rules of chess to appreciate how the following commentary illustrates this important difference:

> [T]he material is equal. White has certainly gained in space, and in time probably. Moreover, his P[awn]'s are better placed, for Black has two isolated P's, one of them, the P at Q[ueen's]R[ook's]4, very weak, since, standing on a Black square, it cannot be defended by the B[ishop], while the Black K[nigh]t cannot come to its support without a great loss of time. The problem for White is how best to attack Black's QRP a second time. *The idea is therefore discovered.* The precise manner in which White wins the pawn is very pretty: 1 Kt-B3, R-B4; 2 Kt-K4, R-Kt4; 3 Kt(K4)-Q6, R-B4; 4 Kt-Kt7, R-B2; 5 Kt(Kt7)xP, and wins. (Znosko-Borovsky 1959: 48–49, emphasis added)

Notice how, when zeroing in, uncertainty is tolerated ("probably"), impressionistic value judgments are allowed ("better placed"), and inductively valid ideas are accepted without rigorous proof ("the Black Kt cannot come to its support without a great loss of time"). All this *precedes* the if/then deductions that verify the sequence of five winning moves.

Computers must be programmed to simulate zeroing in by means of counting out. Strong-AI dogma therefore insists that, at some unconscious level, it is all counting out; that "zeroing in" is just an unsophisticated attempt to describe the brain's "data-processing" operations. This does not seem to be out of the question if one thinks only of games like chess, in which explicit rules cover every possible eventuality, explicit goals completely determine the outcome, and all relevant information is available all the time. Writing in Japanese script, however, takes place under such conditions rarely if ever. If zeroing in (concentration) is a specious concept, how can we explain the real effects it seems to have in the case of written Japanese?

To make these effects clear, let's look at how a computer "writes" Japanese. We will take voice input *(onsei nyūryoku)* as an example for three reasons. It closely reflects the phases of human writing; it is an original goal of the Fifth Generation project that has not been abandoned (Lindamood 1984b); and, like OCR, it is regarded as a way around the typewriter keyboard, which is often mistakenly seen as the real bottleneck of Japanese input (e.g., Panko 1983, Pollack 1984). In voice input, the user speaks into a microphone; the computer's task is twofold: it must transform raw phonetic data into the phonemes of a particular language, and then parse the phonemicized datastream, converting each segment into the written form intended by the user. In Japanese, English, or any other language, it takes hours of "training" time and extremely complex programs to get a computer to do even the first part of this task with a single individual making an effort to speak slowly and consistently in noise-free surroundings; yet secretaries using dictation equipment regularly do it all, and do it well, under much less favorable conditions. This fact alone shows a major difference between concentration and heuristics.

But there is more. Consider what the computer program must do in order to handle the second part of the task in Japanese—all those "decisions" listed above. Some merely require checking various lists of items, but others involve syntactic analysis, and, in the case of genuine homonyms, semantic and pragmatic interpretation as well. All this requires an immense database, of which the equivalent of a large Japanese dictionary is only the most basic component. Take the most obvious example—proper names. How does the computer know that the Nakata Kazuo to whom the boss is writing uses the kanji

名方一雄

rather than

中田和男

to write his name? A secretary might try looking through the boss's file of business cards *(meishi)*[18]; the computer, however, cannot do this unless someone has *previously* created a file containing not just the information on the cards but also how it is all to be read. And if the boss knows two Nakata Kazuo who write their names differently, the computer will need more prestored information in order to tell them apart. Moreover, this is not active information like mathematical equations or rules of grammar, the kind of stuff that, packed into AI machines, is supposed to endow them with the power to solve whole classes of mathematical problems and translate any text from one language to another; rather, it is purely passive, ad hoc data such as telephone numbers, addresses, lines of business, and so on. Heuristic procedures cannot cut the time it takes to search through all these trivia; all they can do is hold the number of fruitless searches to a minimum.

Just as concentration is a prerequisite for writing Japanese script, perspective is a prerequisite for reading it. Readers of Japanese have at their disposal a veritable bagful of tricks for dealing with seldom-used kanji. As long as the reader can supply a satisfactory (not necessarily the intended) linguistic rendition of the written symbols as they go by, the process of reading can continue uninterrupted. This is ambiguity tolerance, or perspective, in its purest form. It is a remarkable human capacity, not a consequence of meanings inherent in so-called ideographs. People can and do make mistakes. They may not supply the readings the writer had in mind; they may get names wrong; they may even take a detour into deciphering, treating unknown or temporarily forgotten kanji as blanks in the hope that they will soon have enough context to fill them in. In every case, however, the assignment of *some* linguistic interpretation takes place; when not even a vague or tentative interpretation can be made, the message is merely being inspected, not read.

Computers lack perspective. At the hardware level, all information is qualitatively uniform; therefore, no matter how high up in software one goes, all information is in principle equally valid. A particular hunk of data can be labelled "vague" or "tentative," but the label itself can be neither; when the program later encounters the label, it either does or does not change course as a result. Even if the program is written to react differently (or randomly!) each time it runs into data carrying a "fuzzy" label, each such encounter results in a completely determined outcome. By contrast, people can put ambiguous information in perspective without "disambiguating" it—they just "live with it."

The Risk of Waiting

If the use of kanji in modern Japan is in fact a cultural property worth saving—and that is debatable—clearly AI will not be its savior. There is no "national genius" or "Japanese spirit" that the abandonment of kanji would imperil, especially if such an abandonment were restricted to computer applications. The one casualty of accepting something other than kanji kanamajiribun as a standard form of writing might be the Ideographic Myth, which has about the same scientific validity as astrology. Nonetheless, MITI shows virtually no interest in non-kanji computerization. Giving up the kanji displays that large-scale integrated circuits have made possible seems like a step backward; the next step forward seems to be AI, which will presumably make it as easy to use kanji on computers as ordinary alphanumerics. MITI is either unaware of or uninterested in investigations of AI by scholars like Dreyfus that call the whole enterprise into question.

Suppose, as Dreyfus argues, strong AI is in principle impossible. As we shall see, nothing short of real artificial intelligence can break the stranglehold of the input problem on effective computer use in Japan. What will happen if the government does nothing and continues to let the manufacturers cater to the prejudices of a nation indoctrinated with the Ideographic Myth? There has already been enough experience with Japanese word processors to supply part of the answer: *users of currently available equipment rapidly lose their kanji writing skills.* A laissez-faire policy can therefore only hasten the already noticeable decline in the ability of the younger generation to use kanji with confidence in their daily lives.

Writing by hand on genkô yôshi may be time-consuming and inefficient, but it does exercise the distinctively human powers of insight, imagination, concentration, and perspective, thereby keeping the skills acquired through years of experience fresh and active. By contrast, the transcriptive Japanese word processors that dominate today's market turn this process into a deadening, passive activity.[19] Professor Kabashima, who thinks that word processors have arrived in the nick of time to rescue kanji from the eroding effects of internationalization, does not dispute this point. Perhaps this is because he is a heavy user of word processors himself. He, and for that matter almost every other Japanese interviewed in 1985 who used word processors frequently, freely admitted that it was increasingly hard to remember how to use kanji when writing by hand. This doesn't bother Kabashima: he looks forward to a time not too far off when people almost never write kanji, just read them (Kabashima 1984: 48).

This assumes, however, that major changes in the technological infrastructure, like the proliferation of computers, won't upset the social and cultural equilibrium, a proposition against which history makes an impressive case. Consider, for example, the enormous impact of the clock (discussed at length in Weizenbaum 1976), to mention only one of a host of inventions that have literally changed the course of human history (see Burke 1978). No one knows whether a generation of Japanese brought up in a world of transcriptive word processing can attain reading skills comparable to their parents', but if our experience with hand-held calculators is any guide, we should expect the worst. Teachers and parents have found it necessary to place deliberate limits on the use of calculators to ensure that children learn the principles of arithmetic and not merely how to push buttons in the proper sequence. Without such restrictions, the new calculators would certainly drive older methods into oblivion: logarithm tables and slide rules, for example, are falling into disuse nearly everywhere. The Japanese abacus *(soroban)* seems to be an exception, but it survives today primarily because of its recognized value in education, which has superseded its previous value as a tool.

Arithmetic is reducible to a terse, absolutely regular set of rules; the great rambling web of kanji and their readings is not. How much more likely it is, then, that unrestricted access to transcriptive kanji interfaces will hasten the decline of real expertise in kanji.

Three Contradictions

As long as Japanese leaders continue to see kanji versus computers as culture versus technology, rather than as a conflict of two technologies, the blithe acknowledgment that active writing skills may deteriorate as kanji-based word processing proliferates is about the most one can expect to hear. To this extent, Miller has a point: most Japanese simply refuse to apply the same practical rationality to their writing practice that they apply with such unrelenting earnestness and spectacular success in business. But Miller errs in implying that this is somehow inevitable, that it is something so ingrained in the Japanese character that nothing can change it. If we review the prevailing outlook on the role of Japanese in the computer age, we find in it three contradictions; the resolution of any one of these could change the course of Japanese computerization.

The first contradiction arises from the emotional conflict between tradition and modernity. On the one hand, the Japanese believe (rightly) that their language is a far more expressive and subtle instrument than any piece of machinery; they love to point out delicate shades of meaning, rituals of politeness, and all the other things that they believe (wrongly) make Japanese unique among languages of the world. On the other hand, they are anxious to prove that their language can be as easily adapted as any other to the latest inventions of high technology; the suggestion that their script (by which they mean language) is a problem for computers strikes them as insulting. Sooner or later, they will realize that language cannot both utterly transcend machines and be totally compatible with them.

The second contradiction is historical. Strong-AI theory holds that intelligence involves nothing more than the manipulation of physical symbols. Yet the Japanese writing system, seen as an expression of human creativity, is one of the most magnificent refutations of this theory that history provides. Academics like Suzuki argue that the Japanese writing system is an essential part of the Japanese language, and has been for centuries. Yet, until recently, full literacy was something aspired to but rarely attained by the great mass of the Japanese population. Sooner or later, myth must give way to fact.

Finally, there is the contradiction—perhaps, in this case, paradox would be a better word—inherent in transcriptive Japanese input. For effective communication, most computer applications simply do not require kanji output, and most people who do computer input are already thinking in terms of kana and rômaji. As more people come to rely on computers for more of their day-to-day writing, their ability to use kanji with facility will almost certainly decline unless something is done to improve methods of input. Sooner or later, those Japanese who want to preserve the orthographic status quo will see that transcriptive input is part of the problem, not part of the solution.

The first contradiction is the one most obvious to the Japanese layman but the least likely to be resolved. Doing so would require distinguishing clearly between the written representation of language and language itself—in short, denying the Ideographic Myth. The second contradiction could come to the surface if the Fifth Generation project fails; Japanese might then start questioning the reasonableness of strong AI. Alternatively, it could emerge as an issue as more foreign students, particularly from less-developed countries, come to Japan and Japanese plays a greater role as an international language; Japanese might then begin to question the assumed indispensability of kanji. But it is the third contradiction that has the best chance of leading to change, for skyrocketing sales of cheap transcriptive word processors may be their own undoing. As more Japanese come to depend on computers, they will learn from experience—just as many Americans learned during the boom years of personal computers—what works and what does not, and demand products that meet their real needs.

There is no permanent myth, as Miller would have us believe, that bars Japan from changing the status quo any more than there was a permanent myth that prevented Western civilization from adopting the physics of Galileo. Aristotelean physics had a lot going for it: "common sense," ecclesiastical and scholarly authority, and a record of accomplishments made by men who believed in it wholeheartedly.

But eventually, the idea that physical theories had to account for all observed data won out, and a fundamental change did take place. Western civilization has certainly changed a great deal since then, but it has not undergone an irreparable break with its past. Japanese attitudes toward language and writing might undergo a similar kind of change if the pressures of computerization bring one or more of the contradictions listed above into sharp enough focus for a large enough segment of the population. Japan could then enter a long, perhaps indefinite period of what DeFrancis (1984a) has called "digraphia," the simultaneous use of two different writing systems. Though even a partial transition to kana or rômaji would certainly take a substantial amount of time to achieve (cf. the resistance to the metric system in the United States), it is just as certainly within the realm of possibility.

Superintelligent computers, however, are another matter.

III

ECONOMICS
AND
TECHNOLOGY

5

The Importance of Efficient Input

It costs more to output information written in Japanese script than in alphanumeric form, because of the large number of kanji and their graphic complexity. The additional expense might take the form of a high-resolution video monitor or printer, extra memory for storing kanji patterns, longer plotting times, fewer characters per page, or some other hardware-related factor. Hardware costs in general can be expected to fall over the years ahead thanks to technical improvements and economies of scale, but Japanese script output will always cost more than alphanumeric. Likewise, the cost of representing and manipulating data encoded to enable output in Japanese script format without further processing will always be greater than the cost of representing and using the same data in alphanumeric format. On a character-for-character basis, kanji take up twice the storage of standard alphanumerics. At the level of whole words and sentences, data stored in a print-ready format require extra storage, extra processing, or both if they are to be sorted, searched, or otherwise handled as linguistically meaningful information. Again, these are hardware-related costs, and we can reasonably expect hardware costs to continue their downward trend. But every advance in design or savings in production of kanji-based hardware can be applied equally well to ordinary alphanumeric-based hardware; hence, the difference of cost can never be eliminated.

Japanese consumers may be willing and able to pay the extra costs of kanji output and computation indefinitely—nobody can say. Input, however, is a fundamentaly different matter because the real work of input occurs on the man side of the man/machine interface. If the promise of a future in which ubiquitous computers help ordinary people solve everyday problems is to be fulfilled, then at the very least the average person must be able to acquire the skills needed to input data quickly, accurately, and with only the minimum of physical and mental stress. Input is the key for four reasons.

First of all, the practical problems easily handled by computers are often data-intensive: the computer does not in itself contribute new methods but rather makes it possible to deal with huge amounts of data, previously unmanageable, in a systematic way. In some cases key data may be collected directly from measuring instruments and sensors, but many applications depend heavily on natural-language data.

Second, useful natural-language data must be distilled and homogenized before it ever gets to the machine. When we write down ordinary speech, we filter out idiosyncratic phonetic variation (how do you pronounce "either"?), reduce the pauses and changes in intonation of continuous speech with a sprinkling of punctuation marks, chop the stream of sounds into conventional words, and dress each in its prescribed spelling. Unless and until computers can consume raw speech unaided, we must cook it for them.

Third, effortless input is the foundation for creative programming and documentation. When computers filled entire rooms and programming was an arcane subspecialty of applied mathematics, hardware costs were the lion's share. In the present age of very large-scale integration, however, the software and integrity of user-accessible databases account for most of a system's value.

Finally, all real-time communication applications depend on fast, error-free, nonfatiguing input. Without efficient input, networking among ordinary citizens becomes difficult or impossible, yet it is precisely in the person-to-person sharing of ideas, not in automatic "expert systems," that the redeeming social value of computerization seems to lie (Roszak 1986: 167–176).

Even researchers who believe that the use of Chinese characters on computers must be retained, no matter what, agree that input is the key issue (e.g., Yu & Xiao 1983). They appear unwilling, however, to face the fact that technical advances and falling hardware costs in themselves will not remedy the shortcomings of existing systems. Considering the beguiling promises of the AI gurus, who can blame them? Machines that will understand spoken language, machines that will "discover" hitherto unknown solutions to complex problems, machines that will not require explicitly programmed instructions—they're all just around the proverbial corner! Unfortunately, work to date, including that of the Fifth Generation project, belies such promises.

In any case, would we *want* to give up the healthy discipline of explicit programming languages? Would we *want* to rely on computers whose "lines of thinking" we cannot always trace? Would we *want* to work with machines endowed with all the foibles of human beings? And even if we did, exactly what could an intelligent machine do that would markedly improve the kanji input problem? It is surprising how few computer scientists and engineers working on this problem have paused to consider that this is a job that requires, not a machine to *simulate* the user's mind, but quite literally a machine to *read* it.

Instead, they are trying to exploit every aspect of kanji in the hopes of finding a miracle cure for the input ailment. There is very little reliable information on the efficiency of the hundreds of systems that have been tried since almost no basic research has been conducted by commercially disinterested parties. A few attempts have been made at developing evaluation criteria (e.g., Chen & Gong 1983 for Chinese), but there is no generally agreed upon way to quantify input performance. Newspapers and trade journals are flooded with claims that system X can produce 99 percent correct Japanese text from raw kana input, or that operators of computer Y can input 160 Chinese characters per minute, but in virtually every instance such statistics turn out to be tainted by tacit assumptions about user training time, the kind of texts to be input, available alternatives (in the case of comparisons with other products), side effects such as physical and mental stress, and so on. In some cases, the figures cited are just plain wrong; the following example recently slipped by a *Newsweek* editor:

> Japan's Matsushita Electric Industrial Co. has developed the Panaword Tegaki word processor, which doesn't even use a keyboard. Operators write characters on a pressure-sensitive square and the machine records them at the rate of 15 per second with 99.5 percent accuracy. (Chin & Martin 1986)

The operator of a Panaword Tegaki uses a stylus to write characters on the machine's working surface, which resembles a child's plastic "magic slate." A person who could handwrite English, letter by letter, on such a contraption at the rate of 15 *letters* per second would be equalling the performance of a typist doing 180 *words* per minute! A rate of 15 characters per *minute* (one every four seconds) is within the bounds of credibility; if the machine records anything 15 times per *second,* it must be *the geometrical coordinates of the operator's stylus* on the writing square.

In the end, all we know for sure is that there are basically three ways to input kanji, each with its strong and weak points.

Inscriptive Input

The Panaword Tegaki just discussed is an example of an inscriptive input device. Its stylus is wired to the machine, and the user inscribes one kanji at a time. (He may also touch labelled cells next to the writing square with the stylus to produce kana, punctuation marks, etc.—an element of descriptive input.) Other makers have come out with larger devices on which a whole sheet of paper covers the working surface and is written on with a ballpoint pen. In either case, as the penpoint moves, its coordinates are relayed to a computer, which calculates the direction of the pen's motion, checks for discontinuities when the pen leaves the paper, and so on. This information is analyzed as it comes in and matched against templates to determine how many and what kind of strokes have been drawn. Further comparisons with more abstract templates allow for the identification of radicals and whole characters. (See Yhap & Greanias 1981 for a lucid explanation of one such system.)

This penpoint-tracing technology is frequently used to aid in the creation of graphic displays on computers. Inputting text this way is far more complex because it requires that each separate character inscribed on the working surface be correctly identified through pattern matching. Ideally, one would like to fill up a sheet of blank paper with ordinary handwriting and have the computer reproduce the text in neat "typed" form. Unfortunately, even in English, which is among the few European languages unencumbered with diacritical marks, this kind of performance still belongs to the realm of science fiction. It should therefore come as no surprise that inscription is the technically most difficult way to input Japanese.

Optical character recognition (OCR) can be regarded as a species of inscriptive input. In this method, instead of a real-time digitizer, one uses a scanning device as the interface with the computer. Rather than having a typist key in the contents of a book, for example, the ideal OCR device "reads" each page and records it character by character. Such machines exist for ordinary alphanumeric script but are expensive ($50,000 and up) and not very "robust," that is, they may fail to do the job right unless the input data meets certain rather severe conditions. Again, the ideal—write a page, feed it in, get back perfectly typed copy ready for on-line editing—is still far off.

In Japan, much of the work on inscriptive input (including OCR) is being carried out at the Musashino and Yokosuka Electrical Communication Laboratories of Nippon Telegraph and Telephone (NTT), a public corporation until 1985. Out of the eight papers on character recognition presented at the International Conference on Text Processing with a Large Character Set held in Tôkyô in October of 1983, six were from teams based at these facilities. (All eight papers on character recognition were by Japanese, as were most of those in other categories dealing with closely allied topics.) The results reported in the NTT papers, as well as those described by Suen in an invited paper at the same conference, are impressive in terms of percentage of kanji correctly identified (often better than 99 percent for 2,000 distinct types of kanji and more). Unfortunately, however, most of the papers concentrate on the structure of various algorithms and do not mention the actual time required to identify individual characters, the other constraints under which the user operates, or the hardware required for supporting the algorithm. The spectacular recognition rates should therefore be interpreted in light of Suen's comments:

> The immense variations in printing styles remain to be the greatest hurdle. In order to enhance the recognition rate, reduce the machine effort and the cost, standards should be developed to minimize shape variations of the Chinese characters. The success in machine recognition of about 1000 characters handprinted according to some given models indicates that *standardization in shapes, strokes, and relations within the character is the key factor in successful operation of Kanji OCR at low cost. This can be achieved by defining the correct position, size and orientation of the basic strokes and radicals which form the Kanji.* This may involve substantial effort of many people in several different disciplines (e.g. computer scientists and engineers, linguists, typographic experts, psychologists and others) to work together to examine and decide the correct shape representations of Chinese characters, reasonable separation of components and strokes, esthetic appearance, and disambiguities of similar characters. Toward this part, the author and his research associates have computed the structural composition of 4,864 most common Chinese characters from 753,941 samples. Statistical distribution of radicals and composition rules have been tabulated [Huang & Suen 1983]. It is hoped that this will form the stepping stone towards standardization and successful Kanji recognition. (Suen 1983: 431, emphasis added)

This call for standardization reveals the magnitude of the gap between practical systems and the experimental results obtained so far. Notice too that Suen is speaking primarily about OCR: real-time inscriptive input is a much tougher nut to crack because of the need to provide the user with virtually immediate feedback and as much freedom in the mechanics of inscribing characters as possible.

Inscriptive input devices are being marketed in Japan today but are not popular because they are expensive. For example, The Handwriter manufactured by Communication Intelligence Corporation (CIC) of Menlo Park, California, a special-purpose microcomputer that serves as a "front end" for several different computers that support Japanese script output, lists for ¥600,000, more than many of the fully programmable computers it supports.[1] Sharp's Nyû Shoin WD-2900T, a complete inscriptive worder processor, goes for ¥3,250,000 and up. With both the CIC and Sharp systems, the user must write neatly and firmly on a surface ruled like genkô yôshi, which limits operating speed to about 20 to 40 characters per minute. Even an inscriptive input system that tolerated the kind of fairly loose writing style most Japanese use on genkô yôshi, and never made a mistake in identifying characters, could not proceed much faster.

On the other hand, the fact that inscriptive input tracks the process of physical writing can also be seen as an advantage. It requires comparatively little training time and, more important, does not lead to a deterioration of ordinary handwriting skills. It capitalizes on precisely those human capacities that make kanji viable for people but unwieldy for machines.

Transcriptive Input

The "method of choice" among Japanese word-processor manufacturers is transcriptive input, in which strings of kana or roman letters are converted piecemeal to kanji. There are many variations. To put it as generally as possible: the user, while typing in phrases and sentences of Japanese, indicates which sections are to be set in hiragana, katakana, kanji, or alphanumeric by pressing special keys or in some other way. When kanji are requested, the computer executes a search through its dictionaries to find all the possible forms that match the readings given. The computer then displays one or more of the matches found, giving the user an opportunity to accept the machine's first choice or select alternatives.

One version of this, frequently mentioned in the Japanese AI literature (e.g., Motooka & Kitsuregawa 1984: 94–95), is a word processor operated entirely by voice. This would be the ultimate in transcriptive input, with the computer not only identifying the distinct words of connected speech automatically, but also figuring out all the typographical changes on its own. The first kind of parsing is hard enough, but the second is even harder because of the inherently indeterminate nature of many of the choices that must be made. One would need a pronounceable syllable that is not a word of the language to serve as an "escape" code for switching the system from dictation to instruction mode and back (use/reference ambiguity again). Then, to instruct the computer to use this kanji instead of that one, some method for naming individual characters would be necessary; in English, one can get by with letter-by-letter spelling, but this would clearly be inadequate for Japanese.

As far as so-called voice input systems on the market today are concerned, such considerations are strictly academic.[2] The "voice" version of NEC's Bungô word processor, for example, requires that the user input a repertoire of sentences, by typing, and record the spoken version of each; later, the computer retrieves these boilerplate sentences by matching the user's spoken input against its prerecorded "index." The fact that the matching algorithm does better with long sentences than with single words shows that it does little in the way of transforming raw phonetic input into anything resembling a phonemic representation. Sharp's Nyû Shoin WD-2900V, which sells for ¥3,450,000 and up, is said to process four moras per second; the assumptions underlying this figure are unclear, however. In any case, it is no improvement over inscriptive methods. Assuming no time is lost for corrections, 240 moras per minute works out to about ten words or 20 to 40 characters per minute.

Because voice input is so primitive, virtually all transcriptive input systems are based on typewriter keyboards and require the user to flag changes of character type. The cheapest machines, for example some of the new lap-held models under ¥100,000, use a kanji-by-kanji look-up procedure. This is painfully slow and tedious for the user but needs only the most modest of look-up dictionaries and searching algorithms. Machines of this type are little more than toys; their displays show only a few characters at a time, and they lack almost all of the features that make word processing an improvement over pencil-and-paper writing, except, of course, for neat output. Higher-priced models attempt to convert the roman or kana version of a multiple-kanji string to that string in one operation but require dictionaries of tens of thousands of words and carefully programmed search-and-retrieve procedures to accomplish this.

Naturally, kanji are not the user's only problem. There are also hiragana, katakana, roman letters (upper and lower case), numerals, Japanese punctuation, Western punctuation, and special symbols to worry about. The most consistent approach is to have the user specify the kind of character desired before typing in the string to be processed. Unfortunately, each "prefix" code also serves to mark the end of the previously typed string; if that happens to be a kanji string, the user, relying on the conversion routine to produce the intended kanji on the first try, is likely to be in the midst of typing the next string before visual feedback is provided. If an incorrect kanji appears in the computer's first choice, going back to fix the error can result in losing some or all of the subsequent (correct) input. In any case, it is confusing to have to go back to repair a kanji string after one has gone on to something else, such as working on a kana string, trying to divide a long kango compound into shorter segments that the computer is more likely to have in its look-up dictionary, or thinking up alternative readings to "help" the computer with an unusual kanji (a common dodge often necessary with names). Not surprisingly, only one of the major manufacturers, Toshiba, now makes machines that use prefix operation; almost all other systems treat conversion to kanji as a separate case. The user selects a default kana mode, hiragana or katakana. (Often there is no choice; hiragana are the default.) Keyboard input appears on the video display in this mode. Whenever he wishes, the user presses one of two keys (a "suffix") to signal that the input up to this point can be left as is or that it should be converted into kanji. This approach works well as long as katakana, alphanumeric, and special punctuation marks, which still require prefix codes, make up only a small percentage of the total characters input. Unfortunately, this is less and less often the case as the vocabulary of modern Japanese changes with the times, especially in scientific and technical writing.

The step up from individual kanji to strings of kanji creates some other problems. The typical system, for example, founders on compounds that involve phonemic variations such as rendaku (see Chapter 1, p. 27) unless they are explicitly listed in its look-up dictionary. Thus, for example, *sanbyaku-en* '¥300' or *nijippun* '20 minutes' must usually be converted one character at a time: *san, hyaku, en* and *ni, jû, fun*. Then there is the problem of names. Virtually all systems provide the user with a way of making ad hoc additions to the computer's store of kanji expressions. Unless a system's database management software is very carefully designed, however, this can create more problems than it solves. Some word processors, for example, have a separate conversion key for proper nouns *(koyû meishi)*; pressing this key accesses a special dictionary. This seems like a clever idea since it prevents "collisions" between proper names and ordinary words; however, it places the burden of maintaining the proper-noun dictionary on the user (how can the machine tell whether a new kanji expression is or is not a proper noun?), and forces the user to distinguish among different kinds of kanji expressions during input. Another approach is to have the computer compile statistics on the frequency with which particular kanji have been selected and update its dictionary, or at least its priorities for offering choices, accordingly; needless to say, this involves another quantum leap in software overhead.

The next step toward transcriptive input efficiency is often called *bunsetsu henkan* in the advertising brochures and fliers dispensed in vast quantities in showrooms and at "data shows" throughout Japan. *Bunsetsu* is the name the linguist Hashimoto Shinkichi gave to the phrase- and clause-like syntactic units on which he based his theory of Japanese grammar; its use in connection with transcriptive input is somewhat misleading. In the context of word processing, a bunsetsu is any string of characters (1) all of the same kind (kanji, hiragana, etc.), or (2) consisting of one or more kanji followed by some kana (on most machines, hiragana).[3] All transcriptive word processors must be able to handle strings of the first type, but only "advanced" systems can deal with strings of the second, which are important because of the inflected endings of Japanese verbs and adjectives and the heavy incidence of noun-phrase-plus-postposition sequences. The idea is to add some analytical power to the system that enables it to divide this second type of string correctly into kanji and kana parts, thereby saving the user a few keystrokes. Unfortunately, the bunsetsu of actual Japanese are not always bunsetsu as defined for the convenience of word processing, so the operator cannot confidently rely on phonological cues like pitch accent (Chapter 1, p. 20) or on grammatical intuition in deciding when to terminate a bunsetsu by hitting a suffix key. Although true bunsetsu that are transcribed with one or two kanji followed by a short string of hiragana do occur frequently in all kinds of Japanese writing, there are other common types that must be reckoned with, such as those that call for hiragana followed by kanji (with or without further hiragana), long kanji compound expressions, short phrases augmented with one-character Sino-Japanese prefixes and/or suffixes, and compound verbs.

Katakana and alphanumeric phrases become particularly troublesome when bunsetsu are the unit of conversion because strings written with these characters cannot be input the same way as strings written with kanji even though they fill the same grammatical "slots" in Japanese sentences. To produce a bunsetsu containing kanji, one types default-mode kana (usually hiragana) or rômaji and then presses a suffix key; to produce the other variety of kana (usually katakana) or alphanumerics in the same grammatical position, one must press the appropriate prefix key before typing, and another prefix key to switch back to default kana to complete the bunsetsu. No manufacturer has attempted to develop a system that treats all kinds of characters in a bunsetsu uniformly because the parsing involved would be prohibitively complex. Many bunsetsu do not end with hiragana, and the possible syllabic structures of gairaigo, unlike kango, are virtually impossible to define—short of listing them all in yet another gigantic look-up dictionary.

Special Keyboards

To reduce the psychological and physical burden of having to remember which control keys to press and when, manufacturers are trying to make their software "smarter." Now on the horizon are look-up dictionaries of more than 100,000 words (more than many printed dictionaries!) with syntactic analysis programs that tackle whole sentences. But all this fancy programming has to run fast in order to keep system response time short—an extra delay of a second may not seem like much, but to a user who must endure it thousands of times while typing a single document, it can be unnerving. Naturally, system designers see this bigger-is-better strategy as an exciting engineering challenge.

Unfortunately, it is more than just a challenge; the whole approach is inherently flawed in two ways. First, it always takes more system resources to resolve the currently most frequent kanji-conversion ambiguity than it took to resolve the last one. This is because each kanji added to the inventory requires more than one new dictionary entry to make it accessible while avoiding "collisions" with other kanji; on the other hand, as the inventory grows larger, the likelihood of the most recent additions occurring in actual texts steadily decreases. Second, "sophisticated" look-up methods have only a narrow range of applicability: because of genuine homonyms, not to mention the extra collisions created by artificial bunsetsu analysis, there is a natural limit to the accuracy of automatic conversion schemes that they can approach but never surpass. In really hard-to-disambiguate (but not uncommon) cases, like names, no amount of context can help determine the choices that must be made, because they are purely arbitrary. In fairly straightforward (and very common) situations, such as guessing that the user probably wants Tôkyô, the place name, and not *tôkyô* 'cephalothorax', a simpleminded procedure (e.g., reproducing the kanji accepted the last time *tôkyô* was typed in) can be as good as a fancy, high-overhead procedure that uses elaborate syntactic analysis. In short, each boost in overhead gives the user less and less benefit, and even a theoretically optimal system would still have to allow for user intervention at all times.

Nonetheless, many Japanese engineers interviewed in 1985 said they believed 100-percent accurate automatic kanji conversion was just around that corner we have heard of so many times. Having thus declared the real problem a moot point, they are busy working on the "next step"—reducing the absolute number of keypresses. To this end they have exercised considerable ingenuity in creating kana-oriented keyboards.

Ordinary English keyboards (Table 10) are, of course, perfectly adequate for roman-to-kanji conversion, and there have been at least two rômaji keyboards proposed specifically for Japanese (Table 11). Most professional word-processor and computer operators who use tran-

Table 10.   Alphanumeric Keyboards for English

A. Typical American Layout (DEC)

Unshifted

```
'   1   2   3   4   5   6   7   8   9   0   -   =
    q   w   e   r   t   y   u   i   o   p   [   ]
    a   s   d   f   g   h   j   k   l   ;   '   \
    <   z   x   c   v   b   n   m   ,   .   /
```

Shifted

```
~   !   @   #   $   %   ^   &   *   (   )   _   +
    Q   W   E   R   T   Y   U   I   O   P   {   }
    A   S   D   F   G   H   J   K   L   :   "   |
    >   Z   X   C   V   B   N   M   ,   .   ?
```

Table 10. *Continued*

B. A "Dvorak Simplified" Rearrangement of the Above

Unshifted

```
'   1   2   3   4   5   6   7   8   9   0   \   =
    '   ,   .   p   y   f   g   c   r   l   /   ]
    a   o   e   u   i   d   h   t   n   s   -   [
    <   ;   q   j   k   x   b   m   w   v   z
```

Shifted

```
~   !   @   #   $   %   ^   &   *   (   )   |   +
    "   ,   .   P   Y   F   G   C   R   L   ?   }
    A   O   E   U   I   D   H   T   N   S   _   {
    >   :   Q   J   K   X   B   M   W   V   Z
```

---

scriptive input prefer typing rômaji even when direct input of kana is available (Becker 1984: 101). One reason for this is that they have to type alphanumerics anyway, and find it difficult to master two different keyboard arrangements. Another reason is that kana typing requires too many keys. True touch typing is difficult on forty-five keys and almost impossible on fifty or more (Yamada 1980a). English typewriter keyboards offer the alphabet and most common punctuation marks in the central thirty keys. As anyone who has learned to touch type knows, it takes special practice to avoid making mistakes when reaching for the lower-frequency symbols and numerals on the fourth row or the other keys the manufacturer may have placed on the left or right. With kana, keys in these locations must be used relatively often. Forty-eight keys are needed just for modern kana (including keys for nigori, handakuten, and bô), plus an assortment of keys for small-form kana, standard punctuation, and toggling between hiragana and katakana, let alone alphanumerics.

The simplest kana keyboards try to get by with a single shift. The

Table 11. Proposed Rômaji Keyboards

A. Tamaru Takurô et al. 1921

Unshifted

2	3	4	5	6	7	8	9	0	"
-	l	y	o	u	m	n	r	b	j	x
,	f	i	a	e	s	t	k	h	q	^
.	w	ô	û	c	z	d	g	p	v

Shifted

"	/	@	%	_	¥	!	(	)	'
§	L	Y	O	U	M	N	R	B	J	X
?	F	I	A	E	S	T	K	H	Q	'
:	W	!	;	C	Z	D	G	P	V

B. Kawakami 1951 (following Dvorak)

Unshifted

7	5	3	1	9	0	2	4	6	8
j	l	f	ô	û	w	m	r	,	.	^
e	i	a	o	u	h	n	t	k	s	-
c	q	v	x	p	y	b	d	g	z

Shifted

#	(	'	"	%	_	/	)	@	¥
J	L	F	?	!	W	M	R	;	:	˘
E	I	A	O	U	H	N	T	K	S	§
C	Q	V	X	P	Y	B	G	Z

Source: Kana Jimuki no Kai 1961: 68–69.

cheapest machines sport a variation on the gojûon arrangement (e.g., Table 12A), easy to learn but hard to use with any kind of speed or rhythm. The Japan Industrial Standard (JIS) kana layout (JIS C-6233 [1980], Table 12B), now found on most computers, has been studied extensively and is known to be poor. It differs little from the dominant kind of kana typewriter keyboard of the pre-microcomputer era, of which there were dozens of variants. Table 13A–D shows four of the less well-known keyboards of that era; Table 13E is a more recent effort. A new, presumably more efficient JIS layout (Table 12C) was announced in late 1985, but it may take years before it becomes a true standard because so many of the older JIS keyboards are already in use.[4]

It is interesting to consider why so many different single-shift kana keyboards had been developed. No doubt part of the reason is that different designers have used different criteria in evaluating the ease of finger and hands motions. This may not be the only source of divergence, however. Japanese script has many more kana (nearly fifty, not counting small kana and kana marked with diacritics) than the language has phonemes (fewer than the number of letters in the alphabet); moreover, very few words are more than four moras long (Hayashi et al. 1982: 318). Consequently, differences in vocabulary from text to text that barely affect the frequencies with which given phonemes are used might nonetheless cause substantial deviations in the frequencies of particular kana.

An analogy with English may be helpful. It is well known that each letter, pair of letters (digraph), triplet of letters (trigraph), and so on, has a characteristic relative frequency of occurrence in English. You can determine these relative frequencies for yourself by counting up the letters, digraphs, etc., in, say, newspaper and magazine articles. In the process, you will discover that the more letters in the unit being tallied, the less likely it is to show up the average number of times in any single short article. One reason is that there are 26 letters, 676 possible digraphs, 17,576 possible trigraphs, and so on; therefore, the longer the units, the less their relative frequencies.[5] Another reason is that the longer units contain more complete words; therefore, differences in the content and purpose of sample texts are more likely to affect the counts. Now the analogy: individual phonemes of Japanese are comparable to individual letters in English; kana, which usually represent consonant-plus-vowel pairs, are comparable to English digraphs; *pairs* of kana, which is what keyboard designers must consider, are comparable to English trigraphs, perhaps even tetragraphs.

Table 12. Common Single-Shift Kana Keyboards

Kana are given in Cabinet Romanization. Lowercase letters appear in the names of keys that produce "small" kana and Japanese punctuation, viz.

j″o j″c	major quotation marks
j′o j′c	minor quotation marks
j·	period
j,	comma
j/	separator

Note also

k	kanji or kanji repeat mark
—	bô, long vowel marker
″	nigori
°	handakuten
F1, F2, &c.	function key
·	blank

A. Typical Gojûon Layout (Brother)

Unshifted

A	I	U	E	O	NA	NI	NU	NE	NO	RA	RI	RU

KA	KI	KU	KE	KO	HA	HI	HU	HE	HO	RE	RO

SA	SI	SU	SE	SO	MA	MI	MU	ME	MO	WA	WO

TA	TI	TU	TE	TO	YA	YU	YO	N	j,	j·

Shifted

a	i	u	e	o	·	·	·	(	)	·	·	·

ka	·	·	ke	·	·	·	·	·	·	·	j″o j″c

·	·	·	·	·	·	·	·	·	·	wa	·

·	·	tu	·	·	ya	yu	yo	·	—	·

143

Table 12. *Continued*

B. One Version of the Current JIS Layout (Sharp)

Unshifted

NU	HU	A	U	E	O	YA	YU	YO	WA	HO	HE	k
TA	TE	I	SU	KA	N	NA	NI	RA	SE	"	°	
TI	TO	SI	HA	KI	KU	MA	NO	SO	RE	KE	MU	
TU	SA	SO	HI	KO	MI	MO	NE	RU	ME	RO		

Shifted

·	·	a	u	e	o	ya	yu	yo	wo	·	£	·	·
·	·	i	·	·	·	·	·	·	·	·	ʃ'o	·	ʃ"o
·	·	·	·	·	·	·	·	·	·	·	ʃ'c	·	ʃ"c
tu	·	·	·	·	·	·	·	·	ʃ.	ʃ,	ʃ/	--	

C. "New" JIS Layout

Unshifted

SO	KE	SE	TE	yo	TU	N	NO	WO	RI	TI	·
HA	KA	SI	TO	TA	KU	U	I	"	KI	NA	·
SU	KO	NI	SA	A	tu	RU	ʃ,	ʃ.	RE		

Shifted

a	°	HO	HU	ME	HI	E	MI	YA	NU	ʃ"o	·
i	HE	RA	yu	YO	MA	O	MO	WA	YU	ʃ"c	·
u	e	o	NE	ya	MU	RO	ʃ/	--	·	·	

Source: (C) Watanabe 1985: 9.

Table 13. Other Single-Shift Kana Keyboards

A. JIS Telex Layout

Unshifted

```
   HE  HI  NE  KE  TO  RA  WA  MU  MO  ME
"     HO  HU  KU  KO  TI  YO  U   N   NA  YA
   RU  HA  TA  KA  SI  I   MA  SA  RI  E   RO
   SU  NI  SE  TE  O   KI  TU  NO  A   MI
```

Shifted

```
      ·     ·    %   #    ·    ·   @   ¥   $   £
   °   1    2    3   4    5    6   7   8   9   0
      ,    --   YU  RE   SO   WI  NU  :   .   WE  =
      /    +    (   j,   WO   )   j"c  ·   *   ?
```

B. Maritime Self-Defense Forces (Toshiba)

Unshifted

```
   q   w   e   r   t   y   u   i   o   p   /
a   s   d   f   g   h   j   k   l   :   (   )
9   7   5   3   1   ~   0   2   4   6   8   MU
   z   x   c   v   b   n   m   ,   .   NU  NE
```

Shifted

```
   --   SU  HO  HI  HU  HE  MA  ME  MI  RO  WA
SE  KU  KI  KO  HA  YU  NO  NI  RI  RU  O   MO
TE  KA  TA  SI  TU  YO  "   WA  I   N   A   °
   KE  SO  SA  TO  TI  YA  WO  NA  RE  RA  E
```

Table 13. *Continued*

C. An Early Kurosawa/Fujitsu Model

```
    YO  RA  RI  RU  RE  RO  WA  WO  N   YU  ME  MI
°   TI  NU  O   TU  TO  NO  NA  KE  SO  TA  HU  MA
"   A   TE  E   KA  KI  KU  KO  SA  SI  MO  YA
HE  HA  NE  U   NI  I   YA  SU  MU  HI  HO
```

D. Dai-ichi Insurance Company Experimental Model (IBM)

Unshifted

```
    NU  HU  N   KI  KA  TA  O   TO  RA  HO
KE  A   TU  I   U   SI  KU  YA  WA  RO
YU  HI  MI  MA  TI  YO  NA  "   HA
RE  E   NE  KO  SA  MO  HE  NO
```

Shifted

```
MU  SO  ·   ·   ·   ·   ·   ·   RU  ·
RI  TE  ·   ·   ·   ·   ·   ·   SE  SU
NI  ME  ·   ·   ·   ·   ·   ·   ·
k   k   k   ·   ·   k   k   ·
```

E. BW-20 Word Processor Keyboard (Hitachi)

Unshifted

```
NU  ME  MU  RO  MI  YA  YU  SE  HI  HU  HO  NE  HE
E   WO  MA  NA  NI  KU  KO  TU  KU  KI  HA  SA  SO
O   U   N   NO  "   I   SI  KA  TA  TE  TO  TI
RE  RI  RA  YO  MO  A   SU  RU  j,  j.  KE
```

146

Table 13. *Continued*

Shifted

·	·	·	·	·	ya	yu	·	·	·	·	· ·
e	·	·	·	·	·	tu	·	·	·	·
o	u	·	·	·	i		·	·	·	· ·
·	·	·	yo	·	a	·	·	·	·

Sources: (A–D) Kana Jimuki no Kai 1961; (E) Kurosu & Nakayama 1983.

Given enough sample text, the law of large numbers must eventually take effect, but designers of kana keyboards may well have underestimated how much text is "enough." The whole idea of an optimal kana keyboard may indeed be more of a theoretical possibility than a practical one.

In any case, one thing is certain: the "perfect" kana keyboard could no more break through the kanji bottleneck than the "ultimate" voice input system. Still, Japanese manufacturers are struggling mightily to prove that their keyboard is the best. Fujitsu reportedly exerted considerable pressure in an attempt to have its OASYS design (Table 14A) declared the new Japanese Industrial Standard. OASYS keyboards use thumbshifts to reduce the number of keys needed to produce kana. The thumbs of both hands are used to operate special keys located where an English typewriter would have a spacebar. The keys struck by the other four fingers of each hand have multiple values depending on whether they are pressed together with the thumbshift of the same hand, the thumbshift of the opposite hand, one of the shift keys located at the periphery of the keyboard, or in isolation.

Fujitsu engineers believe their OASYS keyboard makes efficient Japanese typing a reality (e.g., see Kanda 1986), but this claim is open to question. The thumbshifts and the keys they modify must be pressed simultaneously ("chord-keying"), a mode of operation that seems to be inherently inefficient (Yamada 1983a: 320–321). By contrast, the proposed TRON keyboard (Table 14B) also uses thumbshifts but lets the user press a shift key either while pressing a main key or immediately after. OASYS uses shift keys located in the usual positions to produce moras with initial *p;* TRON provides a separate key for handakuten. The OASYS and TRON distributions of kana differ, yet both are supposed to be based on frequency counts and analyses of typing ergonomics.

The experimental Ricoh system shown in Table 14C can be thought of as a multishift keyboard without shift keys in the ordinary sense.

Table 14.   Multiple-Shift Kana Keyboards

A. OASYS Thumbshift Keyboard (Fujitsu)

Unshifted

```
j.  KA  TA  KO  SA  RA  TI  KU  TU  ,   j,
U   SI  TE  KE  SE  HA  TO  KI  I   N
.   HI  SU  HU  HE  NU  SO  NE  HO  j/
```

Shifted with Same Hand

```
a   E   RI  ya  RE  YO  NI  RU  MA  e   -
WO  A   NA  yu  MO  MI  O   NO  yo  TU
u   --  RO  ya  i   NU  YU  MU  WA  o
```

Shifted with Opposite Hand

```
·   GA  TA  GO  ZA  ·   DI  GU  DU  ·   ·   ·
·   ZI  DE  GE  ZE  BA  DO  GI  ·   ·   ·
·   BI  ZU  HU  BE  ·   ZO  ·   BO  ·   ·
```

B. TRON Keyboard (Sakamura Ken, University of Tôkyô)

Unshifted

```
RI  ,   KU  NO  KI      HA  RU  KO  NA  KE
A   N   I   SI  TO      TA  U   KA  TE  RA
YÖ  tu  .   SU  RE      MO  TU  NI  WO  O
```

Table 14. *Continued*

Shifted with Same Hand

MU	MI	yu	RO	WA		NE	SA	ya	HU	NU
HE	o	yo	--	E		YA	ME	MA	e	SO
o	a	i	j/	yu		TI	u	HI	SE	HO

Shifted with Opposite Hand

·	·	GU	·	GI		BA	ZA	GO	BU	GE
BE	·	·	ZI	DO		DA	VU	GA	DE	RA
·	·	·	·	ZU		DI	DU	BI	ZE	BO

C. Ricoh TX620

Unshifted

·	·	·	·	·	·	·	HO	HI	HU	HE	TI	·
·	·	·	·	·	·	SO	SI	SU	SA	SE	YU	
o	"	F1	F2	·		TU	TE	TA	TO	HA	YO	
o	"	F1	F2	·		KA	KO	KE	KU	KI	YA	

Shifted

·	·	·	·	·	·	·	NU	ME	MI	MU	NE	·
·	·	·	·	·	·	E	I	O	A	U	N	
o	"	F1	F2	·		MA	NO	NI	NA	MO	WO	
o	"	F1	F2	·		RA	RI	RU	RE	RO	WA	

Instead, it uses keys operated by the left hand in the main keyboard area to modify the function of the kana keys, which are all operated by the right hand. The kana are distributed two to a key, but in such a way that only one has a variant form (written small, or with a diacritic mark). After a right-hand key is depressed, a left-hand key is struck that narrows down the previous choice to a single kana. Left-hand "home row" keys signal hiragana, "bottom row" keys katakana. The alternation of hands is an attractive feature of this system, but the heavy loading of the right hand in order to achieve this result may prove to be a drawback.

NEC offers an even more radical departure form the standard keyboard (Table 15A). Morita Masasuke of NEC has created a new keyboard shape: the keys are divided into a central section of eighteen function keys flanked by two clusters of thirty-one keys (including three thumb-operated shifts) for each hand. (Diagrams and photographs can be found in Morita 1983 and Morita 1985.) The clusters have curved rows and are angled toward the center so that the hands need not be turned outward from the forearms. The keys operated by the right hand specify consonants, including Cy combinations, the phonemes Q and N, and the two most common punctuation marks, the comma and period. The keys operated by the left hand are used to complete a sequence begun by the right hand and to specify whether the sequence is to be converted into kana or kanji: five keys (middle row) instruct the machine to register a kana ending in one of the vowels a, i, u, e, or o. The others instruct the machine to register a syllable as part of a kanji reading (on or kun) containing one of the vowels plus (depending on the key) an extra mora, which might be i, u, ki, ku, ti, tu, or N. Since some kanji readings consist of just one mora, separate keys are provided for their vowels (top row), distinct from the "kana vowel" keys. Thus, for example, the Japanese title of Nakayama 1974—*Rekishi to shite no gakumon*—would be typed on Morita's keyboard as

r- -ekV s- -i t- -*o* s- -*i* t- -*e* n- -*o* g- -akV m- -on

with alternating right- and left-hand keystrokes. Italics here indicate middle row vowel keys.

This high rate of right/left alternation (shifts are performed by the thumb of the opposite hand) is a definite plus for the Morita keyboard, as is the clever use of separate vowel keys for kana and kanji, which eliminates the need to press a suffix key in most cases. There are, however, some concealed problems: the left-hand keys for specifying kanji

Table 15. Mora Composition Keyboards

Note that a hyphen after or before a keyname indicates whether it is pressed first or last in a code-pair. V is cover symbol for vowels.

A. "M-Form" Keyboard (Morita Masasuke, NEC)

Unshifted

```
           -i                                r-
      -u   -i   -a                     y-    t-    w-
 -e   -u   -ii  -a   -o         m-    s-    d-    n-    p-
 -e   -uu       -ai  -o         k-    z-          j,    h-
 -ei            -ou             g-                      b-
```

Shifted

```
           -ikV                              ry-
      -ukV -in  -akV                   tu    ty-   N
 -ekV -un  -ikV -an  -okV       my-   sy-   dy-   ny-   py-
 -en  -utV      -atV -on        ky-   zy-         j.    hy-
 -etV           -otV            gy-                     by-
```

B. Proposed NTT Roman/Kanji Conversion Keyboard

```
 j,   w-   r-   m-   h-   -uu  -ai  -ou  j.   -ei
 n-   t-   s-   k-   s-   -u   -a   -o   -i   -e
 p-   d-   z-   g-   b-   -un  -an  -on  -in  -en
```

Table 15. *Continued*

C. The LIPS Keyboard (HS20)

```
-e"  -i"  -a"  -o"  -u"   m-   y-   r-   h-   w-

 -e   -i   -a   -o   -u    n-   0    t-   k-   s-

  -F4  -F3  -F2  -F1  -F5   F6   F7   F8   F9   F10
```

F6 through F10 manipulate the display cursor. F1 through F4 control other program functions; F5 is used for arabic numerals.

D. "Touch 16" (Epson)

```
 y-    m-    k-    F1    h-    ·    -u    -i    ·

 w-    s-    t-    b-    r-    -e   -o    -a    F2         ·
```

E. The "Rainputto" Keyboard

```
ME  MI  MA  MO  MU  WA  HU  HO  HA  HI  HE  F2  F3

-e  -i  -a  -o  -u  NG  p-  m-  n-  r-  w-  F4

-e  -i  -a  -o  -u  b-  h-  t-  k-  s-  y-  F5

 RE  RI  RA  RO  RU  F1  b-  d-  g-  z-
```

Exact method of operation has never been publicly disclosed.

Sources: (B) Shiratori et al. 1985: 19; (C) Tatsuoka 1985: 55; (D) Ohiwa, Takashima & Shibata 1983, Ôiwa, Takashima & Mitsui 1983; (E) Mori 1984:6.

are geared to frequent Sino-Japanese (on) readings of kanji; they are of considerably less help with kun readings, particularly in words requiring okurigana. For example, the input

k- -a k- -e n- -a -i

can only be a verb, *kakenai,* with a kanji for the *ka* and kana for the remainder. There are several such verbs, but the NEC system offers all kanji with a reading (on or kun) of *ka* for selection, not just the kun used in verbs. This is a situation in which it would be better to do what most systems do—wait for an explicit suffix key at the end of the phrase (bunsetsu)—instead of converting to kanji as soon as the input indicates the end of a stretch of kanji. The NEC system has a suffix key that can be pressed to indicate the end of a kanji phrase explicitly (handy for breaking up long kanji compounds), but it is of no help in cases like this. Somewhat less troublesome, but potentially confusing, is the way the system lumps together certain readings that are phonemically distinct; this is because the "kanji vowel" keys for readings ending in $-kV$ and $-tV$ are used whether the final vowel (V) is *u* or *i*. Thus, if you wish to choose among kanji read *shitsu,* you'll be shown the ones read *shichi* as well. Another problem is the assigning of a separate "kanji vowel" key to *-ii;* though this assignment makes the keyboard layout look more symmetrical, there is only one common instance of a kanji with a reading in *-ii,* namely

小 ,

which stands for *chii-* in *chiisai* 'small'. This key ought to signal the more common ending *-ui*. Finally, katakana and standard alphanumerics still must be toggled on and off, and the arrangement of the alphanumerics prevents users who already know how to touch type on a standard keyboard from transferring their skills to the new keyboard.

Table 15B–E show some other mora composition keyboards. The first two are intended for transcriptive input. The Epson keyboard offers two- and three-stroke descriptive kanji input (see below) as an option, and the Rainputto (*Rapid Input*) keyboard is used with a proprietary descriptive coding scheme, the details of which have never been publicly disclosed. Nonetheless, the mora composition principle is employed for typing kana on both systems. Again, each of these different keyboards is supposed to have been designed on the basis of statistical analyses of kana frequencies in actual Japanese texts.

How much improvement do kana keyboards really effect? At a symposium in November 1985, Morita claimed rates of 160 characters per minute for his system but did not describe the test conditions. No manufacturer in Japan supplies catalog performance information for word processors, and most figures quoted are based on results of contests in which the competitors are highly trained and have customized their machines with special look-up dictionaries, complex abbreviation schemes, and so on. Furthermore, tests based on text samples containing only kanji and hiragana, with few or no alphanumerics and katakana, will obviously produce unusually good results. For the sake of simplicity, the keyboard diagrams in this book show only those registers used for producing kana and kanji, but it must be remembered that all transcriptive systems require constant fiddling with kana modes and special overlays for alphanumeric and other symbols.

Checking the Text

No matter how good the keyboard, there is always the chore of checking the display and making choices among alternative kanji. In a typical copy-typing situation, the user must constantly look up from the manuscript, reject or accept the kanji offered by the program, and then find the place in the manuscript where copying left off. On some models, the computer's choices are presented in a separate window on the screen rather than at the current cursor location in the text being typed, making it necessary to check two different screen locations when the preceding context is needed to select the right kanji. Needless to say, all this requires considerable concentration and quickly becomes fatiguing.[6]

Experienced operators try to type fairly large chunks of text without checking on kanji choices; they then go back and correct all the mistakes the program made on the first pass. Unfortunately, on many systems this can only be done by positioning the display cursor manually, deleting the error, and retyping a reading to start the selection cycle again. This, for example, is how the otherwise very sophisticated Xerox STAR system works. The Japanese word-processing package supplied with the IBM 5550 helps the user by "remembering" the default kana rendition of each piece of text converted to kanji, but the user must still reposition the cursor "by hand."

Some other systems in the trans-million-yen range, such as Hitachi's dedicated word processors, go a step further by providing a feature called *ikkatsu henkan,* which might be translated 'one-shot conversion'. Instead of checking on kanji selections immediately, the user inputs as much text as desired, and then presses a key that automatically brings the cursor back to each place where the program made a kanji choice. Unfortunately, once the operator begins to check a section of text in this way, the process cannot be interrupted without the risk of losing track of the kanji that remain to be checked. In addition, this kind of all-at-once conversion does not alleviate the head-swiveling, eye-straining, concentration-breaking process of kanji selection unless the user remembers the kanji that appeared in the manuscript being copied: the longer the passage typed in, the greater the chance that the user will have to check back in the manuscript, thereby losing his place on the screen.

In extemporaneous typing and typing from dictation, no manuscript guides the user's choices. The advantage of not having constantly to shift one's gaze, however, is offset by the disadvantage of having to keep one step ahead of the machine lest it make an incorrect kanji choice. It is said that Mozart composed entire symphonies in his head and considered writing them down merely an exercise in copying, but one can hardly expect such a tour de force of literary composition from even a well-educated Japanese. Moreover, transcriptive word processors tend to encourage the use of rare kanji, unusual readings, and inconsistent okurigana that the writer would never think of without prompting from the machine. In a sense, the word processor interrupts the user's train of linguistic thought to remind him of things best left at the fringes of consciousness.

Unfortunately, the trend in transcriptive input may well be toward even greater complexity. The government has recently opened the door for the return of prewar kana usage; since the dozens of kanji that take the same on reading can often be divided into smaller sets on the basis of these older kana spellings, using them rather than modern spellings might reduce the number of collisions among homophonous kango. For example, the on reading *jô* derives historically from six different phoneme strings: *zyou, zyau, dyau, deu, defu,* and *zeu* (rare). Transcriptive input could be "simplified" if the user learned which of the corresponding kana spellings go with which kanji and used them, instead of the current uniform kana notation, for *jô.* It will be interesting to see if any manufacturer incorporates these prewar kana distinctions into transcriptive input software.

Descriptive Input

The third category of input techniques is by far the broadest. It covers all those methods in which characters are assigned tag-names. This kind of input has a number of advantages: the tags are unique and uniform for all characters; that is, every kanji, kana, and other symbol has its own tag, and all tags are of the same kind. They can be typed with ease. Software support is a matter of simple list look-ups. Much less memory is required than for even the simplest transcriptive input system. The only problem, in fact, is that the sheer number of kanji makes learning such a system seem formidably difficult. Developers and promoters of expensive transcriptive systems pounce on this point (e.g., Becker 1985: 31). They stress the easy-to-learn aspect of transcriptive input, warn of the lack of standards in descriptive codes, and argue that descriptive input demands hundreds of hours of rote memorization.

Tablets

Their easiest target is what Japanese call tablets. These are low, flat boxes with a plastic diagram on top divided into hundreds of small cells; each cell is marked with a kanji or other symbol just as the keys of a typewriter are marked with letters, punctuation marks, and so forth. The operator uses a stylus to touch the cells to "spell out" the desired message; special cells correspond to control functions (e.g., backspace). The stylus can be wired to the box so that each touch is picked up electronically, or the device may be pressure sensitive.

Until September 1984, there was no standard layout for tablets. Each manufacturer developed its own layout; operators who switched machines had to be retrained. Then, after five years of effort, the JIS C-6235 (1984) tablet definition was released (see Philippi 1984). It is designed to handle 2,160 characters: 1,879 kanji, 81 katakana, 80 hiragana, 62 alphanumerics, and 58 other symbols. That is 66 fewer kanji than on the spartan JK list (1,945); moreover, the layout leaves out 104 approved kanji and includes 38 unlisted ones used in some common names

e.g., 阪 the *saka* in Ôsaka.

It remains to be seen whether this new standard will successfully replace the plethora of different inventories and layouts already in use around the country.

Tablet input is the epitome of "hunt-and-peck" typing, little more than an electronic version of the old, mechanical Japanese typewriter. Using a tablet is slow and fatiguing, but its operation is virtually self-explanatory. Many attempts have been made at compromise designs in which slightly fancier software allows for a reduction in the number of cells.

One design has two relatively small arrays of keys separated like the push-buttons on new-model telephones. Rigid sheets punched with holes through which the keys can protrude are secured on rings between the two arrays much like pages in a loose-leaf notebook. The operator changes the values of the keys by turning these pages, which are printed on both sides; the legends exposed to view indicate the current values of the keys. The machine "knows" how many pages lie on each of the two arrays because the inner edges of the pages have identifying tabs, like those found on alphabetic index cards, which engage a row of buttons under the binding rings. The whole affair is a kind of three-dimensional tablet. Though some can still be seen in operation, they are understandably not very popular.

Another design that was around before the current crop of word processors is the multishift keyboard. Each key on the main board can take on any of a dozen different values depending on which of twelve shift keys is depressed on an auxiliary keypad located to the side. Multishift systems are used mostly for newspaper typesetting. They are definitely an improvement over "pure" tablets but still place tremendous demands on the user.

Mnemonics

As already noted in connection with transcriptive input, true touch typing starts becoming difficult when the number of keys exceeds forty: it is beyond the capabilities of most people at fifty keys or more. In the case of descriptive input, however, this limit poses no problem. With just thirty keys one can access 2,700 characters, more than enough for all the jôyô kanji and kana, by assigning a code consisting of three keystrokes to each character. With forty-eight keys (the number specified by the International Standards Organization), 2,304 characters can be tagged with codes consisting of just two keystrokes each. Thus, "all" you have to do to make a workable Japanese touch typing system based on a mixture of two- and three-stroke codes (for high- and low-frequency characters, respectively) is to get typists to learn and use a couple of thousand codes.

"The most common reaction to this statement," according to Yamada Hisao of the University of Tôkyô, "is that it is impossible to memorize such a code table, and that even if the code table could be memorized after much effort, it would not be possible to type Japanese text according to such a complex code correspondence" (Yamada 1983a: 328). But as he and his colleagues have shown in a series of research papers (collected in Yamada 1985), such a level of skill is attainable by ordinary people in roughly the same amount of time required for training in English touch typing, at least in the case of typing from manuscript (copy typing). How this "magic" is accomplished will be explained in detail later, but there is really no trick to it, just basic research on the cognitive aspects of touch typing and a recognition that ease of learning is not necessarily linked with ultimate ease of use.

This is a concept appreciated by few other designers of descriptive kanji input systems. They are desperately seeking the "ultimate" easy-to-learn kanji coding scheme in the hopes of scoring a great marketing coup. The goal is to come up with a simple set of rules the user can apply to any character to determine its unique input code. The rules may be based on the shapes or the functions (readings) of characters, or on some combination of the two. When shape is a criterion, the user may have to be able to identify the number and/or order and direction of the strokes, the overall structural features of the character (e.g., can it be divided into left and right components?), traditional radicals, specially defined graphic components, and so on. The code itself may consist of letters, numbers, or some mixture, and the keyboard used may be anything from a multishift monster to a one-hand calculator-style keypad.

Most work on such mnemonic coding schemes has been done with Chinese in mind, although there are mnemonic systems for Japanese just as there are transcriptive systems for Chinese. There are several reasons why R&D has gone in this direction: multiple readings for kanji and familiarity with kana make transcriptive input more attractive for Japanese than for Chinese; Chinese users need more characters in the machine inventory for ordinary applications than do Japanese; and cost is more of a concern to Chinese consumers (descriptive systems don't need such fancy software). In China alone, "nearly 400 schemes" for encoding characters have been proposed, of which "several dozens" have actually been implemented (Liu 1983: 415). None of these outperforms transcriptive input. Some show considerable ingenuity, but all involve a great deal of arbitrariness, and none is clearly superior to any other. The interested reader can follow up the numerous references in Lackshewitz & Suchenwirth 1983, or delve into any of the *Proceedings* volumes listed in the references.

Even the less technically minded should not pass up these sources, as they provide a wealth of sociolinguistic data. One does not usually think of research reports as being funny or sad, but there are plenty of both kinds to be found in the literature: messianic inventors extol their patented coding schemes as China's ticket to the twenty-first century; dedicated scholars tell of martyred years of hand-counting and classifying thousands upon thousands of characters; corporate engineers trot out every imaginable kind of evidence for the superiority of their company's product except actual performance statistics. There is perhaps no better testimony to the powerful hold that the Ideographic Myth retains in East Asia, despite all the progress of modern technology and linguistic science.

Alternative Approaches

The fact of the matter is that few scientists have attempted to analyze the problems of kanji input with any kind of rigor or objectivity. When one considers that precise measurements of maximum flight for golf clubs are regularly supplied in manufacturer's promotional material, and that actual golf club performance, even more than actual word-processor performance, varies with the skills of individual users, one cannot help thinking that the lack of basic research into the ergonomics of Japanese input is at least partly intentional. More likely, however, it simply reflects the blind spot that most Japanese have for the impact of the writing system on their daily lives. One of the few Japanese who have examined that impact, and the input problem, with scientific detachment is Yamada Hisao.

Patternless Keyboards

Yamada was not the first to come up with the idea of two-stroke coding, but he was the first to subject the hypothesis that mnemonic codes interfere with touch typing skill to rigorous experimentation. He and his colleagues have shown that the premotor region in the right hemisphere of the brain plays a more active role than the premotor region in the left during touch typing from copy, perhaps the most common kind of office work. (The left premotor area is more active during typing of a well-practiced text, when memory comes into play.) In other words, copy typing seems to be a right-hemisphere mapping of the visual patterns of text directly onto the spatial patterns of hand motions without the intervention of language-processing, in which the left hemisphere is usually dominant. Hence, a mnemonic code that causes a detour into linguistic processing may be easy to learn, but ultimately slows down copy typing.[7]

Yamada's approach was to encode all the necessary Japanese characters (including kana, etc.) in what appears at first glance to be a totally patternless array of keystrokes. The codes are in fact assigned so as to minimize awkward finger motions and to maximize alternating hand rhythm. The user learns these codes by means of a special technique that avoids any verbal reference to the readings of the characters. The current system of T-codes (T for University of Tôkyô) uses forty keys: four rows with five keys for each hand. This could accommodate as many as 1,600 (40^2) code pairs, but to avoid difficult fingerings on the top row, only 1,200 basic pairs are used.

The training technique involves a chart divided into four quadrants. The quadrants in which a character is shown indicates the order in which the hands strike the keys:

LL	RL
LR	RR

The display in each quadrant consists of twenty rectangular blocks: four rows of five blocks each. Each block contains twenty characters (there are some blank positions), again arranged in four rows of five. In both cases, the four rows correspond to the four rows of keys on the keyboard and the five columns to the five keys on each row operated by the fingers of one hand. The code of a character is read off this diagram by noting in which quadrant the character lies, then the location of the character within its block, and finally the location of the block in relation to the others in the quadrant. To understand this better, consider Table 16. Assume that it is the first (RL) quadrant diagram. We wish to type the character represented by the letter N. Looking at the position of N within its block, we see that the first stroke is executed by the ring finger of the right hand on the second (home) row. Looking at the position of the block containing N in relation to the other blocks, we see that the second stroke is executed by the left index finger on the third row. If this diagram were in the fourth (RR) quadrant rather than the first (RL), the first stroke would be the same, but the second would be executed by the right ring finger on the third row.

During training the student is introduced to a few new characters at a time, starting with kana, which make up 60 to 70 percent of modern texts. A teaching program called CATT (Computer Assisted Typing Trainer) displays only the characters learned so far in the quadrant diagrams and checks the student as he or she types copy using these characters. For the approximately 1,100 characters beyond the basic

Table 16. One Quadrant of a Character Array for Patternless
Descriptive Input

```
.....    .....   .....   .....   .....

.....    .....   .....   .....   .....

.....    .....   .....   .....   .....

.....    .....   .....   .....   .....


.....    .....   .....   ABCDE   .....

.....    .....   .....   FGHIJ   .....

.....    .....   .....   KLMNO   .....

.....    .....   .....   PQRST   .....


.....    .....   .....   .....   .....

.....    .....   .....   .....   .....

.....    .....   .....   .....   .....

.....    .....   .....   .....   .....


.....    .....   .....   .....   .....

.....    .....   .....   .....   .....

.....    .....   .....   .....   .....

.....    .....   .....   .....   .....
```

1,200 that the 48-key ISO standard can accommodate, the system provides two kinds of codes: for full-time professional typists, the unused two-stroke combinations are exploited; for casual users, a set of partly mnemonic shape composition codes is available. (In any case, the extra 1,100 characters make up less than 2 percent of most texts, often much less.)

It may seem strange that the first stroke of each two-stroke code should be determined by the location of a character within its block and the second by the block's location with respect to its mates, rather than vice versa. Originally, Yamada and his colleagues tried the opposite approach. "We thought this [was] the natural ordering because we have to locate a block before the letter in it" (Yamada 1983a: 363). As it turned out, however, learners had trouble using the "outside-in" chart (e.g., Hiraga, Ono & Yamada 1980: 6) to determine whether a particular pair of strokes would produce a certain character. The discovery that the "inside-out" arrangement (e.g., Yamada 1983a: 378–379) works better provides a nice illustration of the difference between the way men and machines operate. People evidently prefer to take in the chart as a whole, zero in on the desired character, check its local position to verify stroke number one, and then shift their attention to the larger arrangement of blocks to verify stroke number two. A computer program could be written to function in this way. It would search linearly through the whole chart to find the desired character and then check whether its location agreed with the given stroke information. To do this, however, the program would require something that the human user apparently doesn't need—a consecutive numbering for all the rows and all the columns of the chart. In any case, straight linear searching certainly isn't an efficient procedure for a computer to follow, since on average half of all the characters in the chart have to be compared with the search key before the stroke information comes into play at all! The right way for a computer to proceed is to use the stroke information to find the slot that is supposed to contain the desired character and then check what's there against the search key. In this case, to use the first piece of information to locate the block and the second, the character inside the block, is more than just "natural": it is unavoidable.

By 1983 Yamada had established his theory, and throughout 1984 he worked on refining his methods. He was ready to begin research on extemporaneous typing and typing from dictation at the start of 1985 when the Ministry of Education support that had sustained his project up to that time ended. Further Ministry of Education funding was obtained, but only after new applications had been made under different project categories. The contrast with the munificent long-term support for the Fifth Generation project, a brainchild of MITI, is striking. The lack of interest in patternless input systems in all but a few private companies is no less remarkable, but perhaps easier to understand. Yamada's system requires the absolute minimum in software. All the "intelligence" in the man/machine system is concentrated in the man; and it is nearly all primitive, eye-hand coordination intelligence, not the vaunted logical inferences of strong-AI theory. A Japan that adopted patternless input as the standard way to input native script could use dirt-cheap machinery to achieve the same ends now possible only by means of costly hardware. This would obviously be terrible for the computer business—in the short run. Japanese and foreign companies alike are therefore trying their best in their advertising to push "ease of learning" and downplay the frustrations and stress of long-term use after the learning phase is over.

Romanization

If Yamada Hisao were not a full professor at the most prestigious university in all Japan, it is doubtful that his findings would receive even the limited acknowledgment they now enjoy. But there are other reasons why Yamada is considered a maverick. Although he has found a truly efficient way to input Japanese script, he is under no illusions about its limitations and the need for more basic research. He is also an outspoken advocate of romanization (e.g., Yamada 1984).

Not everybody learns to touch type in the West, and not everyone in Japan will want to. The manufacturers would like to jump from this observation to the conclusion that transcriptive (or inscriptive) input systems must become the national standard. This is a non sequitur, but something does have to be done for the hunt-and-peck typists of the world.

Moreover, we still don't know if patternless descriptive input will work as well for extemporaneous typing as it does for copy typing. More work may also have to be done on error recovery: In English, an accidental extra keystroke or the accidental omission of a single keystroke creates a one-letter error, but has no effect on later correct keypresses. But when copy typing with two-stroke codes, the characters generated following such an error will not be those intended. Critics of two-stroke coding often call attention to this phenomenon, though Yamada has found that his typists usually know "by feel" when they have made an error.

The real problem is that there are applications in which touch typing is not by itself enough. Computer-based education provides an excellent example. Imagine a Japanese educational program that solicits a natural-language sentence from a student: he or she uses one of today's typical Japanese word processors to type in the sentence. The very first thing the program must do, to judge the content of the sentence, is sift out and throw away all the information that the transcriptive input dialog introduced and get back to a phonemic representation. This is because the relationship of kanji to the meaning-bearing units of the language is many-to-many, with considerable latitude for free variation in individual usage. If the program merely compares the character codes in the student's response against its response templates, the student's response will be judged as wrong when it fails to match the template's characters even if it represents the same words. Misspellings in English can cause similar problems, but because they are written with just twenty-six letters and a few extra symbols, there are practical techniques for distinguishing misspellings from completely mistaken words (e.g., comparison of derived "hash codes" of words in response and template); such techniques—we can skip over the details—are inapplicable to kanji kanamajiribun texts. With kanji and kana, there is no general, automatic procedure of high reliability for distinguishing intentional from unintentional student input errors.

It is therefore a major programming headache to evaluate Japanese sentences in traditional script of any substantial length. Not surprisingly, most programmers of Japanese educational software don't even try. Instead, they stick to primitive multiple-choice and fill-in-the-blank quizzes, dress them up with flashy color graphics, throw in arcade-game synthesized music, and try to convince customers that this is the state of the art. Unfortunately, multiple-choicing needlessly introduces misinformation into the learning process, and filling in blanks can become an end in itself unrelated to real understanding. If this is all a computer system costing half a million yen or more can do, why not do the same thing with old-fashioned drill books and pencils?

Kanji are not only hard to deal with for programmers but may also be a hindrance to learning itself, at least for less talented students. In 1986, the author met with a team of workers at Waseda University developing a system for high-school students in mathematics. Each work station combines a color television, a programmed microcomputer, and a random-access video disk (with its own microcomputer controller). While using this system, the student is also supposed to have a printed workbook ready to refer to, work problems on paper, take notes, and so forth. Each lesson is a series of multiple-choice problems presented much as they would be on educational television. For example, problem diagrams are photographed from drawings by professional artists, not generated by the microcomputer. (Of course, still shots are stored on the disk as single frames even though they are accompanied by voice-overs.) Noteworthy in this strongly multimedia approach is the heavy use of prerecorded spoken instructions and feedback. The professor in charge of the project explained this by saying that it had been his experience over the years that poor students needed verbal instructions and feedback. *Students who could read and understand the material on their own didn't need computerized coaching,* he said. Indeed, this is truer in Japan than he seems to have realized. PLATO, an American system developed at the University of Illinois and tested over many years, supports prerecorded or synthesized speech output for foreign-language instruction, but judging from the many hundreds of PLATO lessons now available that do not make use of these special features, the consensus among lesson authors and instructors is that verbal output is *not* an essential ingredient for learning at or above the high-school level. The finding that Japanese students in danger of failing math seem to need detailed verbal instruction and feedback therefore suggests that it is not their understanding of math but rather their ability to handle written materials that is holding them back.

At any rate, multimedia seems to be the word of the day. Some Japanese engineers and educators look to facsimile machines as the key to Japanese computer-based education. These machines are somewhat like office copiers connected to a phone line: the markings on a sheet of paper fed into one machine are transmitted to another, which reproduces them on a new sheet. Obviously, "fax" is one way around the kanji problem, but it is a clear case of technological overkill. A key reason for using computers in education is that they allow students to study at their own pace with a "teacher" who, at virtually any time of the day or night, can provide immediate corrective feedback in a wide variety of learning situations. A real teacher has to be at the other end of a fax line; otherwise, we are back to all the problems of inscriptive input, the most expensive and least efficient of the three methods available. Ironically, from an educational viewpoint, inscriptive input may actually be the best approach, because it is the one most like ordinary pen-and-paper writing. No one in Japan, however, seems to be working along these lines. And, of course, fax is expensive. The only media more expensive in Japan are movies and telegrams (Takasaki & Ozawa 1983: 190–192). The typical fax machine must use thermal paper and cost about ¥300,000 at the beginning of 1986.

Thus, although patternless descriptive input does offer a cheap and efficient way to deal with Japanese script *in those applications that require Japanese script output,* one must always consider the application first. Who is going to do the work? What is it they want to accomplish? Clearly, in an educational setting, even the best input system would be counterproductive. Arbitrary codes are simply the wrong format for natural-language data when the linguistic content of the data is what counts. An encoding scheme that represents the linguistic forms of words directly is the obvious alternative. All-kana writing meets this requirement, but demands a number of keys in excess of the limit for good touch typing. Rômaji are thus the logical choice.

In fact, cultural resistance notwithstanding, rômaji are in wider use today than is generally believed. For one thing, the thousands of people who input data via rômaji-to-kanji conversion are, psychologically speaking, *already* working largely in rômaji. Mitsui Bussan, Japan's largest trading company, furnishes a more direct example. It has always used rômaji for its international Japanese telegraphic communications, and continues to do so despite the new crop of Japanese word processors; even some domestic traffic is handled in rômaji. According to Yamazaki Seikô, second in command at Mitsui Bussan's Personnel Department (interview of 9 January 1986), about 20 to 30 messages a day arrive from overseas for each of the two or three thousand employees at the head office in Tôkyô; 80 to 90 percent of these are in English, but that still leaves five to twelve thousand Japanese texts every day. Although some are short (e.g., "Accepted."), the typical message is several pages long. Fax is used only for transmitting charts and diagrams. According to Yamazaki, the only problem with using rômaji is that some high-ranking executives refuse to learn to read romanized texts, which means that many man-hours must be wasted transcribing messages for them.

Costs

It is not clear whether the computer manufacturers have investigated the costs of inputting with kanji in any detail; if they have, they are understandably not eager to disclose what they have lerned. Nevertheless, it is possible to infer from available market and technical information what Japanese script input costs.

One very crude indicator of the cost of input is the overall cost of information distribution in general. From 1973 to 1983, this went up by 252 percent in Japan while the amount of information distributed increased by only 64 percent (further details in Katô 1985: 19–21). Inflation and the "oil shock" of 1973–1974 are not enough to explain the increase in distribution costs. What other long-term trends could be responsible? The most obvious change during this period was the rapid introduction of electronic data transmission and office automation. If greater reliance on Japanese-script input systems in all phases of the production and distribution of information was not the culprit, what was?

Much can be deduced from the prices of what Japanese call *pasokon,* short for *pâsonaru konpyûta* 'personal computers', or simply PCs. PCs deserve special attention because they are being used more and more as terminals for larger systems and instead of "minicomputers" (small mainframes), which they can nearly equal in terms of performance while costing considerably less.[8] Compared with more expensive systems, a greater percentage of the price of PCs necessarily reflects the costs of man/machine interfacing. And what applies to kanji handling on PCs must be equally true of kanji handling on larger systems.

Table 17 is compiled from announced 1986 list prices quoted in a popular Japanese "consumer's report" on PCs. Four kinds of machine were examined. MSX machines are used mostly for audio-visual games, music synthesis, and hobby programming in BASIC. Dedicated word processors (WPs), a dying breed in the West, range from portable machines that can only convert one kanji at a time to sophisticated office machines for transcriptive input; their distinguishing characteristic is that they cannot be programmed to perform any other task. Personal computers built around 8- and 16-bit central processing units (CPUs) need no introduction—they are the workhorses of the current computer revolution.

Notice first the price differences between MSX PCs and WPs. The small difference at the low end of the scale is misleading for two reasons.

Table 17. Comparison of Japanese Personal Computer and Dedicated Word-Processor List Prices for 1986

Machines		Prices			
Type	Number	Highest	Mean	Median	Lowest
MSX PCs	15	¥148,000	¥83,853	¥79,800	¥29,800
WPs	19	¥598,000	¥297,989	¥298,000	¥59,800
8-bit PCs	17	¥997,000	¥301,247	¥168,000	¥84,800
16-bit PCs	19	¥1,048,000	¥538,053	¥400,000	¥195,000

Source: Ôniwa et al. 1985.

One is that the manufacturers are taking a loss on their cheapest WPs. According to the *Asahi Shinbun* of 16 December 1985, the lowest list price for a Japanese word processor with 16-by-16 dot-matrix characters fell from ¥150,000 in December 1984 to ¥40,000 in December 1985; the lowest price for a machine with 24-by-24 characters fell from ¥220,000 to ¥60,000 over the same twelve-month period. (Apparently, there were some price cuts on 16-by-16 dot-matrix machines after Ôniwa et al. published.) These big drops in price are deceptive, however: the retail price is about 59 percent higher than the cost of manufacture (80 percent of which goes for parts and 20 percent for labor and assembly), but the wholesale price to distributors is about 13 percent below cost.

The other reason that low-end WPs seem to be cheaper than MSX PCs is that the latter suffer from an image of being "kids' machines." They do have many limitations: they usually come with a minimum of memory, and no monitor, printer, or peripheral storage device. On the other hand they are, unlike WPs, fully programmable computers, and the newer MSX2 models, such as Matsushita's FS-4000 (¥106,000) and Toshiba's HX-23F (¥103,000), do allow for rudimentary transcriptive input. Therefore, the difference between the cheapest and most expensive MSX machines gives a somewhat more realistic idea of the cost of using Japanese script on a general-purpose computer than the difference between the cheapest WPs and MSX PCs.

Next, look at the big jump between the low- and middle-range prices of WPs. The mean price of a WP is virtually the same as that of an 8-bit PC, but the median price is substantially higher. The 8-bit mean price is pulled up by a couple of unusually expensive models, costing nearly a million yen each; if these are disregarded, the mean price falls to ¥210,080. Since all the 8-bit machines surveyed support kanji at least as an option, and since the ones priced above the median provide JIS Level-1 kanji ROMs (read-only memories) as standard equipment, one may conclude that the overhead of look-up dictionaries and transcriptive input software is substantial.

Finally, consider the 16-bit machines. These are the computers that are capturing the market in Japan today, although their word-processing capabilities are, from the users' viewpoint, about the same as those of the better 8-bit (including some of the MSX) models. The main difference is that a 16-bit CPU can compute faster; this cuts the time required for updating the display screen, speeds kanji look-up procedures, and so on. To take advantage of this, however, one usually needs more sophisticated software than that provided by the manufacturer, and top-of-the-line extras such as built-in hard disk. The IBM 5550, for example, provides almost all of the desirable features that a transcriptive input system can offer, but it lists for around ¥1.3 million. Hands-on experience with Japanese word processors and PCs throughout 1985 indicates that professional-quality transcriptive input software is generally not available on machines costing less than about a million yen (including printers).

Another way to estimate what inputting Japanese script really costs is to look at Fifth Generation work on natural-language processing, most of which is centered on developing machine-readable dictionaries (Ishiwata et al. 1985) and other databases (Ishii 1985). Ishii's work on Japanese text editing (done, incidentally, on a conventional DEC 20 computer) is particularly revealing. He found that it took 4,100 lines of PROLOG code to specify the readings of just the 1,945 jôyô kanji; in all, his system used 73,350 lines of PROLOG for data on kanji kanamajiribun usage (Ishii 1985: 8). Even at a trifling thirty-two bytes per statement (a generously low estimate), that's more than 2.2 megabytes of information (1 megabyte $= 2^{20}$ or 1,048,576 bytes). To this must be added program statements that control the look-up and editing operations, the storage of kanji and kana output patterns, the overhead of system software, and so on. For a Japanese text-editing system that, presumably, could be used as the "front end" of any "machine of the 1990s," this is a staggering read-only memory requirement. The idea that a general-purpose system must devote such enormous resources just to the mechanics of handling script—and Ishii gives no indication of *how well* his system worked—is outrageous. Yet many Japanese would argue that anything less than the roughly 6,000 kanji of JIS Levels 1 and 2 combined, three times more than Ishii's inventory, is unacceptable. A really good Fifth Generation Japanese text editor might well entail even vaster amounts of memory.

And as memory expands, so does the time needed for retrieving information. PROLOG, the language selected for software development by the Fifth Generation project, could well prove to be a poor choice in this regard.

One PROLOG feature that serves it well in some circumstances—a built-in search mechanism that navigates through the complex trees of a program's if/then rules—sometimes works against the language. Because the language itself automatically initiates and performs these searches, it's difficult for the programmer or the system operator to control the search and redirect or limit it. The time required for indiscriminate searches can grow exponentially as the knowledge base grows and the number of facts and relationships increases. For knowledge bases of the size contemplated by the Japanese for their fifth-generation computers, the implications of uncontrollable PROLOG searches can be disastrous. (Harris & Davis 1986: 119)

It is anybody's guess whether parallel processing can prevent computation times from spiraling out of sight, but inasmuch as kanji input is a data-intensive task with no obvious analogy to the mathematics of vector or matrix processing (the operations most accelerated by parallel processing techniques), there is no reason for optimism.

In short, despite all the self-confident talk from the manufacturers about having licked the kanji problem, despite the booming sales of their low-priced word processors, transcriptive input is not a cost-effective technique for handling the Japanese language on computers, and there is no prospect of AI making it cost-effective. If a large number of ordinary Japanese are going to use their own *language* (not merely *script*) on computers with the same freedom that Americans and Europeans enjoy when they sit down in front of a computer, other input methods must be exploited. It's not a question of saving the culture or of complete reform of the writing system. It is simply a matter of choosing the most appropriate way to represent linguistic data in an integrated man/machine system.

6

The Fifth Generation Project

Japan can remove all the obstacles that now prevent it from fully exploiting computer power by taking the following three steps: (1) separating those applications that absolutely require output in native script (e.g., typesetting) from those that do not; (2) adopting national standards for patternless descriptive input for the few applications found to fall into the former category; and (3) fostering public acceptance of rômaji data processing in the majority of applications. It would also be wise to provide long-term support for basic research on the human-factors aspects of computerization; however, this should be regarded as a secondary measure lest calls for "further study" be used as a stalling tactic. Attempts to undertake these steps would certainly encounter a great deal of political resistance. Even today, there are school teachers who refuse to teach rômaji to their students on the lame excuse that this would interfere with learning English! When one considers, however, that billions of yen are going to to be spent on the production and promotion of machinery that not only cannot solve the input problem but actually threatens to undo the very kanji culture it is supposed to preserve, at least an attempt at public education seems worth trying.

Before the advent of microprocessors in the 1970s, hardly anyone claimed that Japan had to computerize with kanji. The introduction of all-katakana output, which is still used commercially, was hailed by the newspapers of the time as a major advance. It was drastic reductions in hardware prices that kindled hopes for machines that could handle kanji kanamajiribun as easily as kana or roman letters alone. In fact, although there are now computer systems to facilitate the output of text in Japanese script, none allows the user to do work in the Japanese language with the kind of freedom that alphabetic script provides. Nevertheless, most Japanese, swayed by fables about language and writing they have heard since childhood, are convinced that it is merely a question of providing the computer with the right logic and the right data. They are only dimly aware that their own ability to use kanji stems not from the welter of arbitrary *facts* about kanji that they have so diligently crammed into their heads, but rather from the *ideas* they have acquired through everyday experience that give the facts relevance and meaning.

That this is the prevalent attitude in Japan today is beyond dispute; it only remains to be established to what extent the planning of the Fifth Generation project was influenced by these attitudes. This is no easy task, for computer scientists and writers sympathetic to strong AI in Japan often react with hostility to the suggestion that something as "trivial" as kanji could be a motive behind something as grand in conception as the Fifth Generation project. The history of the project itself, however, amply shows that the problem of kanji has played a decisive role in shaping the thinking of Japanese about AI. Although there were also important nontechnical incentives for choosing the Fifth Generation path, the desire to use kanji with complete freedom on computers was the one technical dream that everyone involved took for granted.

Concern over Kanji

The need to use Japanese script on computers has often been brought up explicitly during the course of the project. In 1978, "Japanese I/O" *(Nihongo nyûshutsuryoku)* was mentioned in at least two key meetings at which the Fifth Generation concept got its start (Uemae 1985: 13, 37). At the second international Fifth Generation conference (Tôkyô, 1984), which marked the end of the initial phase of the project, Kinoshita Hiroo, director-general of the Machinery and Information Industries Bureau of MITI, obviously had Japanese script on his mind when he said, "[A]lthough I have worked in both Europe and the U.S. and have gained a familiarity with foreign languages, I have often wondered why the alphabet or the English language must be used in the keyboards and the display outputs of computers in use in Japan" (Kinoshita 1985: 16). He continued:

> Estimates put the present proportion of persons capable of using computers in Japan at about 2% of the total population. But for computers to really find their place in society, many more people must learn to use them. Even if not to the extent of the automobile, still not only busi-

nessmen, but also a sizable proportion of all housewives would do well to learn to use them. The age in which only specialists use computers is ended, and I believe we must make efforts to conceive systems which may be used readily by the layman. And in such cases, it becomes essential to strengthen the bond between the computer and its human operator. (Kinoshita 1985: 16)

Kinoshita's comments echoed the thoughts expressed in the reports presented at the first international Fifth Generation conference three years earlier. It was at this conference that the theme of the project was first clearly enunciated: "building the machines of the 1990s"—that is, machines that any ordinary person could use. The late Motooka Tôru of the University of Tôkyô, who led the 1979–1981 study group that wrote the reports, predicted Fifth Generation machines being used in such diverse "areas of social activity" as "economics, industry, art and science, administration, international relations, education, culture and daily life and so forth" (Moto-oka 1982: 4). He specifically cited the "development of systems for helping the physically handicapped get active; development of CAI [computer-aided instruction] system[s] for the lifetime education of the aged; and development of distributed processing systems for enabling people to work at home" (Moto-oka 1982: 15). Karatsu Hajime of the Matsushita Communication Industrial Company, who chaired the study group subcommittee on social impact, envisioned a world in which information surrounds and nourishes everyone "like air."

Everyone may utilize the information unconsciously in the future, dissolved into our society. Today, it belongs to only the specialized field and homogenized society by the result of mass production. (Karatsu 1982: 95)

In setting targets for Fifth Generation computer performance, Karatsu stressed this point again: "The non-professional without training can handle the new machine. This must be placed at first position" (Karatsu 1982: 96).

Although Motooka and Karatsu do not say so explicitly, their machines for everyone are unquestionably machines that use Japanese script, for the report on system architecture promised that the final version of the Fifth Generation Kernel Language (KL) would include, among other features, the "capability of handling kanji and kana letters; programming using [the] Japanese character set" (Uchida et al. 1982: 169). Knowledgeable and influential Japanese observers have stressed the importance of this goal. "The trend towards increased use of Japanese word processors and the development of ultra high level computer language," according to the president of Nippon Electric, "definit[e]ly demand the use of Kanji as input characters" (Kobayashi 1984: 5).

> We Japanese are living in the culture that is based on ideographs and is vague compared with Western logic. In order to develop "Man and C&C [computers and communications]" for people with such cultural backgrounds, we have to challenge research and development of video, voice and knowledge processings in media and concept hierarchy levels. This is why we are working on the development of the 5th generation computer. (Kobayashi 1984: 9)

Makino Tsutomu, director of MITI's Electronics Policy Division, reiterated this point in his comments at the 1984 Fifth Generation conference:

> [A] computer must be something that can be handled by non-professionals, given the fact that it will spread more widely in society for more people. Naturally, future computers must be able to handle instructions *in everyday words and graphics* to become more accessible for end users. (Brandin et al. 1985: 39; emphasis added)

The timing of the Fifth Generation project and its staffing also show that its MITI backers expected that Fifth Generation machines would, in some unspecified way, make the use of Japanese script on computers as easy as that of the alphabetic scripts of the West. The Fifth Generation project was born just as MITI's second large-scale computer R&D effort, PIPS, was coming to an end. PIPS, short for Pattern Information Processing Systems, which ran from 1971 to 1978, had attacked the kanji problem by treating it as a special case of the more general business of processing all kinds of visual "patterns" and "images." As Welke (1982: 123) notes, "Both industry and government made a great effort to develop methods for Kanji processing, e.g. the National R&D Project 'Pattern Information Processing System' (PIPS)." According to Keiô University professor Aiso Hideo, who chaired the study group subcommittee on machine architecture (interview of 9 August 1985), PIPS was severely criticized within MITI immediately after it ended because it had not produced the breakthrough in kanji processing systems that MITI officials had hoped for. Aiso added that PIPS is now praised as the birthplace of the current crop of Japanese word processors.

Interestingly, Aiso traced the roots of the Fifth Generation project back to MITI's first big computer R&D project, which he headed from 1966 to 1971. The goal of this effort was to produce computers to compete with the IBM 370 series mainframes, the supercomputers of that era. Fuchi Kazuhiro, who chaired the study group subcommittee on theory, and is now the research director of the Institute for New Generation Computer Technology (ICOT), rose to prominence in Aiso's project as leader of the team that developed the timesharing operating system for these "very high performance" computers. Aiso's insistence on the continuity between the project he headed, the later VLSI project, and the Fifth Generation is well justified: the strong interest in new kinds of machine architecture (despite a lot of talk about software) that has characterized the Fifth Generation literature clearly reflects the backgrounds of the participants. PIPS, however, is also part of the story. In 1970 Fuchi went to the United States to study, was exposed there to strong-AI theory, and upon his return to Japan the following year, joined the PIPS project working on voice I/O (Uemae 1985: 67–68; Ōyama 1985: 123, 125).

Productivity Crises

There were and still are overt links between concern about kanji and the Fifth Generation project. However much these may be deemphasized by ICOT, they cannot be overemphasized in any objective assessment. For although the project proposes to achieve much more than "just" the solution to the Japanese script problem, these further aims themselves simply reveal the magnitude of the linguistic naiveté of the project's planners.

Motooka's study group members, it will be remembered, came from mostly hardware development backgrounds. Their papers lay great stress on the need to build a fundamentally new kind of computer, a machine that can access "knowledge bases" that will endow it with the equivalent of human experience. Present-day computers, they repeatedly argue, will not be able to meet society's future needs. Thus, for example, speaking of the man/machine interface at the Tôkyô conference of 1981, Fuchi remarked:

> Many voices are raised in dissatisfaction over present-day computers. One of the complaints which perhaps calls for introspection on the computer side is that today's technology is far from the ideal of being truly "handy" for users.

One of the factors concerned with "handiness" is the interface between man and machine. Natural media for communications from the man side are primarily graphical communications and conversations in natural languages. To realize these communication objectives calls not only for expansion of in- and output media, but also for higher performance capabilities, necessarily, of the system itself. (Fuchi 1982: 107)

Many Americans might say similar things about American computers, but in a Japanese context, it is possible to interpret this statement in only two ways. Either high-performance image and voice recognition are necessary for the adequate handling of kanji on computers, or else the "dissatisfaction" that Japanese experience with "present-day computers" is not due to kanji but to some entirely different inconvenience that, nonetheless, will be cleared up by high-performance image and voice processing. If Fuchi did not mean the former, he must have meant the latter. But what can this other inconvenience be? Fuchi does not say, so we are left to conclude that kanji are indeed the problem, and that Fuchi simply takes it for granted that everyone knows this.

The same inference can be drawn from remarks by other Fifth Generation planners. Motooka and Karatsu both put improvements in low-productivity areas of the Japanese economy at the top of their respective 1981 lists of social needs to be fulfilled by Fifth Generation machines. Both identify low-productivity areas as those that are paperwork-intensive (government, administration, service industries, etc.).[9] Motooka points specifically to "documents processing, office management, and decision making in management" (Moto-oka 1982: 14). The first of four "future images of office automation" he offers is "Japanized office automation capable of processing the Japanese languages [sic] in a natural way."[10] Karatsu (1982: 93–94) complains that prices for paperwork-intensive services in Japan tripled over the preceding ten years while those for durable goods increased only 30 to 50 percent over the same period.

How are Fifth Generation machines going to change this situation if not by breaking through the kanji bottleneck? No Japanese working on or interested in the Fifth Generation project interviewed by the author in 1985 was able to say.

A final example of how kanji are indirectly implicated in stated Fifth Generation goals is the emphasis on image processing. Properly speaking, this refers to the very general problem of recognizing figures and objects in a chart or picture presented "whole" to a computer input device. "In its own fifth-generation-computer project, the U.S. Department of Defense has placed a heavy emphasis on these capabilities"

(Ôyama 1985: 128), and references to them abound in the Fifth Generation literature. Yet

> Fuchi has not concerned himself with these problems. As he sees it, the level of hardware needed to process figures is not yet sufficiently advanced, nor is there a sure way to mechanize image processing. When the time is ripe for an image-processing capability, Japan's fifth-generation-computer project will undertake the task. (Ôyama 1985: 128)

Then why all the talk about image processing as a key to future productivity? The answer is that, while Western experts are genuinely interested in the problem of image processing in its full generality, the Japanese have a very important special case in mind—kanji kanamajiribun.

Misunderstandings

Present-day computers are so-called von Neumann machines: they operate under the control of a central processing unit that executes one program instruction at a time. It had been recognized for many years that this type of machine architecture imposes fundamental limitations on the kinds of algorithms that can be used for many tasks of practical importance (e.g., sorting), but it was only with the availability of LSI chips that extensive experimentation with whole arrays of processors became a realistic possibility. The MITI bureaucrats who backed the Fifth Generation concept had picked up terms such as non-von Neumann architecture, parallel processing, AI, expert systems, and knowledge bases at international conferences and from overseas journals, but it is doubtful whether they had more than a superficial understanding of these terms or how they were related to one another.

AI research and development had been, and mostly still is, done on conventional machines. The essential strong-AI claim is that the right program, given the right data, will behave intelligently: all intelligence is reducible to formal rules of logic; it makes no epistemological difference whether the rules are implemented in the "wet" machinery of the brain or the "dry" machinery of a CPU. Hence the emphasis had been heavily on software and programming languages such as LISP, not on machinery. By the end of the 1970s, however, it was clear that anything worthy of the name AI was going to require, at the very least, much faster computers and much larger databases. A few younger experts even began to concede that the models of intelligence on which earlier AI work had been based were, as Dreyfus and others had been saying all along, hopelessly naive. Broadly speaking, two appraoches were suggested to remedy the situation. One was to give AI programs immense encyclopedic "knowledge bases" that would make up for their lack of human experience. The other was to adopt the metaphor of the brain as a "parallel processor" and soft-pedal the orthodox insistence that symbol manipulation per se was the alpha and omega of intelligence. Perhaps AI would have taken this turn even if the prospects for a quantum leap in hardware power had not suddenly brightened around this time, though it seems unlikely it was just a coincidence.

At any rate, this was when the split between weak (cognitive research) and strong (logic programming) AI methodologies began to widen noticeably. Given their hardware bias, it was only natural that the Japanese who developed the Fifth Generation concept fell in with the logic-programming camp. Interestingly, Hall and Kibler, who propose a more elaborate five-way typology of approaches to AI, note that "Feigenbaum provides a clear example of a researcher shifting between perspectives" (1985: 173), from (to use their terminology) an "empirical" to a "constructive" approach. Indeed, it is possible to read *The Fifth Generation* as a manifesto of the knowledge-engineering, logic-programming camp of AI reserach.[11]

The Fifth Generation planners had some acquaintance with work on AI in the United States and in Europe, but they were either unfamiliar with or uninterested in the hotly debated issues AI work had generated. Weizenbaum's famous ELIZA program is a case in point. ELIZA is an interactive dialog simulator that "talks" like a psychotherapist à la Carl Rogers; Weizenbaum wrote it on a lark. He was shocked when it gained notoriety as an AI breakthrough. Particularly appalled by serious suggestions that it could be used to replace human psychiatrists, he wrote his 1976 book *Computer Power and Human Reason* in reaction to what he saw as the excesses of strong-AI dogmatism. Fuchi met ELIZA during his 1970 sojourn in the United States, but, according to Uemae (1985: 160–163), his reaction was quite different: ELIZA was just quackery *(inchiki);* Japanese could and must do honest *(matomo)* AI research—whatever that might be.

Japanese AI

Feigenbaum and McCorduck are delighted that Japanese like Fuchi have paid so little attention to Americans like Weizenbaum. Other AI experts, such as MIT's Marvin Minsky, have shown more caution: "I do not know if the Japanese fifth-generation project will overtake us. *They use the right words,* but that does not mean they are a serious threat" (Winston & Prendergast 1984: 250; emphasis added).

In any society, one can find the well-meaning man who latches onto a new word or phrase, gives it his own interpretation, and goes about using it as if he had invented it himself. The tendency to indulge in this kind of ingenuous repetition of undigested ideas is particularly strong in Japan. A handful of real experts may know that the article in yesterday's newspaper in which Professor X appeared to be on top of the latest developments in the field is a hopeless tangle of confusion, but to criticize one's colleagues publicly "just isn't done" in Japan. This makes it easier for buzzwords to get into the air. If they originate overseas, so much the better, for they are above the endemic faction-alism of Japanese intellectual life, and hence more likely to gain accep-tance. In short, the novelty of an idea is frequently more important than its substance.

Kikuchi Makoto, director of the Sony Research Center, makes this point in his semi-autobiographical account of the Japanese electronics industry (1983). In one case, Kikuchi reports, *IEEE Spectrum,* a jour-nal of the Institute of Electrical and Electronics Engineers, had carried an article by Dr. J. Morton, vice-president of Bell Labs, entitled "From Physics to Function."

> Shortly after the publication of Morton's piece, researchers in Japan began to talk together about functional devices. The consensus was that this represented an important area for research. The phrase spread throughout the research community, and soon anyone giving a talk about work in the field would invariably bring up functional devices. "Research on Functional Devices" began to come in for considerable funding from the Ministry of Finance as one of the items in the Electro-technical Laboratory research plans.
>
> About this time I visited the Bell Laboratories. At lunch I turned to my five or six companions and asked them how work on functional devices was going at Bell.
>
> My American friends looked questioningly at one another.
>
> "Functional devices?" they said. "What on earth are functional devices?"
>
> Now it was my turn to be astonished.
>
> "Your own Dr. Morton wrote an article about them!" I exclaimed.

"Everyone in Japan is talking about nothing else, and you mean to say you've never even heard of them?"

"Morton wrote something like that?" they laughed. "Where? We haven't seen it." (Kikuchi 1983: 133)

An even more dramatic incident occurred in connection with Japan's VLSI project. Around September or October of 1974, after leaving the Electrotechnical Laboratory for Sony, Kikuchi got a call from a journalist friend.

"What do they mean by 'future system?'" he asked.

I was caught off balance.

"I've never heard of it before," I told him. "What is it?"

"That's what I don't understand," said my friend. "It's something I heard from a fellow just back from visiting IBM in the States. According to him, they're planning to make an LSI with almost unbelievable integration. It seems they're calling it the 'future system.' . . . [T]his new device is going to pack a large computer onto a single chip. After all, it's going to be 30 centimeters in diameter."

Here I had to interrupt.

"You mean millimeters, don't you?" I demanded.

"No, it really seems to be centimeters," he replied. (Kikuchi 1983: 135–136)

Although Kikuchi was skeptical, he and others came to take this story of the IBM "future system" seriously; it was the fundamental justification for the VLSI project. Years later, Kikuchi was told by a high-level manager at IBM Japan that the company had never used the words "future system."[12]

But of course, by then the damage was done. The VLSI tidal wave—mediated, as it were, by a single phrase—was quickly amplified throughout the Japanese technological community. Once that had happened, we all had a clear target to aim for. (Kikuchi 1983: 138)

Even allowing for hyperbole, Kikuchi's anecdotes reveal a pattern that was repeated in the case of the Fifth Generation. Feigenbaum and McCorduck assured the world that the Japanese were going to build

AI machines with which they would dominate the economy of the twenty-first century, but at the second international conference in Tôkyô, Fuchi said, "our project is not an artificial intelligence project or an expert system project as wrongly understood by some people" (Fuchi 1985: 20). This was reiterated in an interview with Kusama Hiroyuki, managing researcher at ICOT (30 August 1985), who stressed that any overlap between AI and the Fifth Generation project was purely coincidental.

The fact is that *jinkô chinô,* the Japanese translation of artificial intelligence, is used to mean something rather different from what Feigenbaum and McCorduck have in mind. As Karatsu explained when interviewed on 15 November 1985, the term AI did not even come up in the early planning of the Fifth Generation project. What did come up, according to Karatsu, was the anxiety Japanese engineers and programmers felt at having to do all their work in English and the role of Japanese word-processor technology. It was the advent of Japanese word processors that triggered interest in AI, for kana-to-kanji conversion is, he said, the prototype of inference. (He added that it was Fuchi, while working at the Electrotechnical Laboratory, who introduced the idea of kana-to-kanji conversion to Toshiba, the first company to market such transcriptive input machines; it is uncertain, however, whether Fuchi originated the idea.)

Nonetheless, Fuchi, as just noted, insists that "our project is not an artificial intelligence project or an expert system project." He continues:

> Artificial intelligence research, which is aimed at clarifying the mechanism of intelligence, is an open field requiring a very long period of sustained effort. Expert systems also offer unlimited potential for application. No project can cover all of them. (Fuchi 1985: 20)

This would indeed seem to rule out both weak and strong AI as ICOT fields.

> But our project is closely related to the fields of artificial intelligence and expert systems. The selection of the kernel language is also deeply related to the problem of knowledge representation languages. So, one of the reasons for choosing a predicate logic language as the kernel language is that predicate logic is a promising, if not the only, candidate for a knowledge representation base. (Fuchi 1985: 20)

But why a "knowledge representation base" if one is interested neither in computers as research tools for cognitive science nor in the Physical Symbol System Hypothesis and its ramifications?

The answer to this question is not entirely clear, but in a recent magazine interview, Fuchi gave what seems to be the essence of the answer.

> When you do things like AI or machine translation, it's inevitable that you have to deal with natural language. The origins of ideas differ depending on which language you take as the base, and if we Japanese are going to do these things, freedom of thought will be impossible unless, of course, the base is Japanese.

> The Japanese language is our own, so you could say that it has become a unique reflection of our experiences, or perhaps our thoughts. Though English commands prestige, I can see its limitations. As long as Japanese think in a kind of transplanted language system, they can't use their imaginations. If we make Japanese the base, however, I think there's a possibility of our producing a stream of new ideas, because Japanese provides us with maximum freedom. Moreover, the technological conditions which advance, or should I say encourage, such new ideas will also come along.

> Now I don't necessarily think of these new ideas as Japanese. I have a feeling that, among them, there will be some which will be translatable in some way in the world of technology, and will become considerably universal. I'm a little unhappy when people talk about "Japanese-style AI" in the narrow sense.

> I myself am aiming for a universal base, but I think that the attitude of "well, since it's universal, you might as well do it in English" is extremely weak, at least as a research strategy for Japanese to proceed with on their own. Provided that we bring the Japanese language and Japanese ideas to our work, they will turn into technology and flourish. Only then do I expect them to become part of the universal base. (AI Jânaru 1985: 97–98; trans. JMU)

Other Japanese (e.g., Watanabe & Aida 1985) have written about the Fifth Generation project in more obviously nationalistic terms, and, to take Fuchi at his word, he does not see the Fifth Generation project as a uniquely Japanese endeavor. On the other hand, one cannot help wondering at the extreme vagueness and ambivalence concerning his "universal base" concept. He may not mention the Japanese writing system outright, but it would be most extraordinary if Fuchi did not think of the language and the writing system as inseparable. In any case, whatever he thinks his project is aiming at, it certainly does not sound like the control of the economic power of the twenty-first century.

Nontechnical Motives

Japan has thus misunderstood what the rest of the world means by AI. In the meantime, the rest of the world has misunderstood how and why the Fifth Generation concept got off the ground in Japan.

The first, vague concepts came from a group of four or five young MITI bureaucrats headed by Nakano Masataka in 1978. He got approval to do a preliminary study from Moriyama Nobutada, then head of the Machinery and Information Industries Bureau, but no funding to do it—that would have requried action by the Ministry of Finance. Nakano therefore enlisted the cooperation of a private computer-leasing company called JECC, which in turn approached the American consulting firm Arthur D. Little to do the work (Uemae 1985: 43–44). For similar reasons, the 1979–1981 "study group" that wrote the plans presented at the first international conference of the Fifth Generation project was supported by proceeds from Japan's bicycle races, over which MITI had control and which it could channel to its Japan Information Processing Development Center (JIPDEC) without MOF approval.

Japanese ministries are notorious for their strong sense of territoriality, and the success of MITI officials is often judged on the basis of how much money they can pry loose from the Ministry of Finance for their group's pet project. Thus, the Fifth Generation Study group was not so much interested in evaluating the AI scene and objectively assessing Japan's chances of success in AI research as in cooperating with friendly MITI officials. The study group was dominated by computer engineers eager to do development work at the frontiers of their field, mostly from the University of Tôkyô and the Electrotechnical Laboratory (see Table 18). The official goals of the project were of secondary importance to them—indeed, there were advantages in keeping them broad and vague. The exciting thing was that MITI was willing to go to bat for something unprecedented: big money for a long-term, autonomous, basic research project. "Basic research" here meant simply that the project would not be officially required to produce tangible results. By contrast, the other five MITI computer-related projects that overlapped or dovetailed with the Fifth Generation

Table 18.   Major Organizations That Contributed to Fifth
Generation Project Planning, 1979–1981

Organization	Number of Participants
Electrotechnical Laboratory[a]	14
University of Tôkyô	11
Fujitsû	7
Nippon Telegraph & Telephone	7
Nippon Electric	7
Mitsubishi Electric	6
Tôshiba	5
Hitachi	5
Oki Electric	4
Matsushita	3
Sharp	3
Keiô University	2
Kyôto University	2
Japan Information Processing Development Center	2
Others	16
Total	94

Source: FCGS Proceedings 1981. See Fuchi 1982.

[a]Operated by the Agency for Industrial Science and Technology *(Kôgyô gijutsuin)* of MITI.

(described in Hilton 1982 and summarized in Table 19), as well as the PIPS project, had definite product objectives and were controlled directly by MITI.[13]

When the Institute for New Generation Computer Technology (ICOT) came into being in 1982, it was "the first institute to be specifically established for a national project" and was given an estimated ¥10.5 billion for the first two years of its operation alone (Anderson 1984: 239). Both MITI and the study group representatives had much to gain even if the Fifth Generation project produced few or no results. According to one American observer in contact with project members during its initial phase, the Fifth Generation project was seen as potentially serving at least five nontechnical functions no matter what it achieved technically: it would provide (1) jobs for ex-PIPS workers, (2) a legitimate channel through which MITI could direct development money to Japanese computer manufacturers, (3) an intellectual outlet for junior researchers, (4) encouragement to private companies to fund their own basic research programs, and (5) a basis for university/industry cooperation. Some of the Japanese interviewed during 1985 denied the existence of one or more of these five motives (particularly the first and second), but none denied them all, and all acknowledged the existence of at least one.

A further point should be mentioned in this connection. According to Kimura Shigeru, some MITI officials were having second thoughts about the Fifth Generation shortly after it began. The publication of his translation of *The Fifth Generation,* he claimed, put an end to that!

Where Is the Project Today?

Before ICOT actually "opened for business" in April 1982, the list of project goals had already been pruned back a bit, and further revisions were made in 1983 (Lindamood 1984b). Although some goals have been abandoned, those related to kanji input, particularly voice recognition, are still on the list of objectives. The work, however, is visible not at the headquarters of ICOT itself but rather at such places as the Information Sciences Division of the Electrotechnical Laboratory:

> It is here that much work relating to the fifth generation computer project and artificial intelligence is carried out. . . . The pattern processing section is mainly concerned to develop handwritten *kanji* recognition devices. Research is underway both on different recognition algorithms and on the knowledge base for the matching process. The speech processing section is developing the basic technology by which oral conversation between man and computer, as well as spoken Japanese input to computer, could be realized. Success has been achieved in developing speech synthesis rules using a vocal tract shape model. (Anderson 1984: 254)

Another indication of continuing interest in the kanji problem was Motooka's role as "general chairperson" of the International Conference on Text Processing with a Large Character Set, held at the Keidanren Hall in Tôkyô on 17–19 October 1983. This conference was not an ICOT event, but Motooka evidently believed that its focus was at least as important as AI itself. When asked whether success of the Fifth Generation project was a necessary condition for a complete solution to the problem of large character sets, he candidly remarked that Japanese input would remain a problem *even after* AI machines had been built (Unger 1984a: 247). The majority of Japanese engineers who were asked the same question claimed that the kanji problem had been essentially solved—but then, why the conference?

Table 19. Six Computer-Related Projects Subsidized by the Japanese Government

Project	English Title	Japanese Title	Timeframe and Total Budget	Sponsoring Government Agencies	Private Companies Involved	Overall Goals	Subgoals	Remarks
Supercomputers	High Speed Computer System for Scientific and Technological Uses	Kagaku gijutsuyō kōsoku keisan shisutemu	JFY 1981–1989, $104,545,000	MITI/AIST/ NRDP	Fujitsu, Hitachi, NEC, Toshiba, Mitsubishi, Oki	Create computers that can execute 10 billion floating-point operations per second (10 gigaflops)	High-speed logic and memory; parallel processing	New computer architectures often said to be essential for AI
Optoelectronics	Optical Measurement and Control System	Hikari ōyō keisoku seigyo shisutemu	JFY 1979–1986, $81,818,000	MITI/AIST/ NRDP	Fujitsu, Hitachi, NEC, Toshiba, Mitsubishi, Matsushita, Furukawa, Oki, Sumitomo	Create large-scale industrial control systems using optical elements	Sensing devices; data transmission	Believed that MITI ultimately wants to create a computer that uses light rather than electricity for information transfer
Next Generation Industries (NGI) semiconductors	Next Generation Industries Basic Technologies Research and Development Program, "New Function Elements" section	Jisedai sangyō kiban gijutsu kenkyū kaihatsu seido, shin kinō soshi	JFY 1981–1990, $113,636,000	MITI/AIST/ NGIBT	Fujitsu, Hitachi, Sumitomo, NEC, Oki, Toshiba, Mitsubishi, Sanyo, Sharp, Matsushita	Create new kinds of semiconductors	Ultrafine lattices; three-dimensional elements; elements for extreme environments	Larger NGI program also includes new materials, fine ceramics, and biotechnology

Software automation	Software Production Technology Development Program	Sofutoweä seisan gijutsu kaihatsu keikaku	JFY 1976–1981, $30,118,000	MITI/MIIB/DPPD	Seventeen major and a number of minor companies	Reduce labor costs of software production	Specifics not available	Gave up on automatic code generation, now a Fifth Generation goal; produced instead a library of programming aids
Fourth Generation computers	Promotion and Development of Technology for Next Generation (Fourth Generation) Computers	Jisedai (dai-4 sedai) denshi keisankiyö kihon gijutsu no kaihatsu sokushin	Phase I, JFY 1976–1979, private $190,909,000, MITI $132,263,000; Phase II, JFY 1979–1983, private $111,363,000, MITI $102,272,000	MITI/MIIB/IED	Fujitsu, Hitachi, Mitsubishi, NEC, Toshiba, Oki, Sharp, Matsushita (last three only for Phase II-B)	Develop hardware, hardware operating systems, and peripherals to compete with anticipated IBM "Future Series"	Hardware, OS software, peripherals and terminals (Phases I, II-A, and II-B, respectively)	Phase I also called VLSI project; Phase II included subgoals specifically related to Japanese language
Fifth Generation computers	Research and Development Relating to Basic Technology for Electronic Computers (Fifth Generation Computers)	Denshi keisanki kiso gijutsu no kenkyü kaihatsu dai-5 sedai konpyütä	JFY 1981–1991, $45,455,000 projected for 1981–1984	MITI/MIIB	Fujitsu, Hitachi, NEC, Toshiba, Mitsubishi, Oki, plus two home appliance manufacturers	Develop practical AI computer systems	Machine translation; interactive "expert" systems; automatic code generation	Project goals and stance on AI have changed during course of project

Hierarchy of Government Agencies:

MITI = Ministry of International Trade and Industry/Tsúshó sangyóshó (Tsúsanshó)

    AIST = Agency of Industrial Science and Technology/Kógyó gijutsuin (Kógiin)

        NRDP = National Research and Development Program (Large-scale Project Program)/Ógata kógyó gijutsu kenkyú kaihatsu seido

        NGIBT = Next Generation Industries Basic Technology Planning Office/Jisedai sangyó kiban gijutsu kikakushitsu

    MIIB = Machinery and Information Industries Bureau/Kikai jóhó sangyókyoku (Kijókyoku)

        IED = Industrial Electronics Division/Denshi Kikika (Denshika)

        EPD = Electronics Policy Division/Denshi Seisakuka (Denseika)

        DPPD = Data Processing Promotion Division/Jóhó shori shinkóka (Jóshinka)

ICTP 1983 was just one of many occasions on which foreign and Japanese experts have been able to confer on topics related to Fifth Generation goals. ICOT regularly invites foreign experts to Japan to work with and lecture to its personnel. Indeed, ICOT seems to be turning gradually into an educational enterprise: "The Fifth Generation project envisions instructing 10,000 engineers in the intricacies of software and AI by 1995" (Bylinsky 1986: 31). Many of the publications coming out of ICOT are mostly recapitulations of visitors' lectures. Nonetheless, when interviewed in 1985, more than one foreign observer working at or with regular contacts in laboratories doing Fifth Generation work remarked on the secretiveness and sensitivity to criticism they found there. Although some found this annoying, most thought it amusing, since the Japanese they met were, in their view, somewhat out of touch with current research in the West and gave no signs of having any results worth keeping secret. (See Smith & Brown 1985: 3–4, for a penetrating analysis of this aspect of advanced Japanese research.) Some knowledgeable visitors have been favorably impressed by what they have found at ICOT (see, e.g., Hsiang 1986, Wiik 1986), but more often the reaction is that ICOT is going over old ground. Significantly, there was not a single Japanese name on the advance program for the Third IEEE Symposium on Logic Programming scheduled for Salt Lake City, 21–25 September 1986, which included participants from Australia, Canada, the United States and more than a half dozen European countries. While ICOT remains committed to the strong-AI "expert system" approach, the avant garde of AI in the West is exploring an explicitly weak-AI strategy of using massive parallel processing systems to simulate neural activity at the physiological level (Allman 1986).[14]

This is the paradox of the Fifth Generation project in its middle phase: On the one hand, it is setting a precedent for government-funded basic research; it is stimulating interest in AI in the private companies; it is capturing the popular imagination, and lending prestige to Japanese science in general. On the other hand, it isn't producing the machines of the 1990s, and the idea of government funding for basic research may itself be in jeopardy. Makino Tsutomu, quoted earlier, hinted rather unsubtly later on in his speech that a problem was brewing:

We roughly estimate that 100 billion yen will be required for the ten-year project from 1982 to 1991. Whether it is 100 billion yen or less than that, the amount is still enormous. How will we get this kind of money?

Of course it totally depends upon how we proceed in the negotiation with the financial authority. But it also depends upon how much support the Japanese people give to the understanding of the long-term significance of this project.

I am much impressed with such a large attendance at this conference. I feel we really have to do our best to be successful in negotiations with the financial authority in response to your enthusiasm. (Brandin et al. 1985: 41)

Apparently, Makino's best was not enough:

Unlike the other cooperative R&D projects MITI sponsors, ICOT directs the fifth generation project. The companies involved are left out of the decision-making process. At the same time, ICOT's success depends on these same companies providing manpower and support to stretch a meager budget of $20 million (¥4.7 billion) for fiscal 1985, down 8.3% from 1984.

The slight reduction indicates more than fiscal austerity at the Ministry of Finance. It's more like a warning from within the government bureaucracy to produce some results or face a tougher time next year. But ICOT denies that the decrease is a vote of no confidence. (Murtha 1985: 44)

In fact, ICOT did "face a tougher time" the following year (Sorensen 1986: 35), and the possibility of the Fifth Generation project ending before its so-called final phase starts in 1988 can no longer be dismissed out of hand. It will be most unfortunate for Japan if ICOT gives basic research a bad name, because Japan still underfunds basic research in comparison with applied research and product development. This was, in fact, the key conclusion of a U.S. Department of Commerce study that compared computer science in the United States and Japan (Brandin 1985; see also Davis 1985).

ICOT issues research reports and memoranda in both Japanese and English, but in either language they tend to be rather short on technical details. ICOT's only really substantial achievements have been in hardware. The "game plan" was to produce a sequential inference machine that, together with a special-purpose computer for handling relational databases, would be a stepping-stone on the way to parallel inference and knowledge-base machines (Furukawa & Yokoi 1984: 47). To date, only a "personal sequential inference" (PSI) machine (described in Yokoi, Uchida, et al. 1984) has been built (by Mitsubishi), but what was to become the relational database machine, Delta, is gathering dust in the basement of the building housing ICOT. At the end of August 1985, Delta was, according to Kusama Hiroyuki, six months behind schedule. Confidential sources within ICOT have since reported that the engineer responsible for Delta has left ICOT, and there is no prospect of its ever being completed. This is particularly significant because the programming of the Delta machine would necessarily have set a precedent for the encoding of Japanese-language data. No one at ICOT queried in August 1985, including Fuchi, was able to say with certainty whether Japanese-language data on Delta would be encoded in JIS codes, alphanumerics, or some other format.

The Kernel Language (KL) has also been running into some trouble. It is now a series of languages, KL0, KL1, and KL2. The PSI machine firmware is a "micro-interpreter of KL0" developed on ICOT's DEC 2060 (Uchida & Yokoi 1984: 74). Although KL1 and KL2 come up in discussions of Fifth Generation software, they seem to have no material existence at this point.

This PSI machine is designed to run PROLOG programs because ICOT has chosen PROLOG over LISP as the basis for its software development (see Raloff 1984b for a sketch of the controversy). LISP is used more extensively outside Japan, and even in Japan at the end of 1984 "[t]here was far more LISP in the corporate and university environments than one might be led to believe from ICOT reports" (Smith & Brown 1985: 4). The decision to go with PROLOG, which has some potentially serious shortcomings, is still a sensitive issue among Fifth Generation workers.

PROLOG statements are more like declarative propositions of formal logic than the commands and procedures of most other programming languages, and this is ostensibly the reason it was chosen by ICOT. There may be more to it than that, however, PROLOG was developed (in France) specifically for work on machine translation (MT), and MT is closely related to the input problem in the Japanese view of things. Smith and Brown's comments on Japanese MT are particularly illuminating. They found "a tremendous emphasis on machine translation," but add,

> Current systems aren't very sophisticated. . . . [T]hese projects are being carried on largely without the aid of professional linguists. American researchers are liable to think (correctly) that they aren't based on terribly deep theoretical foundations, and to conclude (not so necessarily correctly) that they won't ever be good enough to do anything useful. . . . [I]t seemed to us eminently possible that the combination of large

resources and heuristics, coupled with relatively modest goals, might produce *what the Japanese would conclude was* a genuine success. At one lab, for example (NEC), we found six employees working full time on adding syntactic and semantic category marks to a 60,000 entry on-line Japanese dictionary, in addition to the researchers working on the translation algorithms proper. This level of effort was not unusual. (Smith & Brown 1985: 5; emphasis added)

As these remarks suggest, there is a definite overlap between the problems addressed in Japanese MT work and transcriptive input.[15]

MT became a point of friction between ICOT and the companies with the changeover of research personnel at the start of the middle stage of the project in April 1985. With ICOT generally complaining that the companies were refusing to send them the researchers it wanted, the companies insisted that MT be removed from ICOT's agenda, since they were all now moving into the market with their systems and MT had ceased to be a basic research issue.[16] One of the researchers at ICOT working on natural-language understanding described it as "a very sensitive political issue with the companies." MT has effectively been lopped off the multibranched tree of goals that graces several ICOT pamphlets; research in the intermediate stage is now strictly confined to continuation of the work on machine-readable dictionaries begun in the initial stage. In early 1986 there was some talk of the possibility of combining results on natural-language understanding with those on machine-readable dictionaries to make some kind of contribution to MT in the final stage, but "MITI and several Japanese companies recently formed a separately funded group to work on natural language technology such as machine translation of Japanese and English" (Sorensen 1986: 35). It is no exaggeration to say that the loss of MT is a serious blow to ICOT.

PROLOG software for handling Japanese script demands prodigious amounts of computer memory. To this must be added the relatively slow execution speed of PROLOG code compared with LISP, even allowing for differences in hardware and implementation. Suzuki Norihisa, then at the University of Tôkyô (currently at IBM), emphasized this point in a recent panel discussion of Fifth Generation results to date (Suzuki et al., 1986: 53). Indeed, the overall tone of the panel, chaired by Aiso, was surprisingly negative.

Of course, no one can predict with certainty what the future holds for ICOT and the Fifth Generation. As Lindamood (1983) notes, in one sense, it does not matter how the project turns out. As an exercise in the politics of Japanese R&D, an effort to enlist the cooperation of government bureaucrats, university faculty, graduate students, and the big corporations, it has already succeeded. As a serious attempt to build strong-AI machines, it will, like virtually all other AI work (Dreyfus 1979, Dreyfus & Dreyfus 1986), produce interesting but limited results, none of which justify the working hypotheses of strong AI. As an attack on the kanji problem, it is guaranteed to fail for reasons that could have been explained in a couple of hours had anyone had the prescience to consult a competent linguist before the whole thing began.

Is this, to use the words of Feigenbaum and McCorduck, "a computer challenge to the world" that deserves a multimillion dollar response?

Epilogue

This book is a first attempt to explore the borderland where linguistics, Japanese society, and technology meet. Since its themes are controversial, it will certainly not be the last word on the subject. Still, even though details may be disputed, the linkage between kanji and the Fifth Generation is clear and should cause us to reflect on our own assumptions about "machine intelligence."

The kanji/Fifth Generation link exists on at least three levels. As a practical phenomenon, kanji usage blocks Japan's way to full utilization of computer power and thus influences the course of Japanese computer development. As a social phenomenon, insistence on kanji usage distorts Japanese attitudes toward language and fosters the illusion that only new, radically different kinds of computers can protect Japanese culture from the assaults of English and international electronic media. And as an intellectual phenomenon, kanji usage entails a reductionist view of knowledge and human intelligence that contributes to Japanese faith in the ultimate success of strong AI.

The truth is, however, that strong AI is neither the only nor the best approach to developing the man/machine systems of the future, and the Japanese would do well to investigate the alternatives thoroughly. As it stands, there are at least four gaping holes in the reasoning behind building the "machines of the 1990s." Most obviously, *AI machines in the strong sense are very likely impossible, even in principle.* Suppose nonetheless that Fifth Generation machines are produced: *they will not lead to a radical improvement in transcriptive kanji input,* the difficulties of which can be removed only by a reform of kanji usage itself. But suppose that Japanese simply resign themselves to the inconveniences of using kanji on Fifth Generation machines: *it will still be cheaper to handle Japanese-language data using rômaji,* combined with patternless descriptive input where appropriate. Suppose nonetheless that the cost of transcriptive-input Fifth Generation machines

193

falls so low that no one bothers with the alternatives: then *the proliferation of transcriptive input systems will bring about the early demise
of the very "kanji culture" that they are supposed to rescue.*

That we can expose these holes, one by one, in the Fifth Generation
rationale does not mean that Japanese have consciously thought
through the matter in this way. On the contrary, the Fifth Generation
planners went wrong largely because of what they took for granted.
Their carelessness was not inevitable, nor is it irreversible. Every society has its blind spots, and no one has ever discovered a law of history
or human nature that prevents a society from transcending them. All
that stands in the way of Japan making full use of computers (without
any sacrifice of cultural continuity) is a lack of insight into the nature
of historical change on the part of a relatively few leaders who have it
within their power to set the wheels of change in motion. Japanese
society has itself produced the guides who can show the way; it has
only to follow them. Instead, it is indulging in a spectacular international game of the blind leading the blind, at public expense, in the
impossible quest for pure, disembodied intelligence.

The real problem is not that the game is wasteful (though it is to a
large extent). Tomorrow's computers will undoubtedly do things that
we will regard as nothing short of miraculous. All the same, they cannot and will not be intelligent in any meaningful sense of the word.
Adherence to a theory that insists otherwise can only hamper progress
in the long run. The true danger of the Fifth Generation project is
therefore not so much that it will fail to produce results (that hardly
matters at this point anyway), but that, having run its course, it may
leave Japan burdened with a need to save face as the rest of the world
moves on to more sophisticated paradigms that dispense with the
notion of "machine intelligence" and focus instead on human needs.

It might be objected that this study is more of an attempt to revive
interest in Japanese script reform than an analysis of the relationship
between writing and data processing in the Japanese context. Why not
write a history of the script reform movement with some concluding
remarks on how modern technology has changed the ground rules
under which the game was played down to the Occupation? Certainly,
such a history should be written. Both Japanese and Western scholars
tend to think of the advocates of Japanese script reform, if they think
of them at all, as naive utopians; in fact, their ranks included some of
the most outstanding intellectuals of the day. Many lessons could be
learned from an unbiased reexamination of the movements for the

elimination of kanji either through romanization or exclusive use of kana.

One lesson, however, is already clear: the golden opportunity afforded by the Occupation was lost because proponents of script reform became entangled in negative political fights, both among themselves and with the government, instead of concentrating on building a positive consensus among ordinary Japanese by getting them to read and write without kanji. Now, when computers have raised the kanji issue anew, is not the time to repeat the same error. The Japanese will cling to kanji, no matter how high the human costs, unless thay perceive a consensus for change that cuts across society. Such a consensus will be possible as long as conservatives see the romanization of data processing as a way to preserve kanji in other areas of life. But once Japan has spent billions of yen tooling up for transcriptive input, appeals to rationality will be too late.

Today, Japan is affluent enough to dabble in AI dreaming. Whether it will always be so well-off is far from certain. China by contrast has no money to play games with. Although the Chinese have even more reason than the Japanese to hang on to traditional writing (for one thing, they do not have kana to fall back on), some, at least, seem willing to view the writing system as a technology rather than a cultural property. In the Chinese world, it is the non-mainland segment that is generally more sympathetic with the Japanese outlook.

Korea has a quasi-alphabetic script, *hankul,* which is very well-suited to the phonological structure of the Korean language and in which Koreans take great national pride. Although many of the same conservative arguments one hears in Japan are repeated in Korea *mutatis mutandis,* Koreans are generally quite happy to dispense with Chinese characters in most areas of daily life, let alone data processing. Korean script, divested of Chinese characters, has a few output problems of its own, but nothing that cannot be solved with simple software, and, more important, nothing that prevents touch typing.

Perhaps, as happened nearly thirteen hundred years ago, it will take a wave of Chinese influence, mediated by Korea, to change the thinking of Japan.

NOTES

Introduction

1. Japanese and Chinese names are given in the customary order, surname first.

2. In this book, *he* is occasionally used to refer to a hypothetical person, and *man* to human beings in general, to avoid unnatural or vague wording. Used in this way, such words refer to women as well as men. (In this particular instance, however, the odds against *he* being a woman are rather high.)

Part I. Linguistics and Orthography

1. To use an analogy, if speech is like pencil-and-paper arithmetic, then writing is like operating a calculator. One can describe the rules for operating the calculator independently of the rules of arithmetic, but clearly calculator operation is not a new, autonomous species of arithmetic. Someone who had learned how to punch the right keys from dictation but remained ignorant of arithmetic—if such a person is possible—would have a very hard time judging his or her performance by inspecting the final result, would not know that dividing by 2 and multiplying by 0.5 yield the same outcome, and so on. In the same way, although some scholars speak of "written language" as an autonomous system that largely overlaps with but is distinct from "spoken language," it is more realistic to see writing not as language but as a technology for recording language.

2. The term *roman letters* in this context means, of course, letters of the Roman alphabet, not roman (as opposed to italic) typeface. Perhaps it would be better to use computerese like *alpha characters;* but how would we translate the verb *romanize* and the noun *romanization* into this jargon? *Alphize* or *alphafy* are monstrosities, and *alphabetize* already means something else. *Latin letters* would be better, but the Japanese term is *rômaji*. Reluctantly, therefore, we will stick with custom and speak of *roman letters* and *romanization*.

3. The whispering (devoicing) of vowels under certain conditions also contributes to this rhythm. (Devoicing is why one sometimes sees words like *sukoshi* 'a little' transcribed as *skoshi* or even *skosh*.)

4. At least this term has the advantage of not being easily confused with "tone," a quite different phonetic phenomenon found in Chinese, Thai, and many other languages.

5. For further historical background in English, see Saeki & Yamada 1977.

6. For the sake of completeness, here are the basic rules of phonetic realization in Japanese. The vowels *u* and, to a lesser extent, *o* are pronounced with slack, unrounded lips. *R* is closer to the sound of *r* in Spanish *pero* 'but' than to any of the sounds represented by *r* in American English, though the *r* in *very* heard in some British speech is a good match. *F* is articulated with the two lips rather than with the upper teeth and lower lip. *G* is often pronounced like the *ng* in *singer* when it is embedded in a word or phrase, although some speakers always use a "hard" *g* sound. *H* before *y* or *i* is pronounced like the *ch* in German *ich* 'I' or *x* of Chinese *xièxiè* 'thanks'.

7. Gairaigo also allow the combinations *bb, dd, gg, hh,* and *zz,* which never occur in native words or kango.

8. And, provided that innovative moras such as Hepburn *si, ti,* and *tu* are written distinctively (e.g., *s'i, t'i, t'u*), it meets those conditions for gairaigo as well.

9. Anyone familiar with Hindi, Thai, or other Indian-based alphabets will recognize the sequences of consonants and vowels here. They are ultimately derived from Sanskrit and came to Japan roughly a thousand years ago as part of Buddhist scholarship.

10. In modern practice, nigori is also used to mark the kana for *u* to indicate the innovative mora *vu;* this new form is used in combination with small kana for *a, i, u, e,* and *o* to represent other innovative moras in *v-*.

11. Occasionally, one will also see single right-to-left rows of characters, on the legends of old maps and such. This is just traditional vertical format with a single character in each column and is still used quite a bit in Hong Kong and Taiwan. In Japan, one might also spot a right-to-left line of characters painted on the right side of a truck or company car, but such writing is hardly more than decorative advertising.

12. Since furigana are often used to indicate which of several possible readings the author intends, many of the 8,011 "compound" characters must have contained the same kanji; perhaps only 4,000 or 5,000 *distinct* kanji were actually involved. Still, this is a large number compared, for example, with the 1,945 currently recommended for daily use. Moreover, kanji that occur frequently tend to be the ones having multiple readings; therefore, on any given page of the newspaper, the number of annotated kanji could well have been close to half the total number of kanji.

13. The Japanese rendering of kanbun was a species of literary rather than colloquial language, anachronistic and often obscure, and the "Chinese" that made it up was not always in conformity with correct Chinese syntax. Conventions varied over the centuries, and early traditions were sometimes forgotten. In many ways, kanbun was to Japan what Medieval Latin was to Europe, and the fact that it survived longer attests to the overwhelming influence of Chinese norms in virtually every area of Japanese learning. Indeed, prior to 1900, efforts at reforming Japanese script (and there were several, including some surprisingly early ones) were stymied largely by the failure of

the reformers to couple reform of the written language with reform of the script (Twine 1983).

14. Japanese write exclusively in kana in braille texts, telegram forms, certain types of computer files, and other media.

15. There are in fact words of completely different meaning in these three languages that are written with the same combination of Chinese characters.

16. These examples, incidentally, do not represent the author's subjective judgment. They come from a survey reported in Kaiho & Nomura 1983: 30 in which Japanese were asked to rank kanji according to perceived degree of complexity, symmetry, "openness," and other subjective criteria. The value of such surveys in understanding the psychology of kanji reading is questionable, but it gives a good indication of how Japanese tend to approach the problem.

17. More than two-thirds of the 1,945 recommended kanji are keisei moji, and the percentage grows as one increases the number of kanji in the sample (Hayashi 1982: 216).

18. Kaiho & Nomura 1983: 40. It is far from clear how confusing these kanji are *in context* for human readers. However, for computers, for which context cannot exist, pairs of hard-to-distinguish kanji can be quite important.

19. Unlike Japanese guides to running-hand and grass-script writing, which show only "correct" forms handwritten by an expert calligrapher, Daniels, for obvious reasons, listed commonly used variants whether "correct" or not. Thus her catalog gives greater insight into actual Japanese writing habits than most, though it is now more than forty years old.

20. Incidentally, there is nothing universal or innate about the colors red and green as signals for "stop" and "go"; see Gamst 1975, Harris 1979: 197–200.

21. Perhaps it also explains why personal checking accounts are virtually unknown in Japan. In any case, the heavy predominance of cash in Japan— where the largest note in circulation, ¥10,000, is worth less than U.S. $100— is astounding.

22. In fact, there are a few—but only a few—earlier medieval and ancient examples of alphabetical lists. Almost of all them make use of only the first one or two letters of the items listed. Even as late as 1604, the compiler of the first English dictionary found the task of alphabetization unfamiliar and taxing; he justified his effort by pointing out to his readers the great utility of the finished product. For further historical details, see Daly's 1967 monograph, or the brief summary in Knuth 1973: 417–419.

23. This ingenious verse, in addition to conveying a Buddhist moral, manages to use each kana once and only once, thus forming an acrostic of the entire language.

24. Further examples and details can be found in Yazaki 1964 and Yokoi 1978; for a rigorous linguistic analysis, see Lovins 1975.

25. Much of the remarkable work the "real human being" does cannot actually be broken down into a neat hierarchy of subtasks; therefore, it is some-

what misleading to speak of "a higher order" as if it were just a matter of building bigger and better machines.

26. A white-collar worker who quits a company may be resented more for the extra work he creates for his colleagues than for any inside information he takes with him. The lifetime employment system is not all altruism and company loyalty.

27. There weren't many libraries in the feudal period, and their function was as much to prevent access to certain information as to perserve it for the ruling elite. As in the Middle Ages in Europe, there was often little concern about the exact authorship of a manuscript. Printing was done from whole-page woodblocks, and hand-copying remained an important means of reproduction. When one considers that all the documents preserved in Japan until only a little more than a hundred years ago were written and circulated under these conditions, the present lack of emphasis on libraries becomes more understandable.

28. For a more detailed discussion of the Japanese book trade, see Sekino 1983.

29. There are, of course, other factors that hold back improvements in Japanese white-collar productivity. For example, "even when companies introduce minicomputers in the office, assistants will be recruited to handle them since such work is beneath any self-respecting manager" (Woronoff 1981: 61); however, the bulk of the problem (which Woronoff misses) lies in the writing system itself.

30. Significantly, although JIS-C6234 [1983] specifies both Level 1 and Level 2 24-by-24 character shapes for dot-matrix printers, JIS-C6232 [1984], which gives 16-by-16 shapes for display devices, stops with Level 1.

31. See Nagao et al. 1981 for the description of one Japanese system that incorporates these and other features. Indeed, for those Japanese interested in natural-language processing, morphological analysis is mostly a preoccupation with problems resulting from the imposition of the writing system on the language rather than problems inherent in the structure of the language itself (see, e.g., Yoshida 1984).

32. Indeed, kanji text processing is the *only* clearly negative factor mentioned explicitly in one of the most recent studies of Japan's transition to an "advanced information society" (Baark 1985: 32, 87).

Part II. Politics and Culture

1. For example, DeFrancis (1984b: 278, 296) has caught Miller putting words in the mouth of none other than Deng Xiaoping.

2. Although Saint-Jacques and Suzuki (1984) are even more severe, most reviewers—for example, Allen (1983), Impoco (1984), and DeWolf (1985)—concur with Chew. Those unfamiliar with Miller's other works may find it comforting to learn that he regularly savages both Westerners (e.g., Miller 1975, 1985) and Japanese (e.g., Miller 1977, 1981) with equal alacrity.

3. Dale (1986: 56–99) notes that some prewar Japanese writers claimed to find a pristine "Yamato spirit" in native words and oral traditions, regarding both kango and gairaigo as equally unwelcome impurities in the Japanese lexicon; however, he greatly overrates the impact of this line of thought on nationalist ideology. His interpretation of the work of Yanagita Kunio (Dale 1986: 208–209), for example, ignores the influence that European folklore studies had on Yanagita's research and the anti-establishment political dimension of Yanagita's love of the common man. The idea that native words are somehow nearer to the Japanese heart never posed a serious challenge to the overwhelming prestige of Chinese writing and learning in prewar Japan. It has primarily been *postwar* writers, such as Watanabe Shôichi and Doi Takeo, who have made much of the "uniqueness" of certain native Japanese words. Indeed, as we shall see later, one postwar writer, Suzuki Takao, has actually turned the alleged "transparency" of Yamato kotoba to Japanese into a defense of kanji.

4. Tsunoda claims to have proven experimentally, through the "Tsunoda Key Tapping" technique, that there is an innate switching mechanism in the brain that governs the processing of sounds, and that the language one speaks between the ages of six and eight determines how this switching mechanism operates (Tsunoda 1985a: 157; 1985b: 138). According to Tsunoda, Japanese and Polynesian languages such as Maori and Tongan lead to one type of switching, and all other languages lead to another. No one has been able to replicate Tsunoda's results except Tsunoda, and even he has been having trouble lately; this he attributes to "the earth's revolution, the lunar motion, and possibly other cosmic activities" (1985b: 139). One wonders what Martin Gardner (see Gardner 1957), whose mathematics column graced *Scientific American* for many years, would say about the recent exposition of Tsunoda's "discoveries" in the Japanese edition of *Scientific American* (Tsunoda 1985c).

5. A further point to consider is that people buy books for various reasons. After 1945, there were people who had received little or no education because of the war but nonetheless subscribed to newspapers lest their neighbors discover that they could not read.

6. But many Japanese believe just that, as shown by a recent international incident. On 22 September 1986, Prime Minister Nakasone was quoted as saying that Japan has an advantage over the United States because it does not have ethnic minorities like blacks, Puerto Ricans, and Mexicans. The major Japanese papers ignored this remark (but did report other parts of Nakasone's speech that day) until it elicited a scathing American reaction, which caught the government by surprise. Although they have since carried some criticisms of the substance of Nakasone's statement (e.g., Kometani 1986), more space has been devoted to clarifying it. Nakasone was speaking at a Liberal Democratic party study group, attempting to explain why the Japanese educational system was more successful than the American.

7. "Examination hell" is not a postwar phenomenon. Nitobe used the term in 1931 (Nitobe 1972: 3.249), and it is doubtful that he coined it.

8. Perhaps pricked by this realization, Suzuki takes a somewhat different tack in more recent writings, such as Suzuki 1977, which contains the startling claim that the Japanese writing system is a synchronic part of the Japanese language, on a par with syntax and phonology. This claim is no more compatible with the findings of linguistic science than creationism is with modern biology. The evidence that Suzuki adduces, mostly historical, simply does not require the far-fetched interpretation he insists on.

9. History as well as common sense shows that Japanese can indeed read and write their language in rômaji. In the early part of this century, Japanese immigrants in Mexico used rômaji in their schools and found that first-year students could read the equivalent of the first three years' textbooks then in use in Japan (Ishida 1973: 126–134). A former member of the Kokugo Shingikai (Japanese Language Council) and a professor at the University of Tôkyô, both interviewed in 1985, have confirmed the existence of a report of similar results obtained during experimental rômaji education in the early 1950s (referred to contemptuously by Trainor [1983: 318–319]). The Ministry of Education seems to have lost all copies of it.

10. Some would not even go this far. Steinberg & Yamada 1979a elicited a blistering rejoinder from Tzeng and Singer (1979), who protested, among other things, what they felt was an attempt to slip the Ideographic Myth in through the back door. Steinberg and Yamada vociferously denied this in their surrejoinder (1979b), but in a Japanese reference to Steinberg and Yamada (1979a), Yamada (1983: 129–130) casually tacks on a statement of the Ideographic Myth.

11. Interestingly, Zheng Qiao himself appears to have appreciated the power of alphabetic writing.

> Now, the writings of Confucius travelled as far east as Korea, as far west as Kansu, as far south as Annam, and as far north as Inner Mongolia. All of these were our ancient feudatories. His writings did not reach beyond these ancient feudatories. How is it that Gautama Buddha's books can penetrate the various parts of China but Confucian writings cannot reach the Airavati River? It is because there are obstacles to the passage of tones and sounds. This is the fault of scholars who came after Confucius! Wherever boats and carts can arrive, there too words and their meanings can extend. Why are there places where boats and carts arrive today but Confucius' words and their meanings do not extend? (Mair 1986: 134)

12. Holtom (1947: 221) says he heard the same opinion (that the blind were more fortunate than the sighted in Japan) from a famous Japanese educator; perhaps he attended one of Nitobe's lectures. In any case, since he was writing *against* script reform, it is noteworthy that he repeated this view without critical comment.

13. Yale University professor Samuel Martin recently suggested that Japan's international reputation for being a "secret club" was largely due to

the Japanese language, specifically Japanese writing, being a "secret code" (Martin 1985: 14).

14. In any event, such claims are invariably based on misinformation about Chinese writing; Logan's "alphabet effect" (1986), for example, rests entirely on the Ideographic Myth. To take a better known case, McLuhan (1962) says that China and other manuscript cultures are "audile-tactile" whereas print culture is intensely visual. Why, then, were Chinese literati so impressed by Matteo Ricci's mastery of the art of visualizing "memory palaces" (Spence 1984)? For that matter, why did the visualization of "memory palaces" flourish in the manuscript culture of medieval Europe and fall into disuse after printed books became common? Evidently, not all manuscript cultures share the same "sense ratios." Nakayama (1984: 78–79) criticizes McLuhan in the same vein. Incidentally, Nakayama and McLuhan (probably under the influence of Pound and Fenollosa) both accept versions of the Ideographic Myth; therefore, their differing views on Chinese culture cannot be due to differing views on the function of Chinese script.

15. Chinese does have some monosyllabic words, and many dissyllabic Chinese words are true compounds (like English "baseball"); however, there are plenty of Chinese dissyllables (like "orange" in English) that cannot be analyzed into independent words. DeFrancis (1984b: 185) quotes the eminent linguist Zhou Youguang (personal communication) as estimating that "only 2,000 or so, or about 30 percent, of the 6,800 'modern standard characters' needed to write contemporary Chinese are free words."

16. Miller has recently put foreward a different interpretation of the famous letter to the American linguist William Dwight Whitney in which Mori broached the subject of jettisoning the Japanese language:

> If compulsory elementary education, and increasingly available higher education, were now indeed conspiring together to make almost everyone talk like everyone else, one could always take refuge in a foreign language, specifically in English, the prestige foreign language of Japan in the late nineteenth and early twentieth centuries. Mori Arinori and the élite that he represented found their long-cherished Japanese sociolinguistic preserve more and more threatened by invasion from the rest of Japanese society. What better way to halt this rising tide of the great unwashed than to declare the entire Japanese language incompetent and inadequate, and to urge instead the wholesale adaptation of a foreign language solely available—and then, only under circumstances of enormous difficulty and expense—to a limited number of the élite? (Miller 1986: 97)

This is just cynical speculation on Miller's part. Mori's writings show no evidence of such a motive.

17. Indeed, as Searle notes, proponents of AI seem to believe in souls, not he. (A favorite claim of the artificial intelligentsia is that talk of irreducible

mental phenomena is just Cartesian dualism in disguise.) For an insightful discussion of what is wrong with strong AI from the viewpoint of linguistics, see Sampson 1980, particularly 97–102.

18. Japanese hand out name cards for a variety of social reasons, but one of the most important is that it saves the recipient the embarassment of not being able to write the donor's name correctly if the need ever arises.

19. This experience-killing effect of transcriptive Japanese word processing is just one example of a more widespread phenomenon documented and explained in Dreyfus & Dreyfus 1986.

Part III. Economics and Technology

1. Because of the wide range of choices in peripheral equipment and extras, differing user needs, the possibility of buying at below list price, and the large number of new models coming onto the market every year, pricing a "fully programmable Japanese personal computer" is a somewhat subjective affair but ¥500,000 (give or take ¥100,000) is probably a reasonable estimate for what a fairly serious user would want. This excludes software and expendables such as diskettes. All prices are stated in yen because the exchange rate varied between about ¥260 and ¥160 to the dollar during 1985 and 1986.

2. An American system for English, to be released in 1986 "at a price under $20,000," is, judging from its technical description (Kurzweil 1986), far more advanced than anything available in Japan. Although Kurzweil, who developed the system, believes "a Japanese machine is feasible," he notes that Japanese poses special problems because many syllables are "distinguished only by the duration of the vowel" and because the nature of Japanese syntax is complex. It should be noted that phonetic and syntactic analysis are both antecedent to the kanji problem.

3. More sophisticated definitions have been developed by researchers working on algorithms for parsing Japanese. See, for example, Yoshida 1981. It is significant that most of the papers in this report on transcriptive input are devoted to syntactic analysis, which would seem to have more to do with machine translation than with input.

4. The same problem is preventing the Dvorak Simplified Keyboard (DSK) from replacing QWERTY as the standard for English. Although some investigators have called the superiority of DSK over QWERTY into question, measurements of performance by trained typists (as opposed to extrapolations from theoretical models) clearly indicate that DSK allows for roughly a 20 percent improvement in typing speed and, even more important, causes less fatigue (Yamada 1983b). Nonetheless, prospects of a switchover to DSK do not look bright (Brookman 1985).

5. This is illustrated by the fact that the index of coincidence, a direct function of relative frequencies used in cryptanalysis, is .066 for single letters but .0084 (nearly ten times smaller) for digraphs in ordinary English text (Sinkov 1966: 63–69, 131–132).

6. Moreover, the general working conditions in Japan's "automated offices" leave much to be desired; see Sumioka 1984; Sôhyô 1985a, 1985b; Nihon Sangyô Eisei Gakkai 1985; Unger 1986.

7. To the extent that this aspect of Yamada's work has involved computers, it might be considered an example of weak AI.

8. It is well known that IBM purposely throttled the operating speed of its PC-AT so that it would not lure customers away from more expensive minis.

9. In a later work (Motooka & Kitsuregawa 1984: 27), agriculture and fishing are also mentioned as low-productivity areas, but this inclusion is highly questionable. Japanese agriculture and fishing are *too* productive; without large government price supports and protective tariffs, much of it would not be economically viable, but that is because the standard of living of Japanese farmers and fishermen is now so high. Furthermore, there is no evidence that *new kinds* of computers are necessary for improvements in the management of farming and fishing, but much evidence that *current kinds* of computers are insufficient for the management of Japanese offices.

10. By "languages," Motooka must have meant different modes of script. This sort of error is quite common in computer science literature relating to kanji handling.

11. According to Kimura Shigeru (interview of 30 September 1985), who translated *The Fifth Generation* into Japanese, Feigenbaum insisted that the technical parts he had written not be cut from the Japanese edition. Significantly, Feigenbaum has recently been quoted as saying that although the Japanese are not making the kind of progress he had foretold in *The Fifth Generation,* his book deserves credit for having put pressure on Americans to invest in AI (Impoco 1987).

12. A former IBM employee has reported that the term was in fact used in some internal company documents, although it was later dropped. And according to Tatsuno (1986: 15), "In 1975 Japanese industry was confronted with yet another challenge from the West. . . . IBM flexed its technical muscle with its Future System computer, which incorporated very large-scale integrated (VLSI) circuits designed with leading-edge electron beam equipment."

13. Table 19 also sheds some light on the question of whether or not ICOT is doing AI research. If it isn't, one can only wonder what it *is* doing, since there seems to be a separate project for virtually every other significant aspect of advanced computer technology. For further information on the panoply of Japanese R&D projects, see Tatsuno 1986: 35–69, 256–258.

14. Recent experimental successes of the "neural net" or "connectionist" approach are particularly important because they call into question the strong-AI insistence that all intelligent activity must be rule-governed. Work in this direction began in the 1960s but was belittled by MIT computer scientists Marvin Minsky and Seymour Papert, two of today's leading strong-AI dogmatists. It is therefore highly significant that Japanese studying biological systems with an aim toward going beyond the Fifth Generation are still locked into the Min-

sky/Papert mentality. "Several U.S. laboratories claim to have produced computers that mimic neural networks. But Japanese researchers dismiss those computers as simply modifications of old technology" (Yoder 1986).

15. Interestingly, William Haas, a British linguist who holds the rather Japanese view that speech and writing are autonomous systems, actually defines the interrelationship between writing and speech as "translation" (Haas 1970: 16–23).

16. Nonetheless, both the quality and sales of MT systems remain poor. For example, the Bravice International Micropak produces English output that must be extensively rewritten by someone highly competent in both English and Japanese, yet "Bravice, as a partner in a company called Career Network, is trying to peddle these ¥1.8 million systems to housewives, aiming their sales efforts not at people who could do the work, but at people who could possibly be convinced to buy the systems" (Lise 1986a). Hitachi has claimed outside sales for a system that it is only using internally on an experimental basis and has forced its subsidiaries to buy (Lise 1986b).

GLOSSARY

This glossary contains the most important Japanese and computer-related technical terms used in the text.

ateji Kanji used to write a native Japanese word in a nonstandard way. There is no etymological relationship between the readings of the kanji and the word represented.

bô The dash-like mark (also called *chôon kigô*) used with katakana to indicate a long vowel.

bunsetsu Units of Japanese sentence structure comparable to phrases and clauses in English. With reference to Japanese word-processing software, any stretch of text composed entirely of one kind of character, or of kanji plus kana (usually hiragana).

furigana Small kana placed next to kanji to indicate their proper reading; "side" kana.

gairaigo Japanese words borrowed from foreign languages, such as English, French, and German, outside the Chinese cultural sphere.

genkô yôshi Japanese manuscript paper.

gojûon The "fifty syllables" of the Japanese sound system; describes the order of kana that begins *a, i, u, e, o, ka, ki, ku,* etc.

handakuten A diacritic mark resembling a degree sign; a kana normally used to represent a mora with initial *h* stands for the corresponding mora with initial *p* when marked with handakuten. Sometimes called *maru*.

hardware The physical elements that comprise a computer system. In the opinion of most software developers, the easy part of the system to fix.

hiragana The principal form of Japanese syllabic script, cursive in style, and used for all functions not filled by katakana.

input The process of entering data into a computer, usually through a typewriter-like keyboard; sometimes, the data themselves.

jôyô kanji The 1,945 kanji presently specified by the government for daily use.

jukujikun The use of a string of kanji to represent a native Japanese word that cannot be divided (except arbitrarily) into readings that can be assigned to the kanji involved.

kana Japanese syllabic script.

kanbun Texts in literary Chinese, or an approximation of it, read in a stylized form of classical Japanese according to fixed rules for glossing kanji and permuting their order; hence, the technique for writing Japanese that makes use of this reading tradition.

kango Japanese words either borrowed whole from Chinese, or created in Japan from Chinese roots.

kanji Chinese characters, specifically those used to write Japanese.

kanji kanamajiribun Japanese text written with a mixture of kana and kanji, with other characters (roman letters, numerals, etc.) interspersed as necessary; the standard form of modern Japanese texts.

kanwa jiten A dictionary in which the main entries are kanji and the definitions are in Japanese; a traditional Chinese/Japanese dictionary.

katakana The auxiliary form of Japanese syllabic script, angular in style. Katakana are used to transcribe foreign loanwords, for emphasis, in telegrams, and for other special purposes.

keisei moji A Chinese character in which an older character, showing a rhyming syllable, is augmented with another character (often in reduced form), called a radical, that suggests the meaning of the word in which the syllable occurs.

kokugo jiten A Japanese/Japanese dictionary.

kun All or part of a Japanese word assigned to a kanji; a native reading for a kanji.

machine translation A computer application in which a program attempts to translate a text in one human language into another without human intervention.

natural-language processing The use of a computer to deal with human languages; machine translation is the classic AI exercise in this area.

nigori A diacritic mark resembling a double quotation mark; a kana normally used to represent a mora with a voiceless initial consonant stands for the corresponding mora with voiced initial when marked with nigori. Properly called *dakuten*.

non-von Neumann Describes any computer architecture that does not depend on a central processing unit that executes one instruction at a time. See parallel processor.

okurigana Kana following a kanji that stands for the initial part of a Japanese word, usually a verb or adjective, to complete it.

on A reading for a kanji based on a borrowing from Chinese into Japanese; hence, a Sino-Japanese reading.

optical character recognition (OCR) A computer application in which a program attempts to determine the characters in a piece of writing.

output The process of displaying, printing out, or transmitting information from a computer; sometimes, the data themselves.

parallel processor A computer system in which many independent processors can operate simultaneously.

real-time application A use of computers in which the timing of user's actions (e.g., input) produce nearly instantaneous results (e.g., output).

rendaku A change of a voiceless consonant to its voiced counterpart in many Japanese compounds. For example, *toki* 'time', *tokidoki* 'sometimes'.

rômaji Letters of the Latin alphabet, particularly when used to write Japanese phonemically.

software Computer programs; the coded instructions executed by a computer. In the opinion of most hardware engineers, the easy part of the system to fix.

sorting Putting computer records in order on the basis of key words or numbers in each record.

strong AI (artificial intelligence) The theory that intelligence is nothing but the physical manipulation of symbols and, therefore, reducible to computer programs.

supercomputers Whatever this year's most advanced computers happen to be; currently, very large, very fast mainframes, usually with parallel processing capabilities.

tategaki Vertical writing; columns of characters running top to bottom cover the page from right to left.

tôyô kanji The set of 1,850 characters specified by the government for daily use in 1946; superseded by the jôyô kanji.

very large scale integration (VLSI) Technology for printing thousands of electronic components on a single chip.

von Neumann machines Conventional computers that process one instruction at a time.

weak AI (artificial intelligence) The use of computers in the study of brain and nervous system function.

yokogaki Horizontal writing; rows of characters running from left to right cover the page from top to bottom, as in English.

REFERENCES

Note that Hepburn romanization is used for Japanese and *pinyin* for Chinese unless a different spelling is given in the source. Japanese and Chinese names are kept in the traditional order, surname first.

In Western Languages

Allen, Louis. 1983. Review of *Japan's Modern Myth,* by Roy Andrew Miller. *Monumenta Nipponica* 38:3 (Autumn), 333–338.

Allman, William F. 1986. "Mindworks." *Science 86* 7:4 (May), 22–31.

Anderson, Alun M. 1984. *Science and Technology in Japan.* In *Longman Guide to World Science and Technology,* vol. 4. Harlow, Essex, England: Longman Group Limited.

Baark, Erik. 1985. *Towards an Advanced Information Society in Japan: A Preliminary Study of Sociocultural and Technological Driving Forces.* Lund, Sweden: Research Policy Institute, Committee for Future Oriented Research.

Bairstow, Jeffrey. 1983. Review of *The Fifth Generation,* by Edward A. Feigenbaum and Pamela McCorduck. *Personal Computing,* October, 207.

Batt, Robert. 1983. "Fifth-Generation Threat by Japanese Overrated, Industry Expert Warns." *Computerworld,* 19 September.

Barrett, William. 1986. *Death of the Soul: From Descartes to the Computer.* Garden City, N.Y.: Anchor Press/Doubleday.

Becker, Joseph D. 1984. "Multilingual Word Processing." *Scientific American,* July, 96–107.

———. 1985. "Typing Chinese, Japanese, and Korean." *Computer,* January, 27–34.

Black, Cyril E., Marius B. Jansen, Herbert S. Levine, Marion J. Levy, Jr., Henry Rosovsky, Gilbert Rozman, Henry D. Smith, II, and S. Frederick Starr. 1975. *The Modernization of Japan and Russia: A Comparative Study.* New York: The Free Press; London: Collier Macmillan.

Boehm, Barry W. 1983. "The Hardware/Software Cost Ratio: Is It a Myth?" *Computer,* March, 78–80.

Bogen, Margaret. 1977. *Artificial Intelligence and Natural Man.* New York: Basic Books.

Booth, Alan, Kunihiro Masao, and C. William Barnes. 1984. *Hell! Hinomaru Eigo no ayamari o tadasu* [Correcting the errors of Rising Sun English]. Tôkyô: Nichibun shuppan.

Bowen, William. 1986. "The Puny Payoff from Office Computers." *Fortune,* 26 May, 20–24.

Brandin, D. H., J. M. Cadiou, T. Makino, B. W. Oakley, F. Salle, and N. Szyperski. 1985. "Panel Discussion: International Research Activities for New Generation Computers." In *Conference Report: International Conference on Fifth Generation Computer Systems, November 6–9, 1984, Keio Plaza Hotel, Tokyo, Japan,* 28–52. Tôkyô: ICOT.

Brookman, Denise C. 1985. "Comfort-crafted Ergonomic Keyboards Increase Efficiency." *Design News,* 20 May, 92–100.

Burke, James. 1978. *Connections.* Boston: Little, Brown.

Bylinsky, Gene. 1986. "Where the U.S. Stands: Computers, Chips, and Factory Automation." *Fortune,* 13 October, 28–32.

Chen Cheng-kuang, and Gong Reng-Weng. 1983. *Evaluating of the Chinese Input Method in R.O.C.* Taipei: Institute for Information Industry.

Chew, John J., Jr. 1984. "The Japanese Language in the Eyes of Postwar Japan." Review of *Japan's Modern Myth,* by Roy Andrew Miller. *Journal of Asian Studies* 43:3 (May), 475–480.

The Chicago Manual of Style. 1982. Thirteenth edition of *A Manual of Style,* revised and expanded. Chicago: University of Chicago Press.

Chin, Paula, and Bradley Martin. 1986. "Solving the Chinese Puzzle: Ancient Characters Finally Meet the Computer Age." *Newsweek,* 18 August, 43.

Cragon, Harvey G. 1982. "The Myth of the Hardware-Software Cost Ratio." *Computer,* December, 100–101.

Dale, Peter N. 1986. *The Myth of Japanese Uniqueness.* New York: St. Martin's Press.

Daly, Lloyd W. 1967. *Contributions to a History of Alphabetization in Antiquity and the Middle Ages.* Collection Latomus 90. Brussels: Latomus.

Daniels, Otome. 1947. *Dictionary of Japanese (Sôsho) Writing Forms.* London: Lund Humphries.

Davidson, Martin. 1980. "Calling Mr. Suzuki, All 39,000 of You." *Winds* (Japan Air Lines), May, 4–8.

Davis, Neil W. 1985. "U.S., Japan Compared in Computers, Research." *Japan Times,* 29 June.

DeFrancis, John. 1947. "Politics and Phonetics." *Far Eastern Survey* 16:19 (5 November), 217–220.

————. 1984a. "Digraphia." *Word* 35:1 (April), 59–66.

————. 1984b. *The Chinese Language: Fact and Fantasy.* Honolulu: University of Hawaii Press.

DeWolf, Charles M. 1985. Review of *Japan's Modern Myth,* by Roy Andrew Miller. *Papers in Linguistics* 18:2.295–316.

Dore, Ronald P. 1965. *Education in Tokugawa Japan.* Berkeley: University of California Press.

Dreyfus, Hubert L. 1979. *What Computers Can't Do: The Limits of Artificial Intelligence.* Revised edition. New York: Harper Colophon.

Dreyfus, Hubert, and Stuart Dreyfus. 1986. *Mind over Machine: Why Computer Programs Can Never Match the Power of Human Intuition and*

Expertise. With Tom Athanasiou. New York: Macmillan/The Free Press.

Duke, Benjamin C. 1977. "Why Noriko Can Read! Some Hints for Johnny." *Educational Forum* 41:2.229–236.

Fallows, James. 1986. "The Japanese Are Different from You and Me." *The Atlantic,* September, 35–41.

Feigenbaum, Edward A., and Pamela McCorduck. 1983. *The Fifth Generation: Artificial Intelligence and Japan's Computer Challenge to the World.* Reading, Mass.: Addison-Wesley.

Fuchi Kazuhiro. 1982. "Aiming for Knowledge Information Processing Systems." In *Fifth Generation Computer Systems: Proceedings of the International Conference on Fifth Generation Computer Systems, Tokyo, 19–22 October 1981,* ed. Moto-oka Tohru, 107–120. Amsterdam: North-Holland.

————. 1985. "Revisiting Original Philosophy of Fifth Generation Computer Systems Project." In *Fifth Generation Computer Systems, 1984,* 18–25. *See* Brandin et al. 1985.

Furukawa Koichi, and Yokoi Toshio. 1984. "Basic Software System." In *Fifth Generation Computer Systems Project: Report on ICOT's Research and Development in the Initial State,* 45–65. Tôkyô: ICOT.

Gamst, Frederick. 1975. "Rethinking Leach's Structural Analysis of Color and Instructional Categories in Traffic Control Signals." *American Ethologist* 2:271–296.

Gardner, Howard. 1985. *The Mind's New Science: A History of the Cognitive Revolution.* New York: Basic Books.

Gardner, Martin. 1957. *Fads and Fallacies: In the Name of Science.* Second edition. New York: Dover Publications.

Gluck, Carol. 1985. *Japan's Modern Myths: Ideology in the Late Meiji Period.* Princeton: Princeton University Press.

Graham, Alan K. 1983. "Re: 'The Myth of the Software/Hardware Cost Ratio,' The Open Channel, Dec. 1982." *Computer,* March, 10.

Gregory, Gene. 1985. *Japanese Electronics Technology: Enterprise and Innovation.* Tôkyô: The Japan Times.

Gregory, Gene Adrian, and Etori Akio. 1981. "Japanese Technology Today: The Electronic Revolution Continues." Advertising supplement. *Scientific American,* October, 97–144.

Haas, William. 1970. *Phono-Graphic Translation.* Manchester: Manchester University Press.

Hadamitzky, Wolfgang, and Mark Spahn. 1981. *Kanji and Kana: A Handbook and Dictionary of the Japanese Writing System.* Rutland, Vt.: Charles E. Tuttle & Co.

Hall, Rogers P., and Dennis F. Kibler. 1985. "Differing Methodological Perspectives in Artificial Intelligence Research." *AI Magazine* 6:3 (Fall), 166–178.

Harris, Larry R., and Dwight B. Davis. 1986. *Artificial Intelligence Enters the Marketplace.* New York: Bantam Books.

Harris, Marvin. 1979. *Cultural Materialism: The Struggle for a Science of Culture.* New York: Vintage Books.

Hilton, Barry. 1982. "Government Subsidized Computer, Software and Integrated Circuit Research and Development by Japanese Private Companies." *ONR Far East Scientific Bulletin* 7:4 (October–December), 1–20.

Hiraga Noburu. 1983. "Seals." In *Kodansha Encyclopedia of Japan* 7:45–46. Tôkyô: Kôdansha.

Hiraga Yuzuru, Ono Yoshihiko, and Yamada Hisao. 1980. "An Assignment of Key-Codes for a Japanese Character Keyboard." University of Tôkyô Department of Information Science Technical Report 80-12 (July).

Hofheinz, Roy, Jr., and Kent E. Calder. 1982. *The Eastasia Edge.* New York: Basic Books.

Hofstadter, Douglas R. 1979. *Gödel, Escher, Bach: An Eternal Golden Braid.* New York: Basic Books.

Holtom, Daniel, C. 1947. "Ideographs and Ideas." *Far Eastern Survey* 16:19 (5 November), 220–223.

Huang Eing-Ming, and Suen Ching Y. 1983. "Computational Analysis of the Structural Composition of a Frequently Used Chinese Character Set." In *Proceedings of ICTP '83, 1983 International Conference on Text Processing with a Large Character Set, Tokyo, 17–19 October,* 292–297.

Hunt, Morton. 1982. *The Universe Within: A New Science Explores the Human Mind.* New York: Simon & Schuster.

Hsiang Jieh. 1986. "Report on a Visit to ICOT." Department of Computer Science, State University of New York at Stony Brook. Photocopy.

Impoco, James. 1984. Review of *Japan's Modern Myth,* by Roy Andrew Miller. *PHP* 15:2 (February), 78–79.

———. 1987. "U. S. Retains Its Lead in Computer Research." *Chicago Sun-Times,* 8 February.

Ishii Kazuo. 1983. "Scholarly Publishing in Japan." In *Proceedings of the AJUP-AAUP Conference on Scholarly Publishing, 1982,* Association of Japanese University Presses and Association of American University Presses, 17–27. Tôkyô: AJUP.

Ishiwata Toshio, Tanaka Hozumi, Amano Shinya, Uchida Hiroshi, Ogino Takano, Miyoshi Hideo, Tanaka Yuichi, and Yokoi Toshio. 1985. "Basic Specifications of the Machine-Readable Dictionary." *ICOT Technical Report TR-100.* Tôkyô: ICOT.

Japan Information Processing Development Center (JIPDEC). 1984. *Computer White Paper: 1983/84 Edition.* Tôkyô: Japan Information Processing Development Center.

Karatsu Hajime. 1982. "What Is Required of the Fifth Generation Computer: Social Needs and Its Impact." In *FGCS Proceedings 1981,* 93–106. See Fuchi 1982.

———. 1985. "Coping with the New Computers." *Japan Quarterly* 32:2 (April–June), 118–122.

Keene, Donald, comp. and ed. 1956. *Modern Japanese Literature: An Anthology.* New York: Grove Press.

Kennedy, George A. 1964. *Selected Works of George A. Kennedy.* Edited by Li Tien-yi. New Haven: Far Eastern Publications.

Kikuchi Makoto. 1983. *Japanese Electronics: A Worm's-Eye View of Its Evolution.* Translated by Simul International. Tôkyô: The Simul Press.

Kindaichi Haruhiko. 1978. *The Japanese Language.* Translated by Hirano Umeyo. Rutland, Vt.: Charles E. Tuttle & Co.

Kinmonth, Earl H. 1981. *The Self-made Man in Meiji Japanese Thought.* Berkeley: University of California Press.

Kinoshita Hiroo. 1985. "Towards an Advanced Information Society." In *Fifth Generation Computer Systems, 1984,* 7–17. *See* Brandin et al. 1985.

Knuth, Donald E. 1973. *The Art of Computer Programming. Vol. 3, Sorting and Searching.* Reading Mass.: Addison-Wesley.

Kobayashi Kôji. 1984. "Man-Machine Interaction in the 'C&C' Age." In *Human-Computer Interaction: Proceedings of the First U.S.A.-Japan Conference on Human-Computer Interaction, Honolulu, 18–20 August 1984,* ed. Gavriel Salvendy, 1–10. New York: Elsevier.

Koestler, Arthur. 1961. *The Lotus and the Robot.* New York: Macmillan.

Kurosu Masaaki, and Nakayama Takeshi. 1983. "Ergonomics of a Japanese Text Entry System." In *Proceedings of ICTP '83,* 118–123. *See* Huang & Suen 1983.

Kurzweil, Raymond. 1986. "The Technology of the Kurzweil Voice Writer." *Byte,* March, 177–186.

Lackshewitz, Christina, and Richard Suchenwirth, 1983. *A Bibliography on Computer Applications in Chinese Language and Script Processing.* Hamburg: Ostasiatisches Seminar, Goettingen University.

Lindamood, George E. 1983. "Update on Japan's Fifth Generation Computer System Project." *ONR Far East Scientific Bulletin* 8:3 (July–September), 16–24.

————. 1984a. "The Great Fifth Generation Episto-Encabulator Project: An Allegory." *Datamation,* 15 June, 193–196.

————. 1984b. "The Structure of the Japanese Fifth Generation Computer Project—Then and Now." *Future Generation Computer Systems* 1:2 (July), 51–55.

Lise, William A. 1986a. "Low-Tech MT Report." *JAT* [*Japan Association of Translators*] *Bulletin* 17 (August), 4–7.

————. 1986b. "Incestuous *Gaihan* [Outside Sales]." *JAT Bulletin* 19 (October), 12.

Liu Yongquan. 1983. "Language Engineering in China." In *Proceedings of ICTP '83,* 412–418. *See* Huang & Suen 1983.

Logan, Robert K. 1986. *The Alphabet Effect.* New York: Morrow.

Lohr, Steve. 1984. "The Japanese Challenge: Can They Achieve Technological Supremacy?" *The New York Times Magazine,* 8 July.

Lovins, Julie Beth. 1975. *Loanwords and the Phonological Structure of Japanese*. Bloomington: Indiana University Linguistics Club.

McCorduck, Pamela. 1979. *Machines Who Think*. San Francisco: W. H. Freeman Co.

McDermott, Drew, M. Mitchell Waldrop, Roger Schank, B. Chandrasekaran, and John McDermott. 1985. "The Dark Ages of AI: A Panel Discussion at AAAI-84." *AI Magazine* 6:3 (Fall), 122–134.

McEwan, J. R. 1962. *The Political Writings of Ogyû Sorai*. Cambridge, Mass.: The University Press.

McLuhan, Marshall. 1962. *The Gutenberg Galaxy: The Making of Typographic Man*. Toronto: University of Toronto Press.

Mair, Victor H., trans. 1986. "Preface to the *Seven Sounds* [of Zheng Qiao]." *Xin Tang* (New China) 7 (August), 134.

Marcom, John, Jr., and E. S. Bowning. 1984. "Japan's Supercomputers: Breakthrough or Boast?" *Wall Street Journal*, 8 August.

Masuda Yoneji. 1980. *The Information Society as Post-Industrial Society*. Tôkyô: Institute for the Information Society.

Miller, Roy Andrew. 1975. *"The Footprints of the Buddha": An Eighth-Century Old Japanese Poetic Sequence*. New Haven: American Oriental Society.

————. 1977. *The Japanese Language in Contemporary Japan: Some Sociolinguistic Observations*. AEI-Hoover Policy Study 22, Hoover Institute Study 58. Washington. D.C.: American Enterprise Institute for Public Policy Research.

————. 1981. *Origins of the Japanese Language*. Seattle: University of Washington Press.

————. 1982. *Japan's Modern Myth: The Language and Beyond*. New York: Weatherhill.

————. 1985. "Comments on Charles DeWolf's Review of *Japan's Modern Myth*." *Papers in Linguistics* 18:2.317–334.

————. 1986. *Nihongo: In Defence of Japanese*. London: Athlone Press.

Mizutani Osamu. 1981. *Japanese: The Spoken Language in Japanese Life*. Translated by Janet Ashby. Tôkyô: The Japan Times.

Morita Masasuke. 1983. "A New System for Inputting Japanese." In *Proceedings of ICTP '83*, 209–214. *See* Huang & Suen 1983.

————. 1985. "Japanese Text Input System." *Computer*, May, 29–37.

Moto-oka Tohru, et al. 1982. "Challenge for Knowledge Information Processing Systems (Preliminary Report on Fifth Generation Computer Systems)." in *FGCS Proceedings 1981*, 3–92. *See* Fuchi 1982.

Murtha, Tom. 1985. "A Lull in the Fifth." *Datamation*, September, 44–45.

Nagao Makoto, Tsujii Jun-ichi, and Matsuyama Takashi. 1981. "Methodologies of Japanese Language Treatment by Computer for Information and Documentation Sciences." In *Scientific Information Systems in Japan*, ed. Inose Hiroshi, 229–236. Amsterdam: North-Holland.

Nakayama Shigeru. 1984. *Academic and Scientific Traditions in China, Japan, and the West.* Translated by Jerry Dusenbury. Tôkyô: University of Tôkyô Press.

Neustupný, J. V. 1984. "Literacy and Minorities: Divergent Perceptions." In *Linguistic Minorities and Literacy: Language Policy Issues in Developing Countries,* ed. Florian Coulmas, 115–129. Amsterdam: Mouton.

Newell, Allen, and Herbert A. Simon. 1976. "Computer Science as Empirical Inquiry: Symbols and Search," *Communications of the Association for Computing Machinery* 19:3 (March), 113–126.

Nishi Toshio. 1982. *Unconditional Democracy: Education and Politics in Occupied Japan 1945–1952.* Hoover Press Publication 244. Stanford: Hoover Institution Press.

Nitobe Inazo. [1929] 1972. "The Use and Study of Foreign Languages in Japan." In *The Works of Inazo Nitobe* (5 vols.), ed. Takagi Yasaka et al., 4.401–474. Tôkyô: University of Tôkyô Press.

―――. [1931] 1972. "Japan: Some Phases of Her Problems and Development." In *Works* 3.3–426. *See* Nitobe [1929].

―――. [1936] 1972. "Lectures on Japan." In *Works* 4.3–368. *See* Nitobe [1929].

Oda Yasumasa. 1977. "Standardization for Cooperative Library Activity." In *Japanese and U.S. Research Libraries at the Turning Point: Proceedings of the Third Japan-U.S. Conference on Libraries and Information Science in Higher Education, Kyôto, Japan, October 28–31, 1975,* ed. Robert D. Stevens, Raynard C. Swank, and Theodore F. Welch, 116–126. Metuchen, N.J.: The Scarecrow Press.

Ohiwa Hajime, Takashima Takaaki, and Shibata Toshihiko. 1983. "Touch Typing of Japanese Text: Input Method and Training." In *Proceedings of ICTP '83,* 203–208. *See* Huang & Suen 1983.

Ohmae Kenichi, ed. 1983. *Japan: Obstacles and Opportunities. A Binational Perspective for U.S. Decision-makers Prepared by McKinsey & Company, Inc. for the United States-Japan Trade Study Group.* Tôkyô: President Inc.

Ouchi, William G. 1981. *Theory Z: How American Business Can Meet the Japanese Challenge.* Reading, Mass.: Addison-Wesley.

Overly, Norman V. 1977. "Why Johnny Reads Differently Than Noriko." *Educational Forum* 41:2.228, 236–245.

Ôyama Shigeo. 1985. "Fuchi Kazuhiro: Making a Computer That Thinks." *Japan Quarterly* 32:2 (April–June), 123–128.

Panko, Raymond R. 1983. "Kanji Keyboard Chaos." *Computerworld,* 28 November.

Paradis, Michel, Hagiwara Hiroko, and Nancy Hildebrandt. 1985. *Neurolinguistic Aspects of the Japanese Writing System.* New York: Academic Press.

Passin, Herbert. 1980. *Japanese and the Japanese.* Tôkyô: Kinseidô.

―――. 1982. *Society and Education in Japan.* First paperback edition. Tôkyô: Kodansha International.

Philippi, Donald L. 1984. "Japanese Keyboard Standardized." *Technical Japanese Translation* 19 (September), 32–34.

Pollack, Andrew. 1984. "The Keyboard Stymies Japan." *New York Times,* 7 June.

Proceedings of the International Computer Conference, Hong Kong, 12–15 October 1980. Chinese Information-Processing and Text Handling: The Next Frontier. 2 vols.

Proceedings of the 1982 International Conference of the Chinese-language Computer Society, Washington, D.C., 22–23 September 1982.

Proceedings of the 1983 International Conference on Chinese Information Processing, Beijing, 12–14 October 1983. 5 vols.

Proceedings of the 1983 International Conference on Text Processing with a Large Character Set, Tokyo, 17–19 October 1983.

Proceedings of the 1985 International Conference on Chinese Computing, San Francisco, 26–28 February 1985.

Raike, William M. 1985. "The Fifth Generation in Japan." *Byte,* April, 401–406.

————. 1986. "Perspectives on Hardware and Software." *Byte,* September, 351–358.

Raloff, Janet. 1984a. "Approaching the Age of Reason." *Science News,* 26 May, 330–333.

————. 1984b. "Swift Mechanical Logic." *Science News,* 2 June, 346–347.

Raphael, Bertram. 1976. *The Thinking Machine: Mind Inside Matter.* San Francisco: W. H. Freeman Co.

Rich, Elaine. 1983. *Artificial Intelligence.* International Student Edition. Singapore: McGraw-Hill.

Roden, Donald T. 1980. *Schooldays in Imperial Japan: A Study of the Culture of a Student Elite.* Berkeley: University of California Press.

Rohlen, Thomas P. 1983. *Japan's High Schools.* Berkeley: University of California Press.

Roszak, Theodore. 1986. *The Cult of Information: The Folklore of Computers and the True Art of Thinking.* New York: Pantheon Books.

Saeki Kôsuke, and Yamada Hisao. 1977. "The Romanization of Japanese Writing: Hepburn Versus Kunrei System Controversies." Reference material, International Standards Organization Technical Committee 46 Subcommittee 2, Paris, November 1977. Tôkyô: Nippon Rômaji Sha.

Saint-Jacques, Bernard, and Suzuki Takao. 1984. "Modern Japan: The Myth and the Reality." *Pacific Affairs* 57:1 (Spring), 90–94.

Sakamoto Takahiko, and Makita Kiyoshi. 1973. "Japan." In *Comparative Reading,* ed. John Downing. New York: Macmillan.

Salthouse, Timothy A. 1984. "The Skill of Typing." *Scientific American,* February, 128–135.

Sampson, Geoffrey. 1980. *Making Sense.* Oxford: Oxford University Press.

Sansom, [Sir] George Bailey. 1928. *An Historical Grammar of Japanese.* Oxford: Clarendon Press.

Scharschmidt, Clemens. 1924. "Schriftreform in Japan. Ein Kulturproblem." *Mitteilungen des Seminars für Orientalischen Sprachen* [Universität Berlin] 26-27:1.163–212.

Schodt, Frederik L. 1983. *Manga! Manga! The World of Japanese Comics.* Tôkyô: Kodansha International.

Searle, John R. 1980. "Minds, Brains, and Programs." *The Behavioral and Brain Sciences* 3:417–457.

————. 1983. *Intentionality: An Essay in the Philosophy of the Mind.* Cambridge, England: Cambridge University Press.

————. 1984. *Minds, Brains, and Science.* Cambridge, Mass.: Harvard University Press.

Seeley, Chris. 1984. "The Japanese Script since 1900." *Visible Language* 18:3 (Summer), 267–302.

Sekino Toshiyuki. 1983. "The Book Market in Japan." In *Proceedings of the AJUP-AAUP Conference,* 42–56. *See* Ishii 1983.

Sinkov, Abraham. 1966. *Elementary Cryptanalysis: A Mathematical Approach.* New Mathematical Library, 22. Washington, D.C.: Mathematical Association of America.

Smith, Brian Cantwell, and John Seely Brown. 1985. "The Research Situation in Japan: Report on an SDF-Supported Visit, October 27-November 9, 1984." Palo Alto: Xerox Palo Alto Research Center.

Sorensen, Karen. 1986. "Fifth Generation: Slow to Rise." *InfoWorld,* 9 June.

Spence, Jonathan. 1984. *The Memory Palace of Matteo Ricci.* New York: Viking.

Steinberg, Danny D., Yamada Jun, Nakano Yôko, Hirakawa Seiko, and Kanemoto Setsuko. 1977. "Meaning and the Learning of Kanji and Kana." *Hiroshima Forum for Psychology* 4.15–24.

Steinberg, Danny D., and Oka Noaki. 1978. "Learning to Read *Kanji* Is Easier Than Learning Individual *Kana.*" *Japanese Journal of Psychology* 49:1.15–21. *See* Oka & Steinberg 1978.

Steinberg, Danny D., and Yamada Jun. 1979a. "Are Whole Word Kanji Easier to Learn Than Syllable Kana?" *Reading Research Quarterly* 14:1.88–99.

————. 1979b. "Pigs Will Be Chickens: Reply to Tzeng and Singer." *Reading Research Quarterly* 14:4.668–671.

Suen Ching Y. 1983. "Computer Recognition of Kanji Characters." In *Proceedings of ICTP '83,* 429–435. *See* Huang & Suen 1983.

Suzuki Takao. 1963. *A Semantic Analysis of Present-day Japanese with Particular Reference to the Role of Chinese Characters.* Tôkyô: Keiô University Press.

————. 1975b. "On the Twofold Phonetic Realization of Basic Concepts: In Defence of Chinese Characters in Japanese." In *Language in Japanese*

Society, ed. Fred C. C. Peng, 175–192. Tôkyô: University of Tôkyô Press.

————. 1977. "Writing Is Not Language, or Is It?" *Journal of Pragmatics* 1:4 (December), 407–420.

Taira Koji. 1971. "Education and Literacy in Meiji Japan: An Interpretation." *Explorations in Economic History* 8:4 (Summer), 371–394.

Takasaki Nozomu, and Ozawa Takahiro. 1983. "Analysis of Information Flow in Japan." *Information Economics and Policy* 1.177–193.

Tanabe Hiroshi. 1977. "Standardization of Bibliographic Information in Japan." In *Japanese and U.S. Research Libraries in the Turning Point,* 101–115. *See* Oda 1977.

Tatsuno, Sheridan. 1986. *The Technopolis Strategy: Japan, High Technology, and the Control of the 21st Century.* New York: Prentice-Hall.

Trainor, Joseph C. 1983. *Educational Reform in Occupied Japan: Trainor's Memoir.* Tôkyô: Meisei University Press.

Tsunoda Tadanobu. 1985b. *The Japanese Brain: Uniqueness and Universality.* Translated by Oiwa Yoshinori. Tôkyô: Taishûkan.

Twine, Nanette. 1983. "Toward Simplicity: Script Reform Movements in the Meiji Period." *Monumenta Nipponica* 38:2 (Summer), 115–132.

————. 1984. "The Adoption of Punctuation in Japanese Script." *Visible Language* 18:3 (Summer), 229–237.

Tzeng, Ovid J. L., and Harry Singer. 1979. "Failure of Steinberg and Yamada to Demonstrate Superiority of Kanji over Kana for Initial Reading Instruction in Japan." *Reading Research Quarterly* 14:4.661–667.

Uchida Shunichi, Tanaka Hidehiko, Tokoro Mario, Takei Kinji, Sugimoto Masakatsu, and Yasuhara Hiroshi. 1982. "New Architectures for Inference Mechanisms." In *FGCS Proceedings 1981,* 167–178. *See* Fuchi 1982.

Uchida Shunichi, and Yokoi Toshio. 1984. "Sequential Inference Machine: SIM Progress Report." In *Report on the Initial Stage,* 67–78. *See* Furukawa & Yokoi 1984.

Unger, J. Marshall. 1984a. "Japanese Orthography in the Computer Age." *Visible Language* 18:3 (Summer), 238–253.

————. 1984b. "Japanese Braille." *Visible Language* 18:3 (Summer), 254–266.

————. 1986. "Japanese Research and Policy on Health Hazards of Video Display Terminals." *ONR Far East Scientific Bulletin* 11:1 (January–March), 4–12.

U.S. Department of State. 1946. *Report of the United States Education Mission to Japan.* Publication 2579, Far Eastern Series 11. Washington, D.C.: U.S. Government Printing Office.

Vogel, Ezra F. 1979. *Japan As Number One: Lessons for Americans.* Cambridge Mass.: Harvard University Press.

Vygotsky, Lev Semenovich. 1962. *Thought and Language.* Edited and translated by Eugenia Hanfmann and Gertrude Vakar. Cambridge, Mass.: M.I.T. Press.

Weizenbaum, Joseph. 1976. *Computer Power and Human Reason: From Judgment to Calculation.* San Francisco: W. H. Freeman Co.

Welch, Theodore F. 1976. *Toshokan: Libraries in Japanese Society.* London: Clive Bingley; Chicago: American Library Association.

Welke, Herbert- Jürgen. 1982. *Data Processing in Japan.* Vol. 1, *Information Research and Resource Reports,* ed. F. Winkelhage and N. Szyperski. Amsterdam: North-Holland.

Wiik, Paul F. 1986. "Report on a Research Visit to ICOT." Artificial Intelligence Applications Institute, University of Edinburgh. Photocopy.

Winston, Patrick H., and Karen A. Prendergast, eds. 1984. *The AI Business: The Commercial Use of Artificial Intelligence.* Cambridge, Mass.: M.I.T. Press.

Wolf, Marvin J. 1983. *The Japanese Conspiracy: The Plot to Dominate Industry Worldwide—and How to Deal with It.* New York: Empire Books.

Woronoff, Jon. 1981. *Japan's Wasted Workers.* Tôkyô: Lotus Press.

Yamada Hisao. 1980a. "A Historical Study of Typewriters and Typing Methods from the Position of Planning Japanese Parallels." *Journal Information Processing* (Tôkyô) 2:5, 175–202.

———. 1980b. "Differences in the Reading Process of Alphabetical and Ideographic Writing Systems." Paper presented at the Second Workshop on the Processing of Language Information by Man and by Machine, Tôkyô, 24 September 1980.

———. 1983a. "Certain Problems Associated with the Design of Input Keyboards for Japanese Writing." In *Cognitive Aspects of Skilled Typing,* ed. W. E. Cooper, 305–407. New York: Springer Verlag.

———. 1983b. "The Dvorak Simplified Keyboard: Practice Belies Theory." *Computer,* March, 80–81.

Yamagiwa, Joseph K. 1948. "Reforms in the Language and Orthography of Newspapers in Japan." *Journal of the American Oriental Society* 68:1 (January–March), 45–51.

Yamazaki Masakazu. 1981. "Social Intercourse in Japanese Society." In *Japan Today,* ed. Kenneth A. Grossberg, 62–69. Philadelphia: Institute for the Study of Human Issues.

Yhap, E. F., and E. C. Greanias. 1981. "An On-Line Chinese Character Recognition System." *IBM Journals of Research and Development* 27:3 (May), 187–195.

Yoder, Stephen Kreider. 1986. "Worms and Slugs Are Research Tools in Japan's Search for New Computers," *Wall Street Journal,* 20 June.

Yokoi Toshio, Uchida Shunichi, and ICOT Third Laboratory. 1984. "Sequential Inference Machine: SIM, Its Programming and Operating System." In *Report on the Initial Stage,* 79–90. *See* Furukawa & Yokoi 1984.

Yu Jinfeng, and Xiao Zhongyi. 1983. "Chinese in the Computer: Efficiency in

Input and the Role of Nested Element Analysis." *Information Processing and Management* 19:5.321–340.

Znosko-Borovsky, Eugene A. 1959. *How* Not *to Play Chess.* Ed. Fred Reinfeld. New York: Dover.

In Japanese

Note that all places of publication are Tôkyô unless otherwise noted.

AI Jânaru. 1985. "Nihon no AI shikakenintachi: Dai 1-kai, Fuchi Kazuhiro [AI Pioneers in Japan: No. 1, Fuchi Kazuhiro]." *AI Jânaru* 1 (December), 93–100.

Brandin, David H. 1985. "Nihon to Beikoku no konpyûta saiensu ni tsuite [On Computer Science in Japan and the U.S.]." Translated by Hiraga Yuzuru. *Jôhô shori* 26:5 (May), 453–457.

Doi Miwako, and Yoneda Kiyoshi. 1982. "Shukanteki oyobi kyakkanteki yominikusa no hyôka [Evaluation of Subjective and Objective Reading Difficulty]." In *Dai 8-kai shisutemu shinpojiumu* [8th System Symposium], 19–21 August, Hokkaidô, 281–286.

Fukuya Masashi. 1969. *Gakureki shugi no keifu* [The Genealogy of School-tie Careerism in Japan]. Reimei shobô.

Hayashi Ôki. 1977. "Kanji no mondai [Problems of Kanji]." In *Iwanami kôza: Nihongo* [Iwanami Lecture Series: The Japanese Language]. *Vol. 3, Kokugo kokuji mondai* [Problems of the National Language and Script], 101–134. Iwanami shoten.

————et al., comps. 1982. *Zusetsu Nihongo: Gurafu de miru kotoba no sugata* [Japanese in Diagrams: The State of the Language Seen through Graphs]. In *Kadokawa shôjiten,* vol. 9. Kadokawa shoten.

Hirai Masao. 1948. *Kokugo kokuji mondai no rekishi* [The History of National Language and National Script Problems]. Shôshinsha.

Hoshina Kôichi. 1949. *Kokugo mondai 50-nen* [Fifty Years of National Language Problems]. San'yô shobô.

Ishida Takeshi. 1973. *Mehiko to Nihonjin: Daisan sekai de kangaeru* [Mexico and the Japanese: Thoughts from the Third World]. Tôkyô Daigaku shuppan kai.

Ishiguro Yoshimi. 1951. *Nihonjin no kokugo seikatsu* [The 'Language Life' of the Japanese]. Tôkyô Daigaku shuppan-bu.

Ishii Satoru. 1985. "Nihongo no kanji/yôgo no kôsei no tame no chishiki [Knowledge Required for Proofreading Chinese Characters and Vocabulary in Japanese]." *ICOT Technical Memorandum TM-0092.* ICOT.

Kabashima Tadao. 1981. *Nihongo wa dô kawaru ka* [How Will the Japanese Language Change?]. Iwanami shinsho 145. Iwanami shoten.

————. 1984. "Konpyûta to kanji no unmei [Computers and the Destiny of Kanji]." *Gengo* 13:43–48.

Kaiho Hiroyuki. 1983. "Ningen wa kanji o dô shori shite iru ka [How Do People Process Kanji?]." In *Kanji o kagaku suru* [Sciencing Kanji], ed. Kaiho Hiroyuki, 35–66. Yûikaku.

Kaiho Hiroyuki, and Nomura Yukimasa. 1983. *Kanji jôhô shori no shinrigaku* [The Psychology of Chinese Character Information Processing]. Kyôiku shuppan.

Kana Jimuki no Kai [Kana Office Machine Society]. 1961. *Kîbôdo no chôsa* [Survey of Keyboards]. Kana Moji Kai.

Kanda Yasunori. 1986. "Hito to konpyûtâ o tsunagu tame ni: Nihongo wâdopurosessâ no gijutsu o kangaeru [Linking People and Computers: Thoughts on the Technology of Japanese Word-Processors]." *Newton*, June, 35–41.

Katayama Asao, comp. 1981. *Asahi shinbun no yôgo no tebiki* [The Asahi Newspaper Handbook of Usage]. Asahi shinbun-sha.

Katô Hidetoshi. 1985. *Denshi jidai no seirigaku* [Filing and Sorting in the Electronic Age]. Chûkô shinsho 772. Chûô kôron-sha.

Kindaichi Haruhiko. 1957. *Nihongo*. Iwanami shinsho 265. Iwanami shoten. *See* Kindaichi 1978.

Kikuchi Makoto. 1982. *Nihon no erekutoronikkusu*. Kôdansha. *See* Kikuchi 1983.

Kometani Fumiko. 1986. "Shokku uketa shushô hatsugen [The Prime Minister's Shocking Statement]." *Asahi Shinbun*, 29 September.

Martin, Samuel E. 1985. "Nihongo no shôrai [The Future of the Japanese Language]" In *Soto kara mita Nihongo, uchi kara mita Nohongo* [The Japanese Language Observed by Japanese and Non-Japanese], ed. Kokugo Gakkai, 9–46. Musashino shoin.

Mizutani Osamu. 1979. *Nihongo no seitai: Uchi no bunka o sasaeru hanashikotoba*. Sôtakusha. *See* Mizutani 1981.

Mori Ken'ichi. 1984. "Nihonbun nyûryoku to sono sôchi" [The Input of Japanese Text and the Equipment It Requires]. In *Nihongo jôhô shori* [Japanese information processing], ed. Nagao Makoto, 1–29. Denshi tsûshin gakkai.

Motooka Tôru, and Kitsuregawa Masaru. 1984. *Gosedai konpyûta* [Fifth Generation Computers]. In *New Science Age*, vol. 4. Iwanami shoten.

Nagao Makoto, ed. 1986. *Jinkô chinô: jitsuyôka no jidai e* [Artificial Intelligence: Into the Age of Implementation]. Shinchôsha.

Nakayama Shigeru. 1974. *Rekishi to shite no gakumon*. Chûô kôron-sha. *See* Nakayama 1984.

Nihon Sangyô Eisei Gakkai [Japan Occupation Health Association]. 1985. "VDT sagyô ni kansuru kentô iinkai hôkoku [Report of the Investigative Committee on VDT Operation]." *Sangyô Igaku* 27:172–194.

Ôiwa Hajime, Takahashi Takaaki, and Mitsui Osamu. 1983. "Nihonbun tatchi taipu nyûryoku no ichi hôshiki [A Method of Touch Typing Japanese Text]." *Jôhô shori gakkai ronbunshi* 24:6 (November), 772–779.

Oka Naoki, and Danny D. Steinberg. 1978. "Kanji to kana moji no yomi no gakushû: Kanji gakushû no yasashisa ni tsuite." *Shinrigaku kenkyû* 49:1.15–21. *See* Steinberg & Oka 1978.

Ôkubo Tadatoshi. 1978. *Ichioku-nin no kokugo kokuji mondai* [The National Language and National Script Problems of One-Hundred Million People]. Sanseidô sensho 45. Sanseidô.

Ôniwa Shunsuke, and the FPC Users Group. 1985. *Yoi pasokon, warui pasokon* [Good PCs, Bad PCs]. JICC shuppan.

Ôno Susumu. 1957. *Nihongo no kigen* [Origins of the Japanese Language]. Iwanami shinsho 289. Iwanami shoten.

Sakakura Atsuyoshi. 1985. "Nihonjin no Nihongo [Japanese for Japanese]." In *Soto kara mita Nihongo*, 47–80. *See* Martin 1985.

Sakamoto Masakata. 1984. *"Watashi no wâpuro taiken* [My Experiences with Word Processors]." *Nihongogaku* 3:7 [July] 62–65.

Sasaki Masato. 1983. "Môjin ni totte kanji to wa [What Are Kanji for the Blind?]." In *Kanji o kagaku suru*, 225–263. *See* Kaiho 1983.

Shiratori Yoshio, Kobashi Fumihiko, and Kimura Hisamasa. 1985. "Nihongo nyûryokuyô shin kî hairetsu to sono sôsasei hyôka [A New Keyboard Arrangement for Japanese Input and an Evaluation of Its Performance]." In *Nihongo bunsho no nyûryoku to henshû: shinpojiumu ronbunshû* [Papers from a Symposium on the Input and Editing of Japanese Texts], 17–24. Jôhô shori gakkai.

Sôhyô Maikon Chôsa Iinkai [General Council of Trade Unions Microcomputer Survey Committee]. 1985a. *VDT rôdô to kenkô chôsa saishû hôkoku* [Final Survey Report on VDT Work and Health]. Nihon rôdô kumiai sôhyô gikai.

—————. 1985b. *VDT rôdô kisei no tame no shihyô* [Guidelines for the Regulation of VDT Work]. Nihon rôdô kumiai sôhyô gikai.

Sorita Yoshio. 1985. "Naze *Mainichi* wa tsuburenai no ka [Why Does the *Mainichi* Not Collapse?]." *Chishiki* 3 (March), 84–90.

Sumioka Takashi. 1984. *OA shôkôgun: Haiteku jidai o shitataka ni ikinuku tame ni* [The Office Automation Syndrome: How to Survive the Hi-Tech Age]. Mikasa shobô.

Suzuki Norihisa, Hayashi Hiroshi, Takeuchi Ikuo, Yamamoto Masahiro, and Aiso Hideo. 1986. "Paneru tôron kai: Dai 5-sedai konpyûta/sûpakonpyûta ga shôyô konpyûta ni ataeru inpakuto ni tsuite [Panel Discussion: What Impact Are Fifth Generation Computers and Supercomputers Having on Commercial Computers?]." *Jôhô shori* 27:1 (January), 49–66.

Suzuki Takao. 1969. "Hyôki to shite no kanji" [Chinese Characters as a Mode of Writing], *Gengo seikatsu* 214:17–25.

—————. 1975a. *Tozasareta gengo: Nihongo no sekai* [Closed Language: The World of Japanese]. Shinchôsha.

Tatsuoka Hiroshi. 1985. "Nihonbun wâdo purosessâ e no kitai: yûzâ no tachiba kara mita kakushu nyûryoku hôshiki [What People Expect from Japanese Word Processors: Various Input Systems from the User's

Viewpoint]." In *Nihongo bunsho no nyûryoku to henshû,* 47–57. *See* Shiratori et al. 1985.

Tôdô Akiyasu. 1982. *Kanji no kako to mirai* [The Past and Future of Chinese Characters]. Iwanami shinsho 205. Iwanami shoten.

Tsunoda Tadanobu. 1985a. *Nô no hakken: Nô no naka no shô-uchû.* Taishûkan. *See* Tsunoda 1985b.

————. 1985c. "Nô no suitchi kikô [The Brain's Switching Mechanism]." *Saiensu,* August, 94–103.

Uemae Jun'ichirô. 1985. *Japanîzu dorîmu: Michi no mori e / gosedai konpyûta* [Japanese Dream: Into the Forest of the Unknown/Fifth Generation Computer]. Kôdansha.

Umesao Tadao. 1972. "Gendai Nihon moji no mondai ten [Problem Areas of Modern Japanese Writing]." In *Nihon bunka to sekai* [Japanese Culture and the World], ed. Umesao Tadao and Tada Michitarô, 196–206. Kôdansha gendai shinsho 280. Kôdansha.

Watanabe Sadahisa. 1985. "Kana kanji henkankei Nihonbun nyûryoku sôchiyô kenban hairetsu no hyôjunka ni tsuite [On the Standardization of Keyboard Arrangements for Use on Kana-to-Kanji Conversion Equipment for the Input of Japanese Text]." In *Nihongo bunsho no nyûryoku to henshû,* 9–16. *See* Shiratori et al. 1985.

Watanabe Shigeru, and Aida Shûhei. 1985. "Haiteku jidai to ningen [The Hi-Tech Age and Human Beings]." *Chishiki* 2 (February), 122–137.

Yamada Hisao. 1984. "*Wâpuro to Nihongo no genjô to shôrai* [The Present and Future of Word Processing and the Japanese Language]." *Nihongogaku* 3:7 (July), 4–17.

————, ed. 1985. *Shizen gengo nyû-shutsuryoku no saitekika* [Optimization of Natural-Language I/O]. Research Report 59101004. University of Tôkyô.

Yamada Jun. 1983. "Kodomo ni totte kanji to wa [About Kanji for Children]." In *Kanji o kagaku suru,* 122–152. *See* Kaiho 1983.

Yazaki Genkurô. 1964. *Nihon no gairaigo* [Western Loanwords in Japan]. Iwanami shinsho 518. Iwanami shoten.

Yokoi Tadao. 1978. *Gairaigo no goten* [A Dictionary of Loanword Errors]. Jiyû kokumin-sha.

Yokoi Toshio. 1985. *Dai-5 sedai konpyûta: jinkô chinô e no kakehashi* [Fifth Generation Computers: The Bridge to Artificial Intelligence]. Ohm-sha.

Yomikaki Nôryoku Chôsa Iinkai [Literacy Survey Committee]. 1951. *Nihonjin no yomikaki nôryoku* [Literacy of the Japanese People]. Tôkyô Daigaku shuppan-bu.

Yoshida Shô, ed. 1981. *Kana kanji henkan o chûshin to shita Nihongo nyûryoku shisutemu no kaihatsu* [Development of Japanese Input Systems Based Mainly on Kana-Kanji Conversion]. Research Report 488007. University of Kyûshû.

————. 1984. "Keitaiso kaiseki [Morphological Analysis]." In *Nihongo jôhô shori,* 86–113. *See* Mori 1984.

INDEX